MAKE WAY FOR LITERACY!

Teaching the Way Young Children Learn

Gretchen Owocki

HEINEMANN
Portsmouth, NH

Washington, DC

Heinemann
A division of Reed Elsevier Inc.
361 Hanover Street
Portsmouth, NH 03801–3912
www.heinemann.com

National Association for the
Education of Young Children
1509 16th Street, N.W.
Washington, DC 20036–1426
www.naeyc.org

Offices and agents throughout the world

Library of Congress Cataloging-in-Publication Data
Owocki, Gretchen.
    Make way for literacy! : teaching the way young children learn /
Gretchen Owocki.
      p. cm.
    Includes bibliographical references and index.
    ISBN: 0-325-00270-3 (alk. paper)
    1. Language arts (Early childhood). 2. Reading (Early childhood).
3. Learning. 4. Literacy. I. Title.

LB1139.5.L35 O87 2001
372.6—dc21   2001039313

Editor: Lois Bridges
Production: Vicki Kasabian
Cover design: Lisa Fowler
Cover photo: Debbra Bohne
Manufacturing: Louise Richardson

Printed in the United States of America on acid-free paper
05 04 03 02 01 RRD 1 2 3 4 5

To David Owocki

and

In memory of Dash
(2/26/90–1/18/01)

CONTENTS

ACKNOWLEDGMENTS

I wish to thank Christian Bush, an extraordinary teacher researcher who believes that all children *can*. Christian graciously welcomed me into her classroom, where, together, we inquired into aspects of literacy that would inform the writing of this book. I also wish to thank Christian's teaching assistant, Laurie Galonska, and her student teacher, Wendy Hogg, who collected data along with us and shared many important insights and ideas.

I am also grateful to Cindy Schultz and Barb Huston for allowing me to write about their work, for helping me understand their processes of conducting teacher research, and for reviewing almost every chapter of the book. Curt Kiwak, Trish Hill, Kathy Meakins, Jacquie Whitmore, and Carol Liss are other teachers with whom I have worked closely and whose collaboration has helped me understand early literacy.

A special thanks to my university colleagues Camille Cammack and Kathleen Clark for their intuitive reviews of chapters, for their ever-knowledgeable perspectives on teaching and learning, and for being such splendid friends.

Thanks to Donna Gail Shaw for helping me find time to write.

Many thanks to the children whose ideas, insights, and even advice on teaching are woven throughout the pages of this book. I am also grateful to their families for their interest and support.

A special thanks also to Lois Bridges, my editor, who is thoughtful in so many ways.

Finally, I wish to thank the graduate and undergraduate students at Saginaw Valley State University and the University of Alaska, whose dedication to quality education gives me inspiration to write.

PART 1

Literacies and Teaching

INTRODUCTION

Arms dance. Legs stir. Young voices whisper, giggle, and scold. Christian Bush's twenty-seven first graders are sitting in a large circle on the rug. It is early in the school year and they are sharing some of their first written responses to a book. It is Zeke's turn to share. Jaw tense, he holds his paper stiffly in front of his face and says very quickly, "I writed a bear combing his hair." He peers around his paper. The other children are leaning forward, looking at the drawing/writing; some are raising their hands. Christian is nodding her head thoughtfully, as if she sees something of interest in his creation. Zeke's face becomes less tense. He lowers the paper and takes questions and comments.

Christian and her children are developing the community that will support them as they live and grow throughout this first-grade year. For now, the children are tentatively emerging from the safety of their protective shells. They are testing the environment, seeing whether it is safe to explore, safe to take risks. If they are threatened, they will pull back, and next time, be even more wary. On this early day of school, however, Zeke finds clear ground to go forth. Because a supportive community has shown itself today, next time, sharing will be easier.

Supportive learning communities don't emerge automatically. Christian will spend much of the early part of the year building and maintaining a safe environment. She will watch her children closely, identifying their interests and strengths and making sure that each child's expertise may shine and grow. She will encourage her children to actively express themselves and will accept all of their efforts as valid. Christian will make sure that there is firm ground for the first steps these children will take in her classroom because she knows that "we learn by reading, talking, writing, listening, experiencing, doing . . . and taking risks. And, we do it better if we are in a safe and secure environment with an adult who cares about us" (Wink 1997, 13).

As a university-based researcher collaborating with Christian, a teacher researcher, I agree with her on this early day of school that there will be more than one starting place in this first-grade journey, more than one road to children's next destinations. Christian, with her understanding of the power that a community has to teach and her attention to variations in learners, will make sure that all of her students can emerge from their protective shells and travel new paths. Building a community will be as important this year as working on academic understandings. A healthy community will provide children with firm ground to try out tentative ideas, to see how others respond to their thinking, and to put their minds together to build new concepts.

This book is for teachers striving to create a classroom community that supports the developing literacies of all children. It describes literacy learning from a developmental, sociocultural perspective, a perspective that keeps at its forefront the connection between children's cognitive processes and their sociocultural contexts for living and growing (Bredekamp and Copple 1997; Wertsch 1991; Vygotsky 1978). My hope is that it will serve as a tool for helping you reflect on your teaching practices and, if you wish, for transforming them. As such, this book is more than reading material. It is also action material. It is designed to help you build on your understandings of early literacy, not only through what you read here but also through conducting literacy inquiries in your classroom. On the following pages you will find a description of how literacy develops, guidelines for evaluating literacy, and strategies for inquiry, as well as practical, curriculum-enhancing ideas that can be used with children ages 4 to 9.

THE STORIES AND IDEAS

The stories and ideas included in this book have come from my own teaching experiences as well as from observations I have made in others' classrooms. Findings from my own inquiries are woven throughout the book, along with findings and insights from the work of many other researchers, including teacher researchers. Some of the research questions I have asked are

- How do children construct literacy knowledge through play?
- How do they construct knowledge through literature discussions?
- What do they learn?
- What do children talk about as they engage in such experiences?
- How are children's home literacies revealed and explored in school settings?

To answer such questions, my typical practice is to observe children and teachers at work in classrooms. I record what I see and hear using a laptop computer and sometimes audiotapes or videotapes. I collect work samples, writing samples, and drawing samples. I also collaborate with the children and the teachers, always seeking to know the whys, the hows, and the whats behind their literacy-related thinking. Analyzing the data helps me better understand teaching and learning and find the answers to my questions. That is what this book will help you learn to do: collect and analyze classroom data, which, in turn, will help you develop insights into teaching and learning.

Before we begin, I want to recognize nine teachers in particular who have supported and informed my work. Throughout the book, you will read about their classrooms and their children. You have already met Christian Bush, who teaches first grade in Michigan. Other Michigan teachers are Christine Eaton (first), Cindy Schultz (first), and Barb Huston (K). Trish Hill (multiage 2–6), Curt Kiwak (multiage 2–6), and Kathy Meakins (preschool) teach in Tucson, Arizona, and Jacquie Whitmore (first/second) teaches in Anchorage, Alaska. I feel that it is important to share the work of these teachers because in their classrooms, children walk with a sense of dignity and work with a sense of purpose that I find extraordinary. These teachers know their stuff about teaching and learning and, on top of that, show an exceptional sense of kindness and respect for their little ones. I believe they have something to teach us all.

1 | HOW LITERACY DEVELOPS

Alex:	[Looking at a map] Mom, I want to show you something. I'm good! I found that little water spot.
Mom:	Oh, yeah, there it is. That's in Sabino Canyon. That's called—
Alex:	Sabino Canyon!
Mom:	No. That's Sabino *Lake*.
Alex:	Sabino Lake.
Cindy:	My mom gave me a card. She gave me a card that said "P.S."
Keith:	Come on!
Brother:	Wait, wait. Back up, Keith [Points to the route sign on a bus]. That says "State Street." That's not our bus.

Because written language plays a central role in the daily workings of our world, children become aware of its significance very early in life. Just as young children find good reason to pay attention to the people, the talk, and the objects in their environments, they find good reason to pay attention to print. Homes, neighborhoods, and communities are filled with print and with people who use it to accomplish their daily tasks of living. Just about wherever children go, they find themselves in the midst of literate activity.

Children's early experiences with written language, both formal and informal, provide essential foundations for all of their literacy learning. Early concepts are formed as children observe and interact with literate members of their communities and as they make their own attempts at reading and writing (Sulzby and Teale 1991; Whitmore and Goodman 1995). Through experiences such as looking at maps, writing notes with family members, and reading the print on city streets, children make myriad discoveries about how written language functions, how it is organized, and what it can mean.

Children's paths to literacy vary greatly. In part, this is because of individual traits. Some children are enormously interested in exploring written language. Any chance they get, they have their hands on paper, pencils, books, maps, manuals, catalogs, computers, or whatever other kinds of literacy materials they have in their environments. They want to know what the shampoo bottle says, what family members are reading, what every sign says, and who wrote it. Other children don't pay much attention to print, either they aren't interested or they're too busy doing other things. Children's unique interests, ways of knowing, and dispositions influence how and to what extent they participate in early literacy events and, in turn, the knowledge they construct.

Families contribute another layer of influence to children's literacy development. Some families actively draw their children into literacy by inviting them to help with grocery lists, share in the reading of mail, listen to storybooks, or talk about the newspaper. They may read advertisements together, sort coupons, follow recipes, or write letters. Other families expose their children to print in more peripheral ways. Their children may see print being used, but for a variety of possible reasons, it remains primarily in the hands of others. Families' literacy practices, interests, resources, and time, as well as their ways of interacting with their children, have a great influence on how and what children come to know about written language.

Wider communities of discourse also influence children's literacy development. For example, if a family's economic situation requires that its members spend most of their time securing food and shelter, then the literacies associated with these events (assessing household finances, developing budgets) will likely become familiar to their children. If a family's social life is centered on going to hockey and football games, watching sports on television, and reading about sports in the newspaper, then the literacies associated with these events (reading sports scores, finding game times in the TV schedule) will become familiar to its children. A family who is practiced in school-like discourses, such as helping children memorize letters of the alphabet or testing their knowledge by asking them questions such as "What does that sign say?" or "What does a rooster say?," will pass these literacies on to its children. The world beyond the household has a great influence on even young children's literacy knowledge.

It is also possible that the broader culture communicates to children—and adults—which literacies belong to them. For example, the literacies associated with nightly news and sports reports may be perceived by children to belong to white males, because they are often the ones who are talking. The literacies associated with service work may be perceived to belong to people, especially women, of color, because they are often the ones who hold these positions. Children's literacies are ultimately shaped by their social, cultural, race, class, and gender identities; their language; their families' values and patterns of domestic organization; cultural forces; history; and the economic, social, and political milieu of their lives (Dyson 1989; Heath 1983; Luke and Freebody 1999; Taylor 1997, 1998; Wink 1997). Given the numerous forces influencing early literacy, we can safely say that no two children's literacies are alike; with each literacy experience, every child creates an increasingly complex weave of literacy knowledge.

We explore in this chapter four key principles for understanding and facilitating literacy, always keeping in mind the complexities just cited. With broad and substantive knowledge of the ways in which literacy develops, you can insightfully observe what your children know about written language and teach toward their likely next steps. You can knowledgeably rethink techniques or practices that are recommended by textbook publishers, journal articles, or mandates but don't seem to meet the needs of your children. And, perhaps most important, you can critically reflect on your teaching. So, go ahead and take the time to grapple with the principles in this chapter. Your knowledge matters and your children will benefit from it.

PRINCIPLE 1: LITERACY DEVELOPS AS A SOCIAL AND CULTURAL PRACTICE

To facilitate literacy effectively, it is a good idea to first think about what this term means to you. Many of us associate *literacy* with knowing how to construct meaning through reading and writing. While reading and writing are two obvious components of literacy, you may find it helpful to think about a third, less obvious component. Reading and writing are always situated within discourse communities—groups of people with socially and culturally determined language practices, behaviors, and ways of thinking about the world (Gee 1996). Thus, a third component of literacy encompasses knowledge of how to negotiate reading and writing within these communities (Dyson 1993). For example, if you were going to place an ad in the newspaper, you would have to know more than how to read and write. You would also have to know what ads are for, who reads them, how to word them, and how to place them. For children living in a print-oriented society, learning to negotiate the literacies of their communities is a part of early socialization. "Children are encultured into the most common and evident forms of literacy in their homes and communities before they even begin school. The accumulated ways of knowing and funds of knowledge of family members . . . are intricately woven into their daily lives" (Taylor 1997, 3). Literacy develops as a social and cultural process.

However, at legislative levels and in school settings, *literacy* is often defined by political discourses alone (Taylor 1997). What counts as literacy in these ideological communities is often that which can be measured on tests, that which can be put into a package by publishing companies, and/or that which has been defined by the dominant culture as worth knowing. What does not count is children's ability to negotiate written language within and across a variety of social and cultural situations; what does not count is their ability to interpret and construct whole texts within meaningful social settings. Defining literacy based only on political discourses limits access to learning for all children but particularly for those whose literacies differ vastly from those of the dominant culture. It pulls our teaching away from children's lived literacies and pushes it toward predetermined sets of goals or standards—those set by individuals far removed from classrooms and with agendas that may not be in the best interest of particular students. Such practices deny children the legitimacy of their own experiences and of using them to learn (Dyson 1993; Lindfors 1991).

You can interrupt this process within your classroom by thinking about what cultural capital—the practices, the behaviors, and the ways of thinking that are valued by the dominant culture—means to you. Are there certain literate behaviors that you value over others? Do these values limit the frames of reference from which your children may approach their learning? What literacies does the school culture promote over others? How can you allow for all children's literacies to become tools for their learning, while at the same time helping them extend their knowledge and gain access to new literacies? Capitalizing on your children's literacies requires conscious reflection on your own teaching practices and may involve unlearning some old ways of thinking (Nieto 1999). We will consider these issues throughout the book. For now, let's proceed by keeping in mind that "there are many kinds of literacy and many kinds of families" (Taylor 1997, 3).

PRINCIPLE 2: LITERACY DEVELOPS THROUGH HYPOTHESIS TESTING

To examine principle 2, we narrow our focus from the social/cultural to the social/internal forces influencing literacy. Many researchers believe that children construct literacy knowledge by generating and testing hypotheses about how written language, but works (Clay 1975; Ferreiro and Teberosky 1982; Goodman 1984; Harste, Burke, and Woodward 1981; Schickedanz 1999). Hypothesis testing is both an internal and a social process (Vygotsky 1978). Internally, children generate hypotheses based on what they know so far about written language, but their hypotheses are continually influenced by their physical (print) and social environments.

For example, one day, I was listening to a group of first graders rehearse a readers theatre script. Archie kept reading, "I could it," instead of the words he had copied on his paper: "I knew it." Finally, he pointed to the tricky word and whispered to me, "What *is* this?" I whispered back, "Knew." He looked at me as if in disbelief and countered, "But it starts with a *k*!" Here's how hypothesis testing works: Based on his experiences with print, Archie had developed a hypothesis about the sound that *k* could make. Because it was somewhat unconventional, it was challenged, in this case, both by print and by his social experience.

When children's current ways of thinking—their current hypotheses—are challenged either socially or by print itself, they modify them and move toward new understandings. Not only does Archie now have a more conventional understanding about what *k* can do, he also has generalizable knowledge about the nature of silent letters.

Archie's example illustrates that internal and social processes are both at work in hypothesis testing and that reasons to refine hypotheses arise as children read, write, and participate socially in literacy events. This thought leads us to our next principle, in which we move our lens even further inward, to a focus on the individual.

PRINCIPLE 3: LITERACY DEVELOPS IDIOSYNCRATICALLY

Karla: Can you whistle?
Amy: No. I used to. Can you?
Karla: No. I just did, but I don't know how.

Development is complex and these children know it! Principle 3 centers on the notion that there is nothing straightforward or simple about learning. Children's growth is idiosyncratic, with each child taking unique paths. Given the personalized nature of hypothesis testing and children's varied familial, social, and cultural influences, it should make sense that no two children are likely to test the same hypotheses at the same time or even in the same order. Children "know their questions in distinctive ways; they generate their answers based on their own context" (Wink 1997, 83). To add further complexity, as Karla and Amy's example illustrates, growth does not always proceed in a steady, forward direction. It often appears recursive, moving back and forth depending on the learner and the task (Sulzby 1985b). To say that literacy growth is idiosyncratic is to recognize that children's progress is unique.

Think about the notion of idiosyncrasy as you read the following example. One day, Kristina, a first grader who usually uses invented spellings, recorded in writing a conversation being had by her whole class. She had a lot to record and she had to be fast, so instead of using letters, she used squiggles. Squiggle writing allowed her to whisper everything that was being said and to experience the challenge of note taking. Kristina's way of approaching this situation is unique because of who she is and what she has experienced. She has seen anecdotal notes taken in her classroom, and she wanted to explore them in her own writing. Although she could write letters, at this point, she needed squiggles to explore this new function.

Children discover literacy in unique and recursive and surprising ways. Sociocultural contexts, personal experiences, and particular literacy events shape what they do with written language, what they know, and how they learn. As a result, even with the same kinds of instruction, children demonstrate different knowledge and learn different things. Literacy develops idiosyncratically.

PRINCIPLE 4: LITERACY CONCEPTS DEVELOP SIMULTANEOUSLY

With the final principle, we turn to an examination of the many paths along which children's literacy develops. To do so, we narrow our focus even further, to hone in on the individual concepts that children explore as they develop literacy. The key principle here is that rather than developing one concept at a time, children develop many concepts simultaneously.

Written Language Functions

Karla, working at the writing table in her preschool classroom, writes a combined string of letters and letterlike symbols. "I'm making a card. 'I'm . . . sorry . . . I . . . been . . . acting . . . this . . . way.' It's a note to my mom."

From a very early age, children develop concepts about the functions of written language. In a print-oriented society, written language serves numerous functions; we use it to accomplish the tasks of daily living, do jobs, satisfy curiosity, gain and share information, make connections with others, regulate behaviors, imagine, remember, and bring pleasure to our lives. Karla's apology note provides one piece of evidence—among many that a teacher might collect—that she is learning about these functions. Exploration of functions is important because it helps children learn to negotiate the uses of literacy in their communities and because it provides motivation for other aspects of literacy learning. When children know what written language can do for them, they want to be able to use it conventionally and they want to explore how it works (Goodman 1986).

Written Language Formats

At the same time as children are developing knowledge about the functions of written language, they are developing knowledge about its formats—its shapes and structures. For example, a letter is typically formatted into a greeting, the body, a closing statement, and a signature. Other examples of formats include lists, graphs, webs, charts, columns, stanzas, and paragraphs. Within these examples, we could be even more specific. For example, a paragraph may be organized into a topic sentence, the body, and a summary statement.

Wide knowledge of formats is important for readers and writers. It is important for readers because it helps them organize their thinking and make predictions about content. For example, when Karla reads from an address book, knowing that it contains an alphabetized list of names increases her ability to predict the kinds of words that will appear and therefore narrows the possibilities for what the print might say. Knowledge of format is important for writers because it helps them organize text in such a way that it is predictable for a reader. Because audiences expect certain structures, knowing how to provide them helps an author communicate effectively. Also, if we know something about format, we don't have to expend effort deciding how to organize.

Written Language Genres

Karla reads to her teacher, Curt, a book she has written: "*What Animals Do At Night.* Coyotes come and howl at the moon at night when dawn is done. At morning they go into their caves . . . for hunters. At night. And for dawn. Mountain lions come and hunt their prey and they kill nice rabbits who are playing on good days . . . Bobcats hunt and do the same thing . . . but they don't have the same prey."

At the same time as children are developing useful knowledge about the functions and formats of written language, they are developing useful knowledge about its genres. Genre is closely related to format; it describes the shape and structure of a piece of written language as well as its content. Because of her exposure to many nonfiction books, four-year-old Karla knows that some books contain factual information, and she has a feel for the structure of language that is used to express such information. She uses this knowledge to produce a text that sounds like expository writing. Today, she uses unconventional symbols to write, but as she moves into more conventional writing, her knowledge of genre will help her organize her work and produce texts that meet reader expectations. It will also help her as a reader, guiding her predictions, expectations, and making of connections to what she knows.

Traditionally, genre has been used to classify a piece of writing into one of three broad categories—poetry, fiction, and nonfiction—with each category containing several subcategories. However, it is important to recognize that genre boundaries are both permeable and subject to individual interpretation (Dudley-Marling and Murphy 1999). Ultimately, the way a reader interprets genre will influence the meaning that is made. The following example from Christian Bush's first-grade classroom illustrates the complexity:

Archie's literature discussion group has read *Sadie and the Snowman* (Morgan 1995), a book about a child who builds a melting snowman over and over again. Christian asks the group to discuss the book's genre.

> **Jake:** This is fiction.
> **Bethany:** Yeah, fiction.
> **Archie:** It *could* be nonfiction. [Jake and Bethany look skeptical.] It could!
> **Christian:** Okay, first, why could it be fiction?
> **Jake:** Because it showed a carrot big to a squirrel. But a carrot is not that big. [Silence]
> **Christian:** Why could it be nonfiction?
> **Hailey:** Because, in lots of places, people like to build snowmans, and they build them over again.
> **Archie:** Yeah, people could make two of something, but they don't need to follow *this* story.

Archie's example illustrates that both the author's intention and the reader's interpretation of genre influence meaning. From one perspective—Jake's, Bethany's, and probably the author's—*Sadie and the Snowman* is a work of fiction and is most logically enjoyed as a story. However, Archie interpreted the piece as if it were nonfiction and, in turn, probably got a much different meaning than his peers. Because readers interpret genre uniquely, within the contexts of their experiences (Fairclough 1989; Kress 1999), it makes sense that no two children would draw meaning from genre in the same way.

Christian teaches her students general distinguishing characteristics of genre, but she knows that if she were to insist on conformity, she might limit the children's meaning-making processes. What is important is that she encourages an open discourse in which children may examine their conflicting viewpoints. Discussing, identifying, and playing around with genre creates "the conditions for enabling learners to operate flexibly and successfully with the wide range of text forms that are available, and, perhaps, to invent new possibilities for others to consider" (Dudley-Marling and Murphy 1999, 457). Only when we treat genre as an active discourse practice can children fully thrive in its potential.

Early Reading Behaviors

At the same time as readers and writers are developing concepts about the functions, the formats, and the genres of written language, they are also developing concepts about books. To explore children's early book-reading behaviors, we will look at some early discoveries of three-year-old twins Madison and Noah. Before we begin, it is important to note that these children have had numerous experiences listening to, reading through, and talking about books. They have learned that books contain interesting information; they know the discourses used to discuss such information; and they have learned to actively partici-pate in book reading by listening and verbally responding to the con-tent. Children who enter preschool or kindergarten with very few such experiences benefit from being socialized into book sharing routines and discourses.

During the first year of their lives, Madison and Noah often sat on their mother's lap as she read books to them. When they pointed toward pictures or made sounds, Jill responded by saying, "Yes, we're reading a book," or "Oh! Do you see the moon in that picture?" With each reading, Jill's voice carried a special cadence—musical, rhythmic, sto-rylike, or serious—depending on the genre. A light, airy tone accompa-nied rhymes and songs, while stories were read in an expressive manner. Concept books were talked through with a more serious de-meanor. With each reading, Jill read the title, turned pages left to right, and finished with "The end."

Researchers have learned much about early reading behaviors by observing children in such situations. Children's earliest responses to books are characterized by their looking at pictures and laughing or smiling when one is recognized or when the adult responds in an in-teresting way (Meow! Vroom!). Children often point to pictures and begin to make vocalizations. Children as young as ten or eleven months begin to choose books based on their content, and in rereadings, they turn to pages they remember or appreciate (Schickedanz 1999). So, by the time they are a year old, some children already have developed con-cepts about books and the routines used to share them.

During their second year, Madison and Noah became less tolerant of sitting through an entire story. At this point, Jill mostly labeled pic-tures as the children browsed. They took over turning the pages, and of course, they knew to turn them left to right, as Jill had done so many times. They also began to label pictures. For example, Noah turned through the pages of a favorite book and read, "Mumma's truck . . . Daddy's truck . . . My truck . . . Poppa's van." Noah's approach is typi-cal: Children's early book reading is often characterized by labeling. Each page is treated as a separate unit, unrelated to the next. Children with more experience begin to form a more cohesive story as they read (Sulzby 1985a). For example, Noah later identified a major conflict in a book as he was reading: "Pooh yummy all gone."

Now that they are three, Madison and Noah point to the print as well as the pictures as they read, often moving their fingers left to right. Although they do not yet read the words, their finger movement shows their developing understanding of directionality. Directionality be-comes important as children begin to connect letters with sounds and sort out letter-sound relationships. Madison and Noah are also devel-oping their ability to make predictions as they read. They have heard so many stories and concept books that they expect the text to say some-thing meaningful and can predict what it might be. For example, when

Jill makes purposeful pauses in her reading, "There was an old lady who swallowed a . . . ," the children fill in the blank.

Prediction is an important strategy for readers. Think about its importance as you read the following line: "When I was little, I couldn't tie my _____ ." Can you see how prediction narrows the possibilities for what a word might be? You can make a pretty good guess about the word before you get to it. If you found that the first letters of the missing word were *sh*, you could confirm your prediction and move on. If you found the first letter to be *r*, you might have to disconfirm and back up to reprocess. Predicting, confirming, and disconfirming are important strategies for readers (Goodman 1993).

Madison and Noah's example shows what the research about early reading shows in general: When children are read to, they develop knowledge about books and the routines and language used to share them (Durkin 1966; Ninio and Bruner 1978; Pappas and Brown 1987; Sulzby 1985a). Over time, they become progressively more sophisticated in their responsibilities and interpretations and they develop dispositions and knowledge that help them enjoy, explore, and learn from books. Figure 1–1 provides a checklist for recording some of the early discoveries children make about reading and handling books. The items are adapted from the work of Clay (1972, 1979), Goodman, Altwerger, and Marek (1989), and Sulzby (1985b).

Written Language Features

At the same time as children are developing knowledge about the functions, formats, and genres of written language, including those associated with books, they are developing knowledge about its features—graphic characteristics, letter-sound relationships, grammatical structures, and meanings. We turn next to an examination of the discoveries young children make about the features of written language.

Early feature-related discoveries

> Ana Celia draws a picture. "This is for my mama." She writes some letters. Her teacher points to the letters and says, "Tell me about this part. What does it say?" Ana Celia responds, "Those are letters! N . . . A . . . A . . . N . . . M . . . C . . . "

Children learn at a very early age that, just like everything else in their worlds, letters can be named. Initially, many children believe that letters are just pictures, rather than something that can represent meaning. Therefore, asking "What does this say?" or "What did you write?" typically results in a response like Ana Celia's: "Those are letters!" Such responses provide evidence that, early on, children hypothesize that print does not *say* anything (Ferreiro 1984).

One of children's exciting early discoveries, then, is that print carries meaning. Those little symbols (letters) that some families

Child's Name: _____

Instructions: Fill in the blanks with the date on which the child was observed demonstrating the particular skill or strategy.

Handling
_____ Holds book in an upright position.
_____ Understands that print proceeds from left to right and top to bottom.
_____ Turns pages left to right.
_____ Reads/views left page before right page.

Surface Feature Knowledge
_____ Appropriately uses terms such as *cover, page, story, title,* and *author.*
       Others: _____
_____ Uses book title and cover illustration to make predictions.
_____ Understands that a book contains an author's message.
_____ Understands that an illustrator creates the visuals for a book.

Print and Punctuation Knowledge
_____ Understands that pictures are read differently than print.
_____ Knows what a letter is (names or points to a letter when asked; uses the term conventionally during conversations).
_____ Knows what a word is (names or points to a word when asked; uses the term conventionally during conversations).
_____ Participates in reading when the language is predictable.
_____ Understands the relationship between oral and written language.
_____ Reads some words conventionally.
_____ Puts great effort into decoding stretches of simple text.
_____ Reads simple text with relative ease.
_____ Understands the functions of punctuation: ___ period, ___comma, ___question mark, ___dialogue markers.
       Others:_____

Interpretive Knowledge
_____ Labels pictures while turning through the pages of a book.
_____ Is aware that books contain stories as well as other kinds of information.
_____ Uses pictures or what is remembered from previous readings to make up a connected story (fiction) or sequence of events (nonfiction).
_____ Discusses/retells stories, referring to ___ character, ___ setting, ___ problem, ___ plot episodes, ___ resolution, ___ theme.
_____ Discusses/retells key concepts and information learned from nonfiction.
_____ Retells in a logical sequence.

Connections (Keene and Zimmermann 1997)
_____ Makes personal connections with books.
_____ Makes connections between books.
_____ Makes connections between books and the world.

FIGURE 1–1   *Observing Book Knowledge*

encourage children to memorize actually mean something. When children develop this understanding, they begin to hypothesize about what those symbols can mean. For example, twenty-two-month-old Jacob pointed to a long string of letters on a cardboard box and said, "Stop!" Jacob believes that all print either says "STOP," a sign his family often reads together, or "Jacob."

Antonia, a three-year-old, is also exploring hypotheses about what symbols can mean. Figure 1–2 shows her drawing of a carrot. After drawing, she wrote her name (an *A* and some *N*s). Then, she wrote a series of small round symbols while saying, "I . . . played . . . with . . . the . . . car . . . rots . . . I . . . played . . . with . . . the . . . car . . . rots."

Like Jacob, Antonia understands that symbols carry meaning. Her example also demonstrates her knowledge that there is a difference between drawing and writing. Her pictures look different than her print and they take up different spaces on the page. When children first begin to differentiate between drawing and writing, they may surround or superimpose their pictures with characters or write characters all over the paper, as with Antonia. Over time, they notice that print proceeds in a linear fashion, and they begin to use this principle in their writing. Many young writers initially use sets of characters—circles, squiggles, lines, crosses, or letters—that are physically similar, as with Antonia's shapes. As they continue to see print in their environments, they notice that the letters in most strings vary, and they begin to apply this criterion to their own writing (+ O + + O).

Ana Celia's, Jacob's, and Antonia's examples can be used to highlight some important early discoveries: letters can be named; print carries meaning; there is a difference between drawing and writing; print proceeds in linear fashion; the letters in a string must vary. Children make these discoveries as they observe and participate in the literate activities of their sociocultural communities.

FIGURE 1–2 *Antonia's Carrot*

Print as a way to label objects

Many children, as they begin to sort out what print can do, initially believe that its primary function is to label objects. That is why children sometimes do things like reading all of the soup labels in the grocery store as *soup* and pointing to a whole sentence while reading a storybook but saying only "Duck." These children, like many, are using print to label objects but not describe them or tell what they do (Ferreiro and Teberosky 1982).

It is interesting that when many children label, they read print as if it can say only the name of what is in the picture but not other words. For example, Angela, working on a play plan one morning, drew a housekeeping area. Referring to her drawing, she said, "This is housekeeping." Then, she wrote letters while saying only, "House . . . keep . . . ing." In her talk, she said, "This is," but she dropped these words in her writing. This is an indication that children's early conceptualizations of what can be written remain somewhat close to the physical object that is being represented.

Print as a physical representation of objects

Children eventually begin to test hypotheses not only about what print can mean but also about how it looks. Because they do not yet understand that words are made up of letters that are associated with sounds, they may make hypotheses that are based on the visual aspects of words (Schickedanz 1999). For example, a child might hypothesize that a long string of letters or large print can represent a big object, like a pond, while a short string of letters or small print can represent a small object, like a tadpole (Ferreiro and Teberosky 1982; Schickedanz 1999). Yetta Goodman (1984) tells the story of three-year-old Josh, who wrote a small *J* to represent himself and a larger *J* to represent his father, Joseph. Goodman points out that from Josh's perspective, the symbols represented people, rather than sounds. He was exploring a visual, rather than a sound-based, hypothesis. Such hypotheses make sense considering that in pictures and real life, ponds are bigger than tadpoles and daddies are bigger than kids (Gundlach 1982). Heaviness, size, length, and age are all criteria that have been observed to play a part in the number or size of letters that children use to represent objects (Ferreiro and Teberosky 1982).

The arbitrary nature of letter strings

As children continue to experiment with written language and participate socially in literacy events, they come to realize that written symbols (letters) are not physically related to the objects they represent. They are arbitrary in nature. However, children still might not know why letters are organized the way they are (Schickedanz 1999). For example, after writing a string of letterlike symbols, Karla pointed to each and explained, "Each one of these is a song. This is 'Jingle Bells,' 'Dashing Through the Snow,' 'Jingle Bells,'—no, this is 'Jingle Bells,' this is a song that I made up . . ." Karla's symbols did not look, in terms of size or shape, like they could represent objects; she understood their arbitrary nature. However, her example confirms that before children think of letters as having sounds that make up words, many think of them as a way to symbolize something meaningful.

Chloe provides a similar example. When she sees the first letter of her name in any word, she hypothesizes that the word is her name. Schickedanz (1999) explains that for a time, children believe that each word has a unique design, a unique sequence of letters that must be learned. If a word begins with a *c*—if it has that design—then it can only belong to *Chloe*. This is not a sound-based hypothesis. Before they understand that letters and sounds are related, many children think of letters as belonging to people, places, or things (McGee and Richgels 1996). Eventually, as children continue to see, use, and talk about print, they realize that relatively few letters (only twenty-six) are used over and over to create all of the different words in our language (Clay 1975; Schickedanz 1999). Their written words, even when using invented symbols, begin to look like real words in terms of length (usually a minimum of three characters) and internal variation (no repeating of a character more than twice in a row) (Ferreiro and Teberosky 1982; Schickedanz 1999). Brent's newspaper page in Figure 1–3 demonstrates this understanding. Notice that children still may not have discovered the relationship between letters and sounds at this point.

Children also begin to hypothesize that there must be variation between words. If words are going to say different things, they must look different. In fact, when writing, if they don't know many letters, they

FIGURE 1–3 *Brent's Newspaper*

may solve the problem by changing the order of those they know to make them look like different words. Brent's example illustrates this strategy.

The relationship between speech and print

I always smile when I see children testing hypotheses about the relationship between speech and written language. We see children working through this hypothesis as they try to match their vocalizations with print. For example, Karla, while writing a long string of letters (she said she was writing the word *rat*), kept her voice going until she stopped writing letters: "Rat. Rat. See, like rat almost. Just like a few more words. Rat!" Similarly, her classmate, Katie, told the story of a book as she pretended to read its print. She moved her finger along the print, adjusting both the rate of her talk and the speed of her finger to ensure a match at the end of each page. Children make discoveries about the relationship between speech and writing as they read and write with literate others, notice and talk about words, see adults pointing to print while reading, and listen to and watch them write while saying words aloud.

The relationship between letters and speech sounds

Eventually, children discover the alphabetic principle—the notion that there is a relationship between letter patterns and sound patterns. In turn, they transition from visual to sound-based hypotheses (Ferreiro 1984; Schickedanz 1999; Wilde 1992). As part of the transition, it is common for children to explore a syllabic hypothesis—the notion that letters correspond with spoken syllables rather than sounds. For example, Ariel, who is syllabic but not alphabetic, wrote her name while articulating it aloud:

Spoken:	Ar	i	el
Written:	E	A	i

Lexy, who is transitioning from syllabic to alphabetic, wrote an entire sentence based on a syllabic/alphabetic hypothesis. She used one letter to represent each syllable, except for the final word, for which she used two:

I	went	to	Myr	tle	Bea . . .	ch
I	W	T	M	T	B	H

It is possible that children make syllabic hypotheses because this is how adults sound when they write. Rather than stressing each phoneme aloud (/c/ /a/ /t/ /n/ /i/ /p/), they stress each syllable (cat-nip) (Schickedanz 1999). A subsequent example from Lexy illustrates that over time, children transition toward increasingly smaller units of sound (Ferreiro and Teberosky 1982; Sulzby 1985b; Wilde 1992):

This	is	a	pic	ture	of	me	play	ing	soc	cer.
FS	IS	A	P	HR	F	ME	PA	E	SA	G

When children first write with an alphabetic hypothesis, they draw from their knowledge of letter names and/or letter-sound relationships. For example, knowing that "*t* is a letter" or that "*t* makes /t/" can help a child spell *to*; they all contain the /t/ sound. Young writers also use their awareness of language phonemes (sounds) as they write. Children who are phonemically aware can "take words apart, put them back together again, and change them" (Cunninghan and Allington 1999, 125). In other words, they can segment, blend, and manipulate their sounds. It makes intuitive sense that being able to manipulate words orally (e.g., derive the syllables cat-nip from *catnip*; the onset-rime combination /c/-at from *cat*; or the individual sounds /c/ /a/ /t/ from *cat*) would be helpful in early spelling.

Lexy's example also illustrates that even very young spellers do not draw only on their knowledge of letters and sounds. Lexy spelled *is* conventionally, but not because of her knowledge of letter names or letter-sound relationships. If she had, she probably would have chosen *iz* or *ez*. It is more likely that she has seen *is* in her environment and used her visual memory to spell it. Children use their visual memories to both generate spellings (Goodman 1993; Graves 1983) and decode text (Pinnell and Fountas 1998).

The following example, taken two months after the previous example, shows Lexy's further growth as a speller. While she is still relying on phonetic spelling to some extent, she is internalizing more commonly used words and spelling patterns:

I	went	to	preschool	and	I	went	to	kindergarten.
I	want	to	PrscaL	and	I	wen	to	KnaGart

As children become more sophisticated with spelling, they can be expected to progress in the following ways (Graves 1983; Read 1975; Wilde 1992):

- move from using initial and final consonants (*sr* for *star*) to incorporating interior consonants and vowels
- begin to spell short vowels conventionally
- use vowel markers (more than one vowel) to spell other vowels sounds conventionally
- spell past-tense endings conventionally
- use double consonants consistently
- internalize spelling patterns such as -ing, -ate, and -ain
- increase their visual memory and repertoires of words they can spell automatically
- recognize when words are misspelled
- continue to invent words when necessary

I chose Lexy's work to illustrate spelling development because it seemed to represent a typical progression. "Typical" does not mean linear or lockstep. No child is likely to fit into any model perfectly. We say "typical" with the understanding that children's growth is idiosyncratic. They may go back and forth between phases, spend a long time in some, zip through others, and skip some altogether. Lexy's spellings have developed this year in a similar progression to those of many of her classmates—from syllables to phonetics to more complex patterns—but the children have taken diverse paths.

Lexy's teacher, Christian, helps her students develop phonemic awareness and phonics knowledge by providing plenty of opportunities for independent, shared, and modeled reading and writing and plenty of time to listen to books and songs, chant and chorally read rhymes and poems, play around with words and tongue twisters, sing songs, study words, and play word games. All along the way, Christian helps them tune in to language and all of its complex features.

Word spacing

As children make discoveries about functions, formats, genres, and features, they are also making discoveries about punctuation. Spaces are one of the first forms of punctuation that children explore in their writing. Although spaces cannot be written, they are a form of punctuation. Like periods or commas, they serve to segment written language. Children do not initially incorporate spaces into their writing because they hear speech in a steady stream (Martens and Goodman 1996). We do pause in speech, but not between each word.

When Amelia stood in front of her class to read aloud her space-free script (Figure 1–4), she had difficulty sorting out which words were which. She started by trying to read what was on the paper but then provided a remembered account: "We should give our—I mean, we should be nice and give people the toys if they had them first or we could get in trouble and be grounded again." Children transition toward convention as it is needed to communicate effectively (Milz 1982).

[Handwritten margin notes:] I maybe that is why some young children don't progress out of — ∅ visual, but auditory

FIGURE 1–4 *Amelia's Advice on Sharing: We should give people the toys if they have the toys first. If we don't give the toys back we could get in trouble.*

FIGURE 1–5 *Zeke's Book Cover: This book is by Zeke M. and the illustrator is Zeke M. and the writer is Zeke M.*

Zeke and Archie, classmates of Amelia's, provide examples of how some children explore this transition. In Figure 1–5, Zeke uses periods to space his words. In Figure 1–6, Archie uses dashes. Children on their way to conventional spacing can be expected to try out a variety of symbols—periods, slashes, squiggles, dashes, commas, lines, or circles.

Amelia, Zeke, and Archie are sorting out the concept of word. As they continue to write and read in social settings, and to be supported by knowledgeable adults who talk with them and teach them about words, they will continue to refine their hypotheses.

Other forms of punctuation

Punctuation can be tricky to teach. The function of punctuation is to help create meaning in writing. In talk, it's easy. We have intonation, gesture, pauses, facial expressions, volume, tone, and other shared cultural understandings. Because these devices are not available in written language, writers must figure out how to use punctuation to convey their meanings (King and Rentel 1982; Martens and Goodman 1996).

FIGURE 1–6 *Archie's Eye Care Script: You take care of your eyes. If you don't, you are in big trouble because then you can't see.*

As with all other aspects of written language, children test hypotheses about punctuation (Cordeiro, Giaccobe, and Cazden 1983; Edelsky 1983; Ferreiro and Teberosky 1982; Martens and Goodman 1996; Milz 1982; Wilde 1992). Although much has yet to be learned about how children construct punctuation knowledge (Dahl and Farnan 1998; Hall 1996), a review of literature conducted by Hall (1996) reveals some points of agreement among researchers: "Learning to punctuate is not a passive process in which children can simply learn a set of rules and can then punctuate accurately" (33). Instead, children actively construct "a view of how the punctuation system works" (33). Children do not make sense of punctuation only by being taught its rules; they must take active part in exploring and constructing the system just as they do with all other aspects of written language.

CONCLUSIONS

Teaching based on the principles described in this chapter begins with a general knowledge of the ways in which children think and learn, and it proceeds as you learn about and support individual children in testing their unique literacy hypotheses. This is no small challenge, but it's a doable one and a positive step toward teaching the way children learn.

2 | EVALUATING CHILDREN'S LITERACY KNOWLEDGE

There is ever a song somewhere, my dear,
There is ever a something sings always . . .

—James Whitcomb Riley

In dynamic early childhood classrooms, comprehensive literacy evaluation is an integral part of teaching. Comprehensive evaluation is about listening to *each* child's songs, primarily as he or she engages in authentic literacy experiences. The process is ongoing and strategic. It involves thoughtfully documenting what children know and can do, and recording information about the ways in which they approach their learning. The major goals of comprehensive evaluation are (1) to construct histories of children's growth; (2) to teach in response to children's demonstrated strengths and needs; and (3) overall, to improve student learning (Goodman 1984; Neill 2000; Pappas, Kiefer, and Levstik 1999; Tierney 2000). In this chapter, we consider eight guidelines that will help you achieve these goals.

OBSERVE CHILDREN AS THEY ENGAGE IN AUTHENTIC EXPERIENCES

The first guideline for achieving the goals of comprehensive evaluation is to observe children as they engage in authentic literacy experiences. Authentic experiences are those that are real, contextualized, and meaningful to children; they "reflect literacy in the community, the workplace, and the instructional activities of the classroom" (Cooper 2000, 526). Because real-life literacy is always embedded within specific linguistic and cultural contexts, it makes sense to collect and evaluate information that comes from such contexts. As you observe, the following set of kidwatching (Goodman 1984) questions can help guide your thinking:

- What do my students know about written language?
- What are their literacies?
- What hypotheses are they testing? What are their ways of approaching learning?
- What do their unconventional uses of written language reveal about their knowledge?
- How can I use this information to inform my instruction?

Barb Huston, a kindergarten teacher researcher, asks these questions on a daily basis. To find answers, she takes anecdotal notes and collects journals, science logs, longitudinal name-writing samples, and writing samples from play and writing centers (grocery lists, sale signs, merchandise, greeting cards, stories). Some of these pieces are produced independently, some collaboratively, and some with teacher guidance (Huston 2000). The diversity of pieces, collected from various meaningful contexts, helps Barb see how children contextually apply the skills and strategies they are learning and ensures that all children have opportunities to reveal their strengths.

OBSERVE CHILDREN AS THEY ENGAGE IN A VARIETY OF EXPERIENCES

The second guideline for comprehensive evaluation is to observe children as they engage in a variety of experiences. Can you imagine how limited your assessment would be if you were to assess writing only through children's written stories or only through worksheets? What if you only were to assess reading only through end-of-unit tests? "The key question in evaluation is not, Can the child perform the specific tasks that have been taught? Rather, the question is, Can the child adjust language used in other situations to meet the demands of new settings?" (Goodman 1984, 221). Answering this question requires that you observe children as they engage in a variety of experiences. You may observe as they

- read and respond to stories, informational text, and poems (independently, collaboratively, or with your guidance)
- use menus, order forms, grocery lists, and food packages
- consult schedules, calendars, and other environmental print
- write stories, informational text, poems, scientific observations, lists, notes, and labels
- listen to books on tape and listen to you read
- engage in shared reading and writing
- discuss texts they are reading for literature circles, content area projects, or just for fun
- dramatize stories, retell stories, and play language games

Focusing on variety ensures that all children have opportunities to shine in their particular areas of strength and to reveal their literacies. It also shows you the extent to which they can apply what they know and what they are learning to new situations and settings. Some further questions that can help you evaluate children's literacies are

- What kinds of literacy experiences do my students seem to prefer or know most about? In what settings do they seem to most easily reveal their knowledge?
- What evidence do I have that children are applying and exploring literacy skills and strategies across settings?
- How can I help my students use what they know to gain access to new literacies?

Developing answers to these questions can help you construct your children's literacy histories and plan thoughtful instruction that is in tune with their interests, their strengths, and their styles of learning.

USE A VARIETY OF ASSESSMENT TOOLS

In order to evaluate children's literacy in a variety of situations, you must use a variety of assessment tools. Using many tools helps you capture both the processes and the products of children's learning. Knowledge of both is necessary in understanding what to teach and how to teach it. Following are some commonly used assessment tools in early childhood classrooms.

Work samples
Work samples include student-written stories, expository pieces, poems, rough drafts, materials from sociodramatic play, notes to friends, responses to literature, journals, logs, drawings, diagrams, webs, maps, and time lines. Kept throughout the year, work samples can be used to track and understand children's knowledge of written language functions, formats, genres, and features; phonics knowledge; spelling development; sense of story; learning in content areas; and personal connections to literature.

Book handling and early reading observations
Structured observations of children's book handling and reading are conducted as children explore a variety of books in a variety of settings. Taken throughout the year, such observations can be used to track and understand children's early reading development (see the form for observing book knowledge in Chapter 1).

Oral reading samples

Oral reading samples, taken using miscue inventories, running records, or informal reading inventories, are used to understand children's decoding and meaning-making strategies. As children read orally, their miscues are documented and then analyzed and used to inform instruction. Reading samples are typically taken as a child reads a whole text, but here, we'll use just one sentence, from a reader named Archie, to briefly illustrate how the process works:

The text said:	"How	much	does	it	cost?"
The text said:	"How	much	does	it	cost?"
Archie read:	"How	much	dollars	it	calls?"

Archie's miscues reveal at least four important strengths. First, he is an active meaning maker. Substituting *dollars* for *does* shows that he is working to make sense of the piece, rather than "just" decoding words. (There were no pictures.) Second, he is predicting what the text will say. Because there was no obvious meaning disruption, he did not self-correct. (Later in the reading, he made a miscue that didn't make sense, and he did self-correct.) Third, in terms of sentence structure, he maintains something that sounds almost like an English sentence, and perhaps it does sound like an English sentence to Archie. Finally, both miscues are graphically similar to the original text, showing that he is paying attention to graphic cues. Done periodically throughout the year, oral reading analyses can be used to identify children's reading strategies, track their growth, and plan instruction based on their demonstrated needs. Retrospective miscue analysis' similar to miscue analysis, involves children in evaluating their own reading processes (Goodman 1996).

Word lists

Word lists may be used to track students' quick recognition of high-frequency words or the strategies used to decode these words.

Text retellings

Text retellings may occur after oral reading, silent reading, or listening. Children may draw, write, act out, or orally express their retellings, and if it helps, you may give prompts. Any genre of text may be used. Retellings help you examine and track children's listening and reading comprehension; sense of story; ability to recall facts and details; and use of inferences (Morrow 1997). Kept over time, retellings show children's progress in learning to make meaning from text (Cooper 2000).

Story retellings may be evaluated by the extent to which they detail and describe the characters, the setting, the problem, the plot episodes, and the resolution. A web or a map may facilitate retelling. Story retellings may also be evaluated to determine whether they are presented in some logical order. To assess several children's retellings at once, you may consider dividing a piece of paper into thirds and asking each of them to draw, write, or dictate something from the beginning, the middle, and the end (Salinger 1998). However, this may constrain the retelling, especially if it seems to the child that there are four or five important parts. Flow maps—half-sheets of paper or boxes drawn in sequence on a page—can accommodate as many story parts as children wish to portray.

Nonfiction retellings may be evaluated by the extent to which children describe the topic, the purpose or the focus, and the main ideas and by how the teller relates the main ideas to one another (Cooper 2000). Webs, maps, or other graphic organizers may be used to facilitate nonfiction retellings.

Anecdotal notes

Anecdotal notes are brief written notes taken as children are writing, reading, playing, performing, collaborating, discussing, and observing. An ideal tool for kidwatching, anecdotal notes are typically taken as children engage in activity that does not require a tremendous amount of support from you. They can be used to document the language children use as they read, write, and collaborate; literacy-related behaviors and actions; approaches to risk taking; responses to assignments; individuals' ways of thinking and working through a task; or specific behaviors such as rhyming words or blending and segmenting their sounds. The notes are descriptive in nature, focusing on what children do and say. Their major purpose is to help you reflect on "children's literacy in action" (Neuman, Copple, and Bredekamp 2000).

Conference notes

Conference notes are notes taken during informal or formal conferences with children and/or families. They are used to track and examine information passed on and discussed by you, your students, and their families. Such notes may include goal statements, plans for working on needs, reflections on growth, responses to questions, and/or families' suggestions for working with their children. Kept over time, they can be used to build collaborative relationships, fine-tune instruction, and determine how children are connecting with and meeting curricular goals.

Developmental checklists

Developmental checklists lay out a typical progression of development in areas such as early reading, concepts about print, writing, and spelling. Checklists can be used to examine children's growth along a continuum and are often designed to represent the district or state competencies children are expected to demonstrate. A somewhat cautious approach is recommended. Although checklists give you a general idea of where children might go next in their literacy-related thinking, they are often based on prescriptive sets of competencies. As such, they may prompt you to compare children's knowledge with the way things "should" be, rather than looking at the way they are (Luke and Freebody 1999). As you use checklists, keep in mind that children's developmental sequences are diverse, and keep your focus on what children *can* do. Also, consider developing your own checklists.

Self-evaluations

Self-evaluations include children's thoughts and ideas about their learning. They are used to help children think about what they have learned and why it is important; to reflect on their participation in projects and activities; and to set goals for future learning.

Family insights

Family members can play an important role in evaluation by reflecting with you on the progress they hope their children will make and have made, keeping logs of their children's literate activity, evaluating their children's experience with homework, and/or engaging in structured observations in your classroom (Pappas, Kiefer, and Levstik 1999). Family insights are collected through interviews, questionnaires, conferences, home-school journals, structured observations, anecdotal notes, and work samples from home.

LET ASSESSMENT EMERGE WITHIN THE CONTEXT OF CLASSROOM LIFE

The fourth guideline for comprehensive evaluation is to let assessment emerge within the context of classroom life. If your approach is to observe children in reading and writing situations that are socially and culturally relevant to them, you may not know exactly how you will assess until class projects are under way. Emergent assessment begins with a basic agenda and a set of possible tools but takes shape in response to children's activities and demonstrated needs. It varies depending on individual children's experiences, on ways of learning and communicating, and on family and community goals and values (King, Crenshaw, and Jenkins 1998; Tierney 2000).

For example, let's say that five of your students have developed an interest in writing and performing scripts. You might decide that this could be a good medium for evaluation. You probably can identify some basic tools that would help you assess what is happening. You might use anecdotal notes to reflect on how children are working in the group, who is willing to take risks, or how they are learning to address audience needs. You might make conference notes with the children to establish goals for their work and discuss their progress. If they are planning a readers theatre script, you might do a running record on one child as the group reads the text aloud. You might collect a draft of the script along with the final product to determine the kinds of mini-lessons that might be appropriate for this group.

With emergent assessment, you maintain a flexibility that allows you to observe what children know and can do in authentic learning situations. You capture both processes and products so that you can examine their literacy in action as well as the kinds of understandings their final products reveal. Emergent assessment helps "ensure that assessment practices keep up with teaching and learning rather than stagnate them by perpetuating the status quo or outdated views of literacy learning" (Tierney 2000, 117).

ENCOURAGE SELF-EVALUATION

The fifth guideline for comprehensive evaluation is to encourage self-evaluation. This is a critical aspect of effective teaching (Neuman, Copple, and Bredekamp 2000; Pappas, Kiefer, and Levstik 1999; Tierney 2000). "[To] be both accountable and empowered, readers and writers need to . . . be inquirers—researching their own selves, considering the consequences of their efforts, and evaluating the implications, worth, and ongoing usefulness of what they are doing or have done" (Tierney 2000, 116). Even very young children can inquire into their own learning by talking about what they have learned, reflecting on why it is important, helping establish goals for their growth, and collecting evidence for their growth.

To get children started with self-evaluation, arrange for them to keep folders of self-selected materials. Encourage them to include conference notes, goal statements, writing samples, and any other artifacts that lend evidence to their growth. Explain that their folders are to be used to track their progress and understand how they learn. They may also be used to plan for and lead conferences with families. Such processes help children develop insight into their own growth, develop a sense of accountability for their learning, and become independent, confident learners (Goodman 1996; Pappas, Kiefer, and Levstik 1999; Tierney 2000).

EVALUATE YOUR OWN PRACTICES

So far we have discussed ways of evaluating by asking questions about children's literate activity. The sixth guideline encourages you to ask questions about your own practices:

- Am I providing materials, conditions, and experiences that allow my students to show what they know?
- What might prevent them from showing what they know?
- How might my notions about literacy influence the opportunities I provide? Am I allowing for exploration of multiple literacies?
- How might my assumptions about children's knowledge influence what I do?

Examining your own assessment practices can help you understand and actively value all children's explorations; reach new ground in terms of what you assess and how you assess it; and ensure that you are making assessment a positive teaching and learning experience. If "the point of literacy is to reflect upon, and be empowered by, text rather than to be subjugated by it" (Tierney 2000, 116), then we have to keep our eyes open to our own potential biases and consciously work toward allowing multiple literacies to become a part of classroom life.

ACTIVELY USE YOUR KNOWLEDGE ABOUT HOW CHILDREN THINK AND LEARN

The seventh guideline for comprehensive evaluation focuses on the importance of developing and maintaining your own professional knowledge. Knowledge about learning theories and literacy development supports literacy evaluation in two major ways. First, it helps you know what to look for in terms of growth and to interpret what you see (Goodman 1984; Salinger 1998). Second, it "permits general predictions within an age range about what activities, materials, interactions or experiences will be . . . interesting, achievable, and also challenging to children" (Bredekamp and Copple 1997, 8–9). Thus, your professional knowledge guides your construction of children's literacy histories as well as your instructional decision making.

For example, many of Barb Huston's kindergartners begin the year writing with scribbles or using just the letters they know. Because Barb knows that many children progress from using scribbles to using random strings of letters to using their knowledge of letter-sound relationships she makes sure to collect pieces that show children's complex progression through these phases. In terms of instruction, her professional knowledge helps her know what and how to teach. For example, she could ask her scribble-writers to sound out words, but she knows that pushing for such a conceptual leap could prove fruitless and even frustrating. It is her professional knowledge that helps her know what to look for in her children's writing and what to emphasize in her teaching.

PULL EVERYTHING TOGETHER

The final guideline for comprehensive evaluation emphasizes the importance of pulling the data together for each child so that it can be used for reflection. Work folders, which may contain any of the tools for evaluation suggested earlier, are a device for organizing information into a manageable whole. It is important that work folders are organized using some rationale, so that you have something more than an ever-growing pile of "stuff." It is difficult to use a pile of "stuff" to track and interpret growth and to inform your instructional decision making. One way to organize is to start with a set of goals. These goals could be informed by best practices literature; standards set by national or state organizations; district or school curriculum guides; and/or the goals that you have established with your families and children. The goals serve as a framework for what to collect.

For example, the National Association for the Education of Young Children has a very broad set of goals: "The goals of the language and literacy program are for children to expand their ability to communicate through speaking, listening, reading, and writing and to develop the ability and disposition to acquire knowledge through reading" (Bredekamp and Copple 1997, 172). This statement could be turned into five work folder categories—speaking, listening, reading, writing, and reading dispositions—and pieces could be collected to help you examine and document growth in each. As you develop your framework, ask yourself, your families, and your children which goals are most relevant to your setting. The framework can be adjusted as necessary, and it's likely that you will refine your approach as you go.

The point of the work folder is to showcase and reflect on children's literacy and literacy growth. We want children and families to play an active role in this process and see the folder as a tool for affirming children's literacies, tracking and understanding their growth, and highlighting what they know and can do.

CONCLUSIONS

On one hand, working with the guidelines described in this chapter makes evaluation complex; on the other hand, "an approach to assessment with a new openness to complexity, respect for diversity, and interest in acquiring a rich picture of each student" (Tierney 2000, 124) may be the only way to adequately meet the needs of all children. We saw in Chapter 1 that children's familial, social, cultural, racial, linguistic, class, and gender identities all influence what they know and how they learn. To take sensitive action on this understanding requires that we struggle with complexity.

3 | INQUIRING INTO CHILDREN'S LITERACIES

> My journey was neither linear, solitary, nor sequential but was instead a messy process of coming to know myself, my questions, and my work. (Sims 1993, 284)

When reflecting on your teaching, or your students' learning, do you ever find yourself thinking, "I wonder why . . ." "I wonder how . . ." "What would happen if . . .?" "I wish I better understood . . ."? Teacher inquiry often begins with just such sentiments.

Cindy Schultz is a first-grade teacher who decided this year to try out partner reading. Early in the year, she had seen some of her children engaging in rich interactions while reading together and wondered if formally organizing partner reading might contribute to all of her children's developing literacies. She used inquiry to find out. To guide her inquiry, she formed a research question: "How does partner reading foster literacy development?" Two subquestions helped narrow her focus: "How do children interact when engaged in partner reading? . . . What practical support do they give one another" (Schultz 2000)?

Barb Huston, whom you met in Chapter 2, is an urban kindergarten teacher who has created a developmentally appropriate teaching-learning environment in her classroom. Her children regularly engage in authentic literacy events, collaborate often, and are instructed based on their individual needs. However, one area of Barb's teaching life has remained unsettling. Every so often, she hears, "Urban kids need more structure," "My child can't deal with choices," "Developmentally appropriate practices don't work." Because of statements such as these, Barb decided to take a closer look at the literacy learning and teaching in her classroom. She wanted to further develop her understandings about literacy and further her ability to advocate for developmentally sensitive teaching. To guide her inquiry, she developed a broad research question: What does development look like when developmentally appropriate practices are implemented in an urban kindergarten classroom (Huston 2000)?

In this chapter, we explore ways of taking your literacy "wonderings" (Bissex 1987) through an inquiry process that leads to improved teaching and learning, with Cindy's and Barb's work, as well as that of other teacher researchers, serving as examples of this process.

WHAT IS TEACHER INQUIRY?

Teacher inquiry is the systematic study of your practices and your students' learning. The process begins with a tension or wondering, as Cindy's and Barb's examples show, and then moves through a continuing cycle of observation, reflection, and action. For example, now that Cindy has put partner reading into place, she uses this time of day to observe and document her students' language and ways of interacting. Her documentation helps her reflect on her children's demonstrations of knowledge—to "re-see" and "re-search" those moments that shed light on their learning (Patterson 1996). Among other things, Cindy reflects on the reading strategies her children are using, asking herself, "What are they doing well? How are they solving problems? Where could they use help?" She takes action by using what she learns to help her children build on their strengths and to teach strategies they may not be using. And then, the cycle continues. She observes again, reflects again, and teaches again, with ever-growing insights into her students' developing competencies.

Teacher inquiry both draws from and informs theory. When Cindy observes partner reading, she draws on her theoretical knowledge of the strategies that effective readers use. She knows what strategies to look for and has a good idea of how children develop strategy knowledge. But, theory always takes new shape as it is applied to particular instances of teaching. Because each partner-reading situation is unique, Cindy is always building theory.

Any time a teacher applies theory to a particular, a new perspective results. This means that you are in a unique position to provide perspectives on teaching and learning that are not accessible to outside researchers. Because your research is embedded in practice and draws on understandings and ways of knowing that have developed out of the history in your classroom, you offer a distinctly exclusive contribution to the field's knowledge base (Cochran-Smith and Lytle 1993).

HOW DOES INQUIRY ENHANCE
TEACHING AND LEARNING?

Now let's take a deeper look at how inquiry enhances teaching and learning. We will focus on its ability to help you (1) fine-tune your teaching; (2) develop awareness of your children's literacies; and (3) critique your ideologies and assumptions (Cochran-Smith and Lytle 1993; Davis et al. 1999; Grady 1998; Isakson and Williams 1996; Mc-Farland and Stansell 1993).

A Way of Fine-Tuning

Inquiry is an exceptional tool for fine-tuning your teaching. We saw earlier that by engaging in the cycle of observation, reflection, and action, Cindy continually sharpens her teaching insights. What she learns from her observations during partner reading she uses to inform her teaching of reading throughout the day. Because she has taken time to learn about individual children's strategy use, her teaching is in tune with what they know.

But Cindy learns about much more than reading strategies as she observes her students. She learns about a range of things, including their ways of interacting and collaborating, their genre and topic preferences, how they make decisions, and how they build friendships. These learnings, too, help her fine-tune her daily teaching. For example, an analysis of her anecdotal notes revealed that some children were rarely chosen as partners and that when these students were the choosers, the people they chose often expressed disappointment. Cindy reflected that the unchosen children were those who had frequent trouble with relationships; she didn't feel she could help them by merely assigning partners. "What I really wanted," she reflected, "was to begin to change the way the other students felt about [these] children" (Schultz 2000, 49). And so began a new strand of inquiry.

You may be wondering, in an already busy teaching day, how you could possibly find the time and energy for inquiry. Undoubtedly, unless you have administrative, district, and even public support—in other words, time and opportunities for collaboration—you face a challenge. But, I have seen time and again that it is a doable challenge, and those who have taken it wouldn't trade for anything the new insights they've developed. If you approach inquiry as a way of fine-tuning, rather than adding to what you do already, it becomes part of the daily rhythms of the classroom. However, this may take some thoughtful reconsideration of what you do with your teaching time. Start to ask yourself—and others—whether the time you spend observing children for inquiry purposes could be a worthwhile and even essential part of your work as a teacher.

A Way of Developing Awareness

As you watch children with the purpose of understanding what they can do, you learn things about them that you never could have known without taking time to observe.

—Cindy

Another asset of inquiry is that it offers a systematic framework for developing your awareness of children's literacies. For example, as part of their inquiry processes, Cindy and Barb collect samples of children's work and document how they use written language, what they use it for, the strategies they use, and the interests they show. Teacher inquiry is about documenting both what children know and how they demonstrate and construct their knowledge. Such observation and documentation reveals children's strengths today and how they develop over time. "Revealing students' practices with language is critical activity for us as educators if we want to understand what our students learn from our teaching and how to build upon what they know" (Landis 1999, 210).

A Way of Critically Reflecting

I discovered that writing provokes thinking I otherwise would not do and prods me into uncomfortable areas that I would otherwise dismiss.

—Marne Isakson (Isakson and Williams 1996, 15)

A final asset of inquiry is its ability to provoke critical reflection on your own beliefs and assumptions. "Teachers bring to their research projects those beliefs and assumptions they hold as individuals at a particular moment within the context of all previous, current, and anticipated experiences" (Smith 1993, 39). Although often implicit, beliefs and assumptions have a great influence over what you do as a teacher. They shape the research questions you ask, the way you document knowledge, the kinds of knowledge you document, and the ways of knowing you promote. Therefore, beliefs and assumptions warrant careful attention. Inquiry elevates your awareness of your beliefs and assumptions by putting you in a position to consciously reflect on how your theory and practice inform each other; to purposefully discuss beliefs and practices with other teachers; and to critically evaluate what you are doing and why. As you design and carry out your project, asking yourself some particular questions can provoke these processes:

- Why am I doing _____ this way? How is this informed by theory? How does it inform theory?
- How do I know what my students know?
- What counts as knowledge in my classroom? Whose knowledge is recognized and valued both by the children and by me?
- What are my students' ways of knowing? How can I tell?
- How do I make use of their many literacies in my teaching?

Cochran-Smith and Lytle assert that "teachers and students negotiate what counts as knowledge in the classroom, who can have knowledge and how knowledge can be generated, challenged, and evaluated" (1993, 45). Teacher inquiry can help you systematically examine your ways of approaching knowledge issues and make any desired transformations in your teaching.

Many teacher researchers report stories of transformation. For example, Barb reflected, "Teacher research made me better. How? I became a better kidwatcher; I was able to better scaffold my students' writing. Before this research . . . I thought I understood how young children evolve into writers. Not true. . . . Observing my students' successes was enlightening whereas traditional assessments can be stressful and confusing . . ." (Huston 2000, 66). Christian Bush, taking field notes one day as her children were playing, said, "I get it now. This is how they learn about the functions of print." A student had just written a note to her requesting that her seat be moved. Other children were writing police and weather reports, sign-up sheets for soccer, biographies, scientific observations, and newspaper articles. Christian later reflected, "I didn't really understand how diverse and meaningful [functions] could be until then. Just like with children, sometimes it takes a simple moment of involvement to say, 'Aha! I get it.' "

Now let's take a look at some ideas for getting started with inquiry. We'll explore some basic techniques and tools here, and then, in Chapters 4 through 10, you will find inquiry ideas related to the topics in those chapters.

RECOGNIZING AND DEVELOPING INQUIRY QUESTIONS

A beginning step in inquiry is to form your issues, wonderings, and tensions into questions. "Teacher researchers look for questions . . . that can lead to a new vision of themselves as teachers and their students as learners" (Hubbard and Power 1993b, 21). This means that questions for inquiry arise from real classroom issues. What piques your interest? What makes you wonder? What would you like to fine-tune? Focus on issues that are real to you. Your research questions need to be important to you because they will guide you through the entire inquiry process.

Research questions help focus both your data collection and analysis, and if you are writing up your research, they can guide the organization of your report. Many research questions begin with *how* or *what*. *How* and *what* questions lead to descriptions of phenomena; description is the way that teacher researchers answer their questions (Hubbard and Power 1993a; 1999). When I frame a question, I play around with a lot of wordings and, most important, try to imagine myself answering that question. Given my circumstances, is it answerable? Is it something I can observe? Do I have access to the kind of data I need to answer it? Do I know the answer already?

Thinking about the following set of general questions may help you shape your own, more specific questions:

- What is happening here?
- What might explain what is happening?
- What use can I make of this information to support the learners in my classroom? (Isakson and Boody 1993, 34)

Consider also working with the following set of questions:

- What specifically am I doing in my classroom?
- What does it mean that I choose to do it this way?
- How are the students responding?
- What does it mean that they respond in these ways?
- How did I come to do and see things this way?
- What do I intend to change? How? (from Patterson and Shannon 1993, 8)

As you can see, teacher inquiry puts you in tune with your teaching practices and the learning that is happening in your classroom.

Your questions most likely will change throughout the inquiry cycle. First, it's hard to know exactly how to focus before you start collecting data. When my friend Liz had just defended her doctoral dissertation, she told me, "The committee said everything's fine. I just have to change my question." She explained that she really hadn't been answering the question she had initially intended to answer. Second, you will find that questions naturally evolve and change as your understandings evolve and change. Third, you may find that as your questions are framed, they are not quite answerable. Keep playing with the questions.

DEVELOPING A PLAN FOR INQUIRY

To organize for inquiry, try laying out a plan of action, which, of course, can change as you go. Figure 3–1 offers a general format for planning.

Research Question(s)	Include questions and any subquestions.
Rationale	How will this study benefit you and your children?
Readings	List important readings and what they will contribute.
Participants	Who will participate in the study? (If you are focusing on a subgroup, tell which children you will focus on and why.)
DataCollection/ Analysis	List the kinds of data you will collect; when you will collect and for how long; and how you might analyze.
Time Line	Sketch out a rough time line of events.

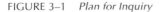

FIGURE 3–1 *Plan for Inquiry*

Keep family members informed throughout the process. Let them know what you are attempting to learn and how it will enhance teaching and learning in your classroom. When possible, invite them to make informal observations, help collect writing samples, answer interview or survey questions, and respond to tentative findings. Before beginning a project, consult with your principal or district office to determine the permission guidelines for your district.

READING AND WRITING FOR INQUIRY

Books are like worlds to me, and time after time they collide with my own world and, having done so, change it. (Fecho 1993, 265)

Like any other researchers, teacher researchers read extensively to inform their work. Given an already full schedule, extensive reading may seem like a colossal task, but you can make it manageable. You do not need to conduct a comprehensive review of literature to conduct inquiry, but it is important to read as much as you can. Once you have an area of interest, plan a trip to the library and come home with a few articles and a few good books. Or, if you haven't taken classes in a while, stop in a college bookstore and see what and who your colleagues are reading in classes. Reading a small number of pieces that speak to you and seem particularly relevant to your work is a good way to begin. Then, along the way, continue to seek pieces that directly inform the questions you are asking and contribute to the new visions you are developing.

Like any other reader, you read to meet your particular needs and objectives. We all approach our readings with certain goals in mind. Teachers typically read to examine theories and see how they hold up in light of their particular practices. But they don't just succumb to theory; they adapt it, rethink it, and filter it through their classrooms (Cochran-Smith and Lytle 1993; Fecho 1993). By working with theory as you teach, you transform it, giving it meaning and taking meaning from it. When it comes back out of your classroom, it is refined, and so is your thinking. As you read, continuously think about how this is happening.

You also read to find out about currently recommended practices and to see what other teachers are doing and why. Again, rather than taking everything you read into your classroom, you take the parts that you judge relevant to your work; you generalize selectively, as a result of your personal experiences (Donmoyer 1990). If you are writing up your findings, your readers will generalize in this same way—selectively. So, as you write, rather than making generalizations about all children, describe what *your* children do, and readers can make their own generalizations.

If you are writing a literature review as part of a research report (or even if you aren't), asking yourself a few guiding questions as you read journals and books may help you organize your thinking and pull together some useful information:

- What theories contribute to my work? How do they hold up in my classroom?
- What are other teachers doing in my area of study? Why are they doing it this way? What research questions are being asked in their classrooms? What methods are being used to answer the questions? What has been found? What are the implications?
- How do these findings connect with other findings?
- How does all of this inform my work and my thinking?

GATHERING AND ANALYZING DATA

Many of the tools you use for gathering inquiry data are the same as you use for assessment and evaluation. As you conduct inquiry, you may simply have in mind different questions or a different focus. As Cindy points out, "data gathering is really something you do *already*. You just do it more so with inquiry, and with more structure and dedicated time. But, it's *all* about getting to know your students better, seeing what they know and how they use it, and seeing how they learn best." We look first at some tools for gathering data and then at some tools for analyzing it.

Field Notes

Field notes serve as a major tool for collecting inquiry data. They can be used for many purposes: to record writing, reading, talk, actions, behaviors, strategies, or questions. Some teachers write field notes in folders or binders; some use clipboards; some carry sticky notes in their pockets. Christian suggests placing sticky notes on an old wall or desk calendar and assigning each child a number on the calendar to keep track of who needs to be observed.

Field notes typically include both descriptive material (verbatim accounts of what you observe) and interpretive material (your reflections). Figure 3–2 shows an example from Christian's notes taken during a literature circle. You can see how both descriptive and interpretive notes inform the inquiry cycle. Both help her understand how her children use language to construct meaning, and both help her fine-tune her teaching.

Amelia- my grama and grapa cam to vist.

A: <u>My grandma and grandpa came to visit</u>. Does anyone
        have a question?
Max: How long did it take you to write?
A: I'm not sure. 5 or 6 or 7 minutes. Does anybody want
        to know about the pictures? Does anybody want to know
        who these people are?
Evan: I do.
A: Mom, Grandpa, Grandma and- uh-oh. I forgot my dad.
        I'd better put him in.

* Amelia is using vocabulary from the story.

* It seems like the children are picking up the vocab. auditorially and using it
before I show it to them. After I show them on the chart and they see it will their
writing change? Will they attempt to use conventional spelling?

FIGURE 3–2   *Christian's Literature Circle Notes*

To keep descriptions separate from interpretations, try using an as-
terisk (as Christian does), parentheses, or a column for each type of
note. As an important rule of thumb, the notes you collect should be
useful to you; they should help you answer your questions, reflect on
your teaching, learn about your students, and/or track students' growth.

Cindy usually takes field notes as her students partner read, but
sometimes she fills in information later. She visits each pair of readers
for a few minutes each day and sometimes observes from afar. Because
she is trying to learn how children interact with and support one another
during partner reading, her notes are focused on social and intellectual
exchanges between children. As Barb takes notes (remember, her goal is
to characterize development), she focuses on children's demonstrations
of what they know, their interests, and their views of themselves as writers. Cindy, Barb, and Christian each have a different focus as they take
notes because they are interested in learning different things. What is
important is that their notes are focused on what they are trying to learn.

A well-worded question will help you focus. For example, think
about the following question: Does talk during journal writing help
children develop literacy? This question does not suggest a particular
focus, and it will ultimately result in a yes or no answer. Remember that
your question should help you describe phenomena. Changing the
wording to What do my children talk about during journal writing? or
What information do they share while writing? gives you more focus
and leads you toward descriptions that can inform your teaching. As

you begin to collect data, keep playing with your questions, and know that they are likely to evolve.

You may find that it is easiest to take field notes when children are working collaboratively, without a great deal of assistance from you. Many teachers choose to observe as children are writing, working on projects, discussing literature, working in centers, or reading in pairs. If your language and actions are central to the data you need to collect, you may wish to try audio- and videotapes.

Audiotapes and Videotapes

Audio- and videotapes offer explicit portraits of your classroom that may be reviewed again and again. They are particularly useful if you want to explore brief events in detail. Rather than doing complete transcriptions, you may wish to transcribe some sections and review and take notes on others. Sally Meyer (1998), a preschool special education teacher, uses videotapes to inquire into the functions of oral language her children use as they play. She transcribes some of the notes word for word, and takes brief notes on others, just enough to help her identify which functions are being explored.

Work Samples

Work samples are another important source of data. They can include just about anything your children produce: writing, drawings, paintings, webs, sculptures, sketches, products from collaborative projects, or materials produced during play. Christian, to understand what her children do during literature circles, collects individual literature response journals as well as charts, webs, and illustrations that the groups produce together. Combined with her field notes, these materials provide a good picture of the knowledge her children are constructing and the progress they are making. Barb, to understand her students' writing development, collects all kinds of writing samples.

Checklists

Checklists are another way to collect data. Checklists can focus on anything from reading and writing strategies, to language functions, to ways of participating in groups. Taking anecdotal notes on the checklist helps round out what a simple check means. It is important that you create your own checklists. Otherwise, the items become prescriptive, and teaching and learning begin to lean in a direction that may not be relevant for your children or answering your questions.

Barb uses a checklist to track and make sense of the concepts of print her children explore. On it, she includes book concepts, reading concepts, word and letter concepts, and punctuation. The checklist reminds her of what to look for as she observes and helps her track the range of concepts her children are exploring. Many teachers, once they have thought through and become familiar with checklist items, abandon them in favor of narrative summaries (Short, Harste, and Burke 1996).

Interviews and Surveys

Interviewing or surveying students and their family members can help you develop insight into their viewpoints and perspectives. Cindy reserves time for planned, one-question interviews to understand her children's attitudes toward partner reading, their preferences for partners, and what they value in partners' ways of interacting. Children's answers help her confirm what she observes. Interviews can also be very informal, conducted on the spot. For example, "How did you two decide to work together today?" "When you are reading, what makes you decide to stop and talk about the book?" "What did you do when you got stuck on that word?" Responses to such questions become part of the field notes. Even if you are not conducting an interview, talking with students about their learning on a daily basis helps you and them develop important insights.

As part of her literature circle inquiry, Christian conducts whole-class interviews. She asks a preplanned question and follows individual responses with probing and further questioning. For example:

Christian: What went well in your literature circles today?
      Jay: We had smooth writing and not a lot of capitals.
Christian: Tell us what smooth writing is, in case there are people here who don't know.
      Jay: It means—when writing—[Shows a flowing movement with his hand] it's just like that and has no mess-ups.

Christian typically gets ten or twelve perspectives when she asks such questions. If several children respond like Jay, she may conclude that smooth writing is important, and she may want to find out why. Christian also regularly asks what didn't go well. Her questions enable her to reflect on and fine-tune her instruction. Figure 3–3 shows a coded response to one of Christian's questions.

Coding

Coding is a way to organize, reflect on, and make sense of your data. It typically begins with looking for patterns and teasing out interesting trends (Guba and Lincoln 1981). As you read through your data, certain words, behaviors, events, or ways of thinking will begin to repeat themselves and stand out to you (Bogdan and Biklen 1998). These are your coding categories. As they begin to stand out, create one- or two-word descriptors for them, as in Christian's example. If you find that you have too many categories, either prioritize them by importance

Christian:	What didn't go well in your literature circles today? What would you like to change?	
Hailey:	Some people in our group were talking when they shouldn't have been.	*out of turn talk*
Archie:	And the noise level should stay down.	*noise*
Zeke:	Somebody had bad questions.	*questions*
Christian:	Can you tell us what you mean?	
Zeke:	They need to have a better question than the bad one- the kind that hurts people's feelings. The person that was reading had bad feelings because it was a bad question.	
Amelia:	Sometimes some people were talking so sometimes we had to stop and wait for them to give us our attention.	*out-of-turn talk*
Stuart:	I don't like when a lot of people take a lot of questions because then we can't hear everybody's story.	*time*
Jake:	Some people had a lot of [silly] questions like, "Two thousand? Two million?" They <u>should</u> say, like, "Did you have fun being a pirate."	*questions*
Jay:	Yeah, I didn't like when people were saying goofy questions like, "Did you ever live in a watermelon's village?"	*questions*

FIGURE 3–3 *A Coded Interview Response*

(Guba and Lincoln 1981) or combine them until you feel you have a workable set.

In Figure 3–3, we see a coded interview question. Figure 3–4 shows a coded section of field notes taken by Christian that was used to understand the functions that written language serve in her students' play.

Another option for coding is to begin with an already-existing set of categories. For example, Sally Meyer, who, as we saw earlier, uses videotapes to examine her preschoolers' oral language, uses Halliday's (1975) functions of oral language to code her data (Meyer 1998). Figure 3–5 shows how a grid provides a helpful visual for her analysis. Sally lists language functions across the top and field note page numbers down the left side of the grid. She places a check in each box of the grid to easily locate instances of each function. This allows her to see which, and how often, functions are used. Remember, Sally also transcribes sections of videotapes to reflect in more detail on how her children use language functions.

Collecting and analyzing classroom data will lead you to develop myriad new understandings. When you develop new teaching understandings,

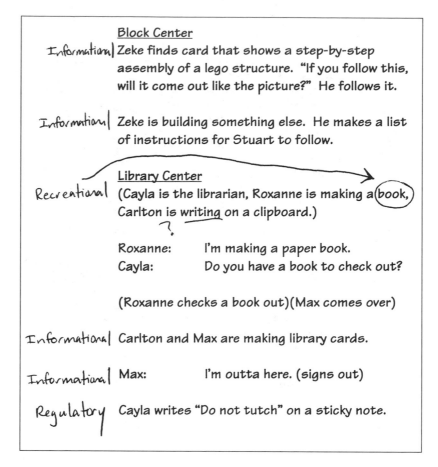

Block Center

Information Zeke finds card that shows a step-by-step assembly of a lego structure. "If you follow this, will it come out like the picture?" He follows it.

Information Zeke is building something else. He makes a list of instructions for Stuart to follow.

Library Center

Recreational (Cayla is the librarian, Roxanne is making a book, Carlton is writing on a clipboard.)

Roxanne: I'm making a paper book.
Cayla: Do you have a book to check out?

(Roxanne checks a book out)(Max comes over)

Informational Carlton and Max are making library cards.

Informational Max: I'm outta here. (signs out)

Regulatory Cayla writes "Do not tutch" on a sticky note.

FIGURE 3–4   *Coded Field Notes*

you are in a strong position to "write a new identity" for yourself and take new action (Short, Harste, and Burke 1996, 369). Go ahead and become the teacher that your inquiry suggests you can be. Put your new ways of teaching and viewing children permanently into place. Continue your cycle of inquiry. Help others discover for themselves what you have learned through your inquiry. And in so doing, you will continue to grow as a teacher.

SHARING YOUR FINDINGS

As your new identity reveals itself to others, you may find that they are interested in what you have been doing. It is likely that one of your major goals is to develop a principled set of ideas that fosters the improvement of learning in your classroom. Thus, you and your children

9C notes/tape	Instrumental	Regulatory	Interactional	Personal	Heuristic	Imaginative	Informative	Appendix pg 5
1/29-39						✓		
-40					✓	✓		
-41							✓	
-42					✓-A			
-43						✓	✓	
-44	✓					✓		
-45							✓	
-46		✓				✓		
-47			✓			✓		
-48						✓	✓	
-49						✓	✓	
-50		✓				✓		
-51						✓	✓	
-52	✓				✓			
-53			✓					
-54			✓			✓		
-55					✓	✓		
-56						✓	✓	
-57			✓					
	2	3	4	0	3/1	13	6/1	33

FIGURE 3–5   *A Teacher-Developed Analysis Grid*

are likely to be the primary beneficiaries, and sharing your findings may not be as significant to you as the value of your experiences themselves (Fischer et al. 2000; Pappas, Kiefer, and Levstik 1999). However, several audiences may benefit from knowing about your work, and sharing it can be an act of advocacy.

Your students and their families will be delighted to be privy to summative reports of your findings. Teachers I know have shared their findings through captioned photo albums, freestanding tri-fold boards, posters, bulletin boards, one-page written reports, and newsletters.

Study groups and/or other teachers may also want to read your work. A second-grade teacher in Cindy's building read a final report from Cindy's research and found it useful and encouraging. This teacher had used partner reading for years and knew it was worthwhile, but she hadn't gathered evidence that could help her articulate why. Cindy's work helped her do so, but this teacher also had perspectives that gave Cindy new insights. Both benefited from the exchange. Even if you can find only one other person with whom to share, think, and inquire, bouncing around ideas and constructing knowledge together may prevent the sense of isolation that teacher researchers often feel, and it could make a world of difference in what you learn. Too often, teacher work is viewed by administrators, families, and even some teachers as something that happens only when you are with children in the classroom, rather than when you are talking with other teachers (Cochran-Smith and Lytle 1993). For many, little time is available for collaboration. If you find yourself in this situation, you may wish to begin a dialogue with your colleagues and administrators to work toward an institutional commitment to inquiry in your setting.

The media, whether district- or community-based, can be an excellent venue for sharing your work. Whether through special interest reports or editorials, media can get word out to families and the public about the inquiries happening in classrooms and can be a tool for gaining support. Anything you do to counteract the negative views of education that are often portrayed by the media is an act of advocacy for children.

Boards of education and building administrators may also be interested in your work. If your inquiry sheds light on the kinds of instruction or curricula that help children learn, or on what teachers need to do their jobs well, it just might be worth sharing. Unfortunately, teacher researchers are often excluded from the discourse that surrounds educational decision making (Cochran-Smith and Lytle 1993; Routman 2000). You've heard it: "I know this isn't the best way, but our district is trying it." "We're required to do this computer program, but my kids are choosing books they don't care about and reading to answer multiple-choice questions." "My principal said she doesn't want to see kids inventing spellings." Teacher inquiry is a step toward advocating for children and breaking down these barriers, even if it helps create support only in your own classroom for what you know is best. However, if you have developed insights from working with your children, you have important knowledge worth sharing.

Wider audiences may also be interested in your work. Many state and national conferences include poster sessions for informally sharing research. Posters, typically put together on freestanding tri-fold boards, highlight the rationale for conducting the study, methods of data collection and analysis, and major findings and conclusions. Other options at state and national conferences include roundtable discussions or more formal sessions ranging from fifteen minutes to an hour and fifteen minutes. Professional journals are another medium for sharing your work. *Language Arts*, *The Reading Teacher*, and *Young Children* are widely read and accept numerous pieces from teachers.

Do share your findings in some way. I know of no researchers who are more in tune with the ways in which children think and learn than teacher researchers. Who could be in a better position to understand children's learning? You have observed children, documented their knowledge and ways of knowing, and used your professional knowledge to reflect and draw conclusions. Your knowledge, however you decide to use it, is of value to the field.

PART 2

Literacy Engagements

Chapters 4 through 10 are full of literacy engagements—classroom experiences for supporting children's literacy growth. The engagements are designed to help you create an environment in which children may use their "hundred languages" or "multiple sign systems" to construct and demonstrate their literacy knowledge (Houck 1997). This means using story, discussion, listening, writing, drawing, painting, carpentry, collage, sculpture, block construction, dance, movement, drama, music, and more to communicate, play around with, and develop literacy-related understandings.

A multiple sign system approach makes sense when it comes to teaching and learning. First, it draws on multiple domains and intelligences, allowing all children to use their strengths as they learn, as well as to develop strengths in new areas. Second, the act of shifting thinking from one sign system to another, called transmediating, "is intellectual functioning of a very high order" (Hendrick 1997, 50; Short, Harste, and Burke 1996). As children interpret through sculpture or movement what they have listened to in a book, or as they interpret through talk or writing what they have seen in a piece of art, they mentally reconfigure what they know, creating for themselves a new way of seeing.

Recent research (Morrow et al. 1999; Koskinen et al. 1999) has shown that exemplary literacy instruction involves children in a variety of literacy events including silent, oral, shared, independent, collaborative, performed, and guided reading; independent, collaborative, and guided writing; and wordplay and word analysis. Content area connections (science, math, social studies, physical and health education) are pursued through all of the language arts. The literacy engagements discussed in this section address all of these elements.

As you work with the engagements, it will be important to find ways to connect them with your curriculum and classroom. For example, if you try literature circles (Chapter 7) or readers theatre (Chapter 8), use these engagements to help your children explore curriculum and inquiries that are already going on in your classroom. If you use them in an isolated fashion, they may teach children skills and strategies for reading and writing, which is not a bad thing. But if you connect them with other curricular efforts, they are most likely to help your children not only develop their reading and writing but also use their knowledge to understand and act upon the world.

Along with literacy engagements, each chapter includes ideas for teacher inquiry. Chapter 3 described the tools you would need to engage in inquiry; each of the following chapters gives examples of inquiry directions you might take as you work with the specific engagements.

4 | EXPLORING CHILDREN'S LITERATURE

Kiara: [Browsing through a book about insects] Mrs. Bush, how come the mother bird brings them the food—and there's bird breath on it and slobber on it—and they eat it?

Christian: [Looking at the book] Because baby birds can't get food, and that's how she feeds them.

Kiara: You mean she cuts it up in pieces?

Christian: No. [Pointing to picture] See? She just brings it up for them.

The National Association for the Education of Young Children maintains that appropriate curriculum "promotes the development of knowledge and understanding, processes and skills, as well as the dispositions to use and apply skills and to go on learning" (Bredekamp and Copple 1997, 20). We begin this chapter by exploring how these characteristics of quality can be used to shape a literature-based curriculum. Then, keeping these characteristics in mind, we will look at some ways to use literature as a tool for facilitating literacy and content knowledge.

KNOWLEDGE AND UNDERSTANDING

Archie: [Listening to a biography of Helen Keller] Is Helen Keller going to, like, how could she see roses to pick them and smell them?

Using literature to foster the development of knowledge and understanding requires that we focus our use of books on more than just teaching children to read. We must also use books as tools for helping children learn about the world. Through books, children can explore science, social studies, and math concepts, develop multicultural understandings, learn how to do and make things, and learn more about topics of personal interest. Learning from books becomes customary when a program offers children the flexibility to read, listen, and be instructed in areas that are interesting and familiar to them. An appropriate curriculum "builds upon what children already know and are able to do (activating prior knowledge) to consolidate their learning and to foster their acquisition of new concepts and skills" (Bredekamp and Copple 1997, 20). It makes sense, then, to develop a collection of books that reflects a wide variety of topics so that all of your children can personally connect with them and use their prior knowledge as a starting point for building new concepts and interests.

Of course, books must also be available for children to explore whole-class topics, whether they are studied because they are of importance to your group of children and your community or because they are a required part of your curriculum. Whole-class topics provide a context for children to construct curricular concepts together and an opportunity for you to model how experts learn from books.

Including a variety of genres is important to facilitating knowledge and understanding, too. Fiction provides a delightful, contextualized way for children to learn about all kinds of things. Unfortunately, most of the material read by young children in classrooms *is* fiction, with little effort made to teach them to read nonfiction (Duke 2000; Tonjes, Wolpow, and Zintz 1999). As a result, children miss out on reading about many topics and do not develop the knowledge or dispositions to effectively read nonfiction. Reading in varied genres helps children develop the capacity to learn all kinds of things, from all kinds of text.

PROCESSES AND SKILLS

Mitchell: [Discussing insect body parts] Do *we* have three body parts?
Christian: Good question. Do we have a head? Abdomen? You know, I really don't know. We *have* these parts, but they're all connected. How could we find out?
Mitchell: Research.

Depending on your children's experience and knowledge, you can use literature and literature response to help them develop myriad processes and skills. For example, literature can be used to support children's development of reading strategies. As children read, help them acquire strategies such as predicting, confirming, disconfirming, self-correcting, and monitoring comprehension. Also promote their automatic word recognition, word identification, and use of picture clues.

You can also use literature to help children learn to negotiate meaning. Focus on processes known to be used by effective readers, such as reading and listening with a purpose; predicting outcomes, drawing conclusions, inferencing; synthesizing; determining what's important; creating mental images; problem-solving; self-questioning; interpreting illustrations; using information such as title pages, tables of contents, headings, bold print, glossaries, charts, photographs, maps and indexes; and making text-to-self, text-to-world, and text-to-text connections

(Keene and Zimmermann 1997). Be sure to teach children how book-handling behaviors for fiction and nonfiction differ. Fiction readers typically read a book cover to cover. Nonfiction readers may read to answer particular questions, to satisfy a general curiosity (Tower 2000), or to learn how to do something. Prior knowledge needs differ as well. With fiction, meaning construction is enhanced when children activate prior knowledge about the story line. With nonfiction, meaning is enhanced when they focus on the topic, the central ideas, and the text structure (Cooper 2000).

Finally, you can introduce strategies, processes, and skills for response. *Visual response*, such as drawing, painting, modeling, or sculpting, is especially important in early childhood classrooms because it provides children with opportunities to construct understanding about books and "to communicate what they are thinking at any stage of knowing. Before they can . . . write [readable text] children are encouraged to express their understandings in symbolic languages they *can* use" (Houck 1997, 33–34). Working multiple times with the same media helps children develop the skills necessary to use them for expressive purposes. *Written response*, such as predicting, reflecting, and retelling, is equally important because it, too, compels children to revisit their thinking and organize it in a new way. Like visual response, writing is a way of knowing for children, even before adults can read what they have to say! *Drama* (reenacting, puppet shows) is another way of constructing and expressing knowledge. As children contextualize what they have read for a new audience and present it through their own language, they see in new ways. *Talk* is perhaps the most natural format response for children. Talk allows children to articulate impressions, clarify for themselves and you what they have understood, and use others' interpretations and ideas to build their knowledge.

DISPOSITIONS

Amelia: I love *No, David!* I have this book at home, and my dad's name is David.

Lastly, we want to ensure that children's experiences with literature support their development of healthy learning dispositions. In terms of a literature curriculum, we can think of dispositions as attitudes, perspectives, understandings, and preferences that shape children's approaches to literature, their sense of what it can do for them, and their ideas about how to use it in their worlds. Dispositions carry a lot of weight. Because they have such a powerful influence over what children do with books, we want to ensure that they are positive, characterized by an emotional engagement with literature that enables learning to happen, including being receptive to the skills needed to learn.

Children who are emotionally engaged enjoy listening to and reading books. They understand that literature can enhance, influence, and inform their personal and academic lives. One way to help students become emotionally engaged is to bring the stories of *all* children into the classroom. Does your classroom library include stories about children with special talents, needs, and interests? Does it include books representing varied family structures and economic situations? Does it include children of color; children who speak more than one language; and children from other countries? Do your students relate to these characters? Do they find the plots socially relevant? It is also important that your collection offer a variety of topics and genres. For all children to find books that appeal, variety is key. Finally, it is important to ensure that your children understand what they are listening to and reading. Offering numerous ways of exploring books along with well-designed process and skill instruction, supports children's understanding. An appropriate book curriculum is "socially relevant, intellectually engaging, and personally meaningful to children" (Bredekamp and Copple 1997, 20). It draws children into reading, keeps them interested, and keeps them wanting to read more.

The following engagements incorporate the characteristics of a quality literature program.

STRATEGIES FOR READING A PICTURE BOOK

Before Reading

Look at the cover. Begin by asking your children to describe the information the cover provides. Ask: "What do you see here? What does this cover tell us? What clues does it give for what might be inside?"

Talk about pictures and text. Next, turn through the pages, inviting children to describe what they see in the pictures, the text, and the text format. Picture and text talks give children a general sense of what they are about to read and familiarize them with the language and vocabulary they will encounter (Clay 1985).

Activate prior knowledge. Continue by inviting the children to read the title and examine the illustrations again. Ask whether they think the book is fiction or nonfiction. With fiction, invite children to predict and discuss what they think will happen in the story. With nonfiction, invite them to predict and discuss what they think they will learn (Cooper 2000).

Personal connections. To help your children personally connect with the book, ask them about the experiences they've had with the topic at hand. Allow for children's personal stories to be a way of connecting with literature.

Set a purpose. Engage children in a general discussion about the topic of the book, particularly if it's nonfiction. Ask what they know about the topic and what they hope to learn. Having a purpose helps readers focus on what they want to learn and connect new understandings to old knowledge (Cooper 2000). Keep in mind that children are very good at setting their own purposes; the purpose for reading does not have to come from you.

During Reading

Make predictions. Read aloud part of the book, stopping at a strategic point. Invite children to discuss, write about, or create a visual representation of how the piece might end, or of what they think might come next. Then, read further, allowing children to confirm or disconfirm their predictions. Predicting helps readers to stay focused on content and to explore the ways in which authors structure their writing.

Pause and reflect. Invite students to listen to the book as they sit in small groups, each with a large piece of paper in the middle. Occasionally, stop reading and invite children to write or draw graffiti (observations and reflections). Early on, model or give specific suggestions, such as "Write or draw about something you have learned so far/found interesting/noticed about the illustrations" and so on. After the reading, allow children to use their graffiti either as a discussion starter or to create a new, unified piece such as a web or a chart. The common focus provides a good context for constructing knowledge together (Short, Harste, and Burke 1996).

Create mental images. Help children take their experiences with books to a deeper level by encouraging them to occasionally pause to consider the sights, sounds, smells, tastes and physical sensations that come to mind as a result of the listening or reading.

Synthesize and summarize. Help children learn to use brief syntheses and summaries to enhance and monitor their comprehension. First, team them up for a read-aloud with you. As you read, occasionally pause to model the way effective readers occasionally synthesize or think through the gist of what they have read so far. Point out that synthesizing helps readers track their comprehension and better understand text. Then, as you read subsequent texts, invite teams to synthesize or summarize together what they have heard and learned so far. Although you will be reading to the whole class, choose two to four children to observe each time you engage in this activity. Use anecdotal notes to document and evaluate their language.

Conduct oral cloze. After reading and enjoying a predictable big book with children, read it again while pointing to the words. As you read, occasionally pause, so that children may fill in missing words or phrases. You may want to cover words or phrases with a sticky note or your hand. For example, "Brown bear, brown bear, what do you see? I see a red bird looking at _____" (Martin 1967). When the children say "me," ask them how they knew the word. Have a little fun: "I don't know . . . it starts with an *m*. Do you still think it's *me*?" Or, "Let me uncover the first letter . . . It's an *m*. Do you still think it's *me*?"

Oral cloze can also be used with less predictable language structures. For example, "The hole had twigs and leaves and owl _____ in it" (Waddell 1992). Looking at such a sentence with children, ask them to hypothesize about the missing word. Asking, "What would make sense?" and "If you read on, can you figure out what the word might be?" draws on semantic knowledge. Asking "What would sound right?" draws on syntactic knowledge. Then, showing the first letter (*f*) and asking, "Can we confirm our prediction, or should we make a new guess?" draws on graphophonic knowledge. Hence, oral cloze supports children's use of cueing systems, facilitates their letter and phonics knowledge, and helps them use prediction as a strategy for reading. Point out to children that these strategies can help them when they are reading independently.

After Reading

Make personal connections. As you read, help children personally connect with literature by modeling your own connections and helping them make their own. Then, after reading, invite them to discuss, write, or construct a visual artifact in response to directions such as: "Talk about/write about/show (one of the following): what you are thinking or feeling now that you've heard this text/a part of the story you liked/a connection between what we've read and your own life/a particular character you identified with/something you have learned."

Make text-to-text connections. Invite students to use a three-column chart (Book 1/Book 2/Both) to reflect on similarities between two texts. A Venn diagram may also be used. Exploring connections between texts helps children build their concepts about the world (Keene and Zimmermann 1997).

Sketch to stretch. Invite students to read or listen to a selection and then draw a picture of what it means to them. Rather than sketching a particular event, children portray the meaning of the story or a personal connection they have made. In small groups, participants first guess at possible meanings, then listen to the sketcher tell what he or she had in mind (Short, Harste, and Burke 1996).

Create reenactments. Invite children to reenact a story you have read to the class. Reenactments allow children to try on the roles of various characters and personalities and to thereby develop insights into their feelings, their motivations, and the ways in which they change over time. To introduce reenactment, read your children a story and reenact it together. A story web or flow map may help guide you. Once your children know the process, encourage them to do their own reenactments. Simple costumes may help them get into character.

Perform retellings. Retellings are closely related to reenactments but are somewhat more formal and do not always involve dramatization. Like reenactments, retellings help children rethink their way through a text, thereby enhancing their understandings. To introduce the following forms of retelling, (1) model your own retellings, thinking aloud about how you decide what to tell and (2) engage with your children in whole-class retellings.

> *Visual retellings* are created through drawing, painting, coloring, or sculpting. They may be used with fiction or nonfiction. Captions or a narrative may be added and read chorally as a class, or by teams, as a center choice.
>
> *Story webs* are used to organize and re-present fiction. Figure 4–1 shows a simple story web laying out the characters, setting, problem, and resolution for *Harry the Dirty Dog* (Zion 1956).
>
> *Exposition webs* are used to retell nonfiction events. To create a web, ask children what they learned from the book. As you record their responses, categorize them in some meaningful way (what insects look like/what insects eat).
>
> *Flow maps* are used to retell or revisit a sequenced story or a nonfiction event. Children may create a flow map by drawing boxes on a piece of paper and using arrows to connect them, or by working with half-sheets of paper that will eventually be stapled together. Key events are drawn or written in each box.
>
> *Prop retellings* enable children to draw on concrete, visual information as they structure and restructure their thinking. Children can make their own props with paper, colored pencils, crayons, chalk, paint, or markers, or you can provide the props. Laminate the pieces and allow children to fasten self-stick Velcro (for felt boards) or strip magnets (for cookie sheets or magnetic boards) to the back. Or, to create puppets, attach paper characters to popsicle sticks. Make materials available for children to retell during play or center times.

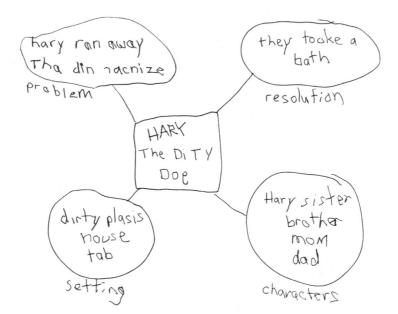

FIGURE 4–1 *Story Web for* Harry the Dirty Dog. *Problem: Harry ran away. They didn't recognize. Resolution: They took a bath. Setting: Dirty places, house, tub. Characters: Harry, sister, brother, mom, dad.*

In assessing story retellings, listen for reference to the characters, the setting, the problem, and the resolution and notice whether the sequence of events is maintained. With nonfiction, listen for an understanding of key concepts presented in the text. However, young children need experience with retelling predictable texts—those with clear plot structures, repetitive phrases, familiar characters, and familiar sequences—before they can move into retelling more complex text and before retelling can be used as a tool for evaluation (Morrow 1997). You can help children learn to retell by modeling and by retelling stories together, using any of the techniques described previously. Some predictable stories for helping children learn to retell include the following:

Goldilocks and the Three Bears, by James Marshall
The Three Little Pigs, by Paul Galdone
The Three Billy Goats Gruff, by Paul Galdone
The Very Busy Spider, by Eric Carle
Brown Bear, Brown Bear, What Do You See?, by Bill Martin Jr.
Polar Bear, Polar Bear, What Do You Hear?, by Bill Martin Jr.
Why Bear Has a Short Tail, by Cass Hollander
Who's in Rabbit's House?, by Verna Aardema
Why Mosquitoes Buzz in People's Ears, by Verna Aardema
The Mitten, by Jan Brett
Bit by Bit, by Steve Sanfield

Play. After sharing a book with your children, invite them to gather props to play with what they've read. Playing with ideas from books helps children contextualize them and see them in new ways. Following are examples of book-play sets to give you an idea of the kinds of materials you or your children might match with books.

Too Many Tamales, by Gary Soto
As Maria helps make tamales, she tries on her mother's ring, which turns up missing.
Materials: Play dough, bowls and platters, toy rings.

Rumplestiltskin, by Paul Zelinsky
Crafty little Rumplestiltskin helps the miller's daughter spin gold—in exchange for her first-born child.
Materials: Spools, golden yarn, wooden spoons, toy necklaces, rings, dolls, and masks for costumes (for miller, miller's daughter, king, Rumplestiltskin, servant). Children may make their own masks.

A House for Hermit Crab, by Eric Carle
Hermit Crab outgrows his old shell, moves into a new one, and is joined by a host of sea creatures.
Materials: Large boxes (for Hermit Crab's shell or for the ocean), paper and fabric scraps, markers, crayons, tape, glue (for making sea creatures or decorating the boxes).

Stone Soup, by Marcia Brown
Three soldiers outwit the people of a little village, convincing them to stir up a fine feast for all.
Materials: A large pot, a ladle, and plastic vegetables (or provide construction paper for children to create their own vegetables).

Tillie and the Wall, by Leo Lionni
A little mouse seeks to discover what is on the other side of a stone wall.
Materials: Sand tub or table, blocks, toy mice.

Dolphin's First Day, by Kathleen Weidner Zoehfeld
The story of a dolphin's first day of life.
Materials: Water tub or table, toy dolphins.

Ibis: A True Whale Story, by John Himmelman
A young whale is entangled by a fishing net.
Materials: Water tub or table, toy boats, toy whales, pieces of netting.

The Ladybug and Other Insects, by Gallimard Jeunesse and Pascale de Bourgoing
A basic introduction to ladybugs.
Materials: Play dough, pipe cleaners, and construction paper for making insect models; popsicle sticks and toothpicks for carving; masking tape and pens for labeling.

Weather Words, by Gail Gibbons
Learn about weather and the words used to describe it.
Materials: Weather words (magnetic or felt), a hand pointer for reporting the weather, materials for making new words and writing reports.

Bread, Bread, Bread, by Ann Morris
Learn about bread from all over the world.
Materials: Aprons, play dough, rolling pins, pans, empty plastic seasoning containers, empty containers labeled *flour*, *salt*, *yeast*, and *sugar*.

TASTES AND PREFERENCES

Personally connecting with literature draws children into reading, promotes their critical and reflective response, and helps them understand text better (Cullinan and Galda 1998; Keene and Zimmermann 1997). A good way to foster personal connections is to help children develop their tastes and preferences. Consider the following options.

Advertisements. Invite children to each create a brochure, a poster, or a television commercial to advertise a favorite book or set of books to the class. Allow time for sharing.

Book reviews. Read several books and their reviews with children and then write one together as a class. Then, invite children to write their own. Give them time to browse the class library for books they have read and liked—or not liked. Individual reviews could be included in a class newsletter or magazine or a compiled set could be bound together and placed in the class library. Allow time for sharing.

Polls. Invite children to conduct opinion polls. Equip each team of two with a list of initials or names of all the children in the class. Pollsters write their question on the page, with the possible answer choices. For example, "Which genre do you prefer—fiction or poetry?" When interviewers ask a classmate the poll question, they circle his or her initials to keep track of whom they have polled and write them again under the choice the classmate has made. This process continues until all initials are circled (Graves 1989). Children may conduct polls about preferred books, genres, authors, topics, or response activities. You can use the information to form groups based on the preferences they have indicated.

EXAMINING CHARACTERS AND PERSONALITIES

When children purposefully study fictional characters and real personalities they develop insight into their perspectives, points of view, and ways of thinking about the world.

Character/personality webs. After reading or listening to a text, make a web that describes a particular character or personality. Consider including physical characteristics, personality traits, actions, feelings, ways of approaching problems, likes and dislikes, strengths, and relationships with others. Use the web as a tool for discussion; writing a biography; or comparing with other characters or personalities.

Picture points. As you read with children, discuss the facial expressions of book characters. On occasion, after listening to a book, invite children to draw a picture of a character or personality *at a particular point in time*. Encourage them to include a label, a caption, or a speech bubble. Try the activity in small groups and then ask the children to place their portraits in time order and discuss how the character or personality changed over time.

Portrait gallery. Maintain a portrait gallery of characters from books. Write labels or descriptions for the characters. As a center activity, or during play time, children may play as gallery visitors, curators, designers, and tour guides.

Interviews. Invite your children to play at interviewing. They can take on the roles of interviewers and characters or personalities and either play spontaneously or plan their questions in writing. Model the process in a whole-group setting with volunteers, and then try this activity in pairs or small groups.

Point of view studies. Read aloud a picture book; enjoy and discuss as always. Then, before reading the book again, invite children to each choose a character and imagine that they are that character as you read the book again. Last, children write, draw, or discuss what happened from that character's point of view, noting the different perspectives (Glazer 1997).

Perspective pictures. Share a picture book. Invite children to discuss and then draw a picture that shows the visual or spatial perspective of one of the characters. For example, "What would the world look like through a hole in a tree/from a spider web/from outer space/through the eyes of a baby?"

ILLUSTRATION STUDIES

Exploring book illustrations helps children appreciate the creative, imaginative work that illustrators do and develop insight into their artistry. It also helps them understand text better.

Media and technique explorations. Invite students to observe and describe illustrations in terms of color, line, shape, and texture (Kiefer 1986). Then, encourage them to explore these devices in their own creations. Plan to have them try watercolors, tempera, ink, chalk, crayon, charcoal, pastels, pencil, collage, cut paper, fabric, and tissue paper.

Comparisons. Invite children to observe the illustrations in two or more books by the same illustrator that contain similar artistic media or techniques. Help them articulate the ways in which the art is similar and different across books and describe trends in the illustrator's work (Cullinan and Galda 1998). A Venn diagram may be useful.

Visual literacy. Help your children appreciate and interpret illustrations by engaging with them in the following thinking processes (Ivener 1997):

1. Observing: What do you see? What do you notice?
2. Comparing: How is this picture/book like another?
3. Classifying: What moods does the author want us to feel? Would you consider this book a favorite?
4. Hypothesizing: What will the story be about? What media do you think this illustrator has used?
5. Organizing: Use illustrations to tell the sequence. Illustrate a part of the story.
6. Summarizing: Use illustrations to summarize the story. Illustrate the theme.
7. Applying: Use a certain media to illustrate a lived experience.
8. Criticizing: What do you like/dislike about the illustrations? Do they complement the story? What other techniques might be considered?

WORDLESS PICTURE BOOKS

Christian: If these are wordless picture books, who's the author?
Roxanne: We can pretend we're the author.

Wordless pictures books foster children's use of oral language, familiarity with book handling, visual literacy, and knowledge of stories and their sequences. Try the following as you use wordless picture books:

- Demonstrate your own readings, thinking aloud about how you decide what to say.
- Be an audience to children's readings. Use anecdotal notes to help identify and reflect on their strengths. What language and vocabulary are they using? Are they labeling or have they developed a sense that pictures tell a connected story? Does their reading present a complete account of the pictures?

- Audiotape and videotape children's readings. Encourage children to listen to and evaluate themselves. Did they speak clearly? Would a listener know when to turn the page? Does the reading make sense? Place their tapes with the books in the listening center.
- Invite children to write words for wordless picture books and read them to the class.

GENRE STUDIES

Genre studies help children develop insight into the content and structures of various categories of literature. In a typical study, children read a genre-based text set, engage in response activities, and compose their own pieces in that genre. To organize, collect a text set (three to twenty books) that will appeal to your children and connect with your curricular goals. The books may be read in whole- or small-group settings and should also be made available for individual reading and browsing. As you read the books with children, discuss both format and content. Also, arrange response activities that help children (1) connect with and learn from the individual books in the set and (2) make connections between books. Following are some ideas for getting started.

Alphabet books. After reading, discussing, and responding to several books, help children choose themes for writing their own books. Consider encouraging them to choose themes that connect with a classroom inquiry topic. Talk about the number of pages the books will have and why. Less experienced children may wish to write only the letters of the alphabet, while older children may write words or sentences.

Autobiographies. After reading a few autobiographies with your children and engaging in response activities that help them explore their content and format, invite children to write their own. To construct their own autobiographies, children write about or draw early memories, stories they have heard about their early lives, and special life events. A time line can be used to plan, or children may write one event per page and then organize the pages in some meaningful sequence.

Biographies. A good biography tells the story of another person's life and helps the reader understand the historical context in which that life was lived. Emphasize these characteristics as you share biographies with your students. To help them construct biographies of their own, discuss possible subjects. It might be easiest to write about a classmate or a family member—someone with whom they feel comfortable. Children can get their information by interviewing both their subjects and the subjects' acquaintances. To remember what they hear, they can audiotape, take notes, or draw pictures. A time line can be used for planning, or suggest that children write one event per page and then organize their pages in some meaningful order. Remind them that biographies are not always presented in time order. For example, they may begin in the present or they may include flashbacks.

Number books. Share a number book text set, discussing the variety in format and content. Invite children to create books of their own, appropriating the style (or combination of styles) of the authors they are reading.

All About _____ books. Read some of the "All About . . ." books in Jim Arnosky's series (see Appendix). Invite children to write individual or class books about topics of general interest: *All About Me/Our Class/Our Families/The Foods We Eat/Our Hands.* Or, they may write books connected with content inquiries: *All About Water/Insects/Community Life,* and so on. For class books, each child contributes one page.

Storybooks. Engage children in a genre study of fiction, fantasy, fairy tales, folktales, tall tales, or fables. Bring several to browse; discuss their distinguishing characteristics and write a storybook as a class or allow children to write their own. Possible planning devices include time lines and story webs.

Recipe books. Bring in a set of books for browsing. As a group, discuss their content (you'll find more than just recipes!) and formats. Help children write recipes for a class book. Try to include the kinds that children can actually make on their own—with edible results. For example, they could concoct numerous versions of recipes for the following:

> *Hors d'Oeuvres:* Try various combinations and amounts of crackers, celery, cheeses, cheese spreads, peanut butter, jelly, raisins, and olives.
> *Trail Mix:* Try various combinations and amounts of nuts, cereals, dried fruits, pretzels, popcorn, pumpkin seeds, crackers, peanut butter chips, and chocolate chips.
> *Fruit and Vegetable Salads:* Try various combinations and amounts of carrots, celery, cauliflower, bell peppers, cucumbers, water chestnuts, raisins, nuts, cheeses, apple chunks, seedless red and green grapes, banana chunks, pineapple chunks, oranges, kiwi, figs, and strawberries. Children may wish to develop recipes for fruit kabobs.
> *Yogurt Drinks:* Try various combinations of yogurt, berries, bananas, peaches, fruit juice, honey, and cinnamon.

OTHER KINDS OF BOOKS

Children benefit from opportunities to make all kinds of books, even if they aren't part of a genre study. The following types of books may be constructed individually or as a class, with each child contributing a page. When books are finished, encourage children to read and reread them and share them with friends and families.

One- and two-word books. Write a one-word book based on a theme you are studying (heroes, insects, people, water, homes, weather, time). Each child creates a page of the book by writing a word and illustrating a page. For example, if you are studying water, each child could write *water* but draw a pond, a lake, a stream, and so on. Or, each child could write a different water word. For two-word books, add an adjective: *mucky water, blue water.*

Things children can do books. Children choose photographs from magazines that show interesting things kids can do and write captions beginning with, "Children can . . ." (Derman-Sparks 1989). Or, children may create their own illustrations.

Environmental print books. Invite children to bring in pieces of print they can read. (A note home will facilitate this process.) Children may collect their print from magazines, food packages, coupons, the newspaper, or whatever they find in their environments. Place the materials in an album or a scrapbook; read it as a class and make it available in the class library.

Class histories. Record the history of your year together. Set up a schedule so that one child per day records something. Or, you could do the recording with help from the class. For example, "We used mirrors to draw pictures of ourselves," "Kiara found a beetle in the parking lot," "Our families came for a poetry reading," "Mollie's great-grandpa died."

FAMILY READING NIGHTS

One final way to help your students develop knowledge from and about books is to invite families to school for reading nights. Use reading nights to share what you are doing with reading at school and to discover the kinds of things families are doing at home. All children are welcome. Here's a sample program for a reading night:

6:00   *Greeting Time.* Families chat, browse a display of books, choose a book from the display, and find a seat. On subsequent reading nights, families may bring their own books or other print material from home to display and share.

6:10   *Introductions.* Each person introduces him- or herself and shares one thing he or she enjoys doing. Include the children. On subsequent reading nights, families may share a special family object, offer an idea for helping children learn to read or write, or recommend a good book.

6:20   *Discussion.* Ask family members if and how they read and talk about books with their children. Find out what books they like to share at home. Children may participate in this conversation or browse books in another part of the classroom. On subsequent reading nights, you may discuss what, other than books, families read with their children (recipes, food packages, street signs, mail). You may also wish to use this time to take suggestions for future reading nights.

6:30   *Demonstration.* Read a good book (a short one), demonstrating how you model reading strategies and talk with children about books. On subsequent reading nights, you may use this time to share other types of literature: a recipe book (discuss reading and following the recipe and reading food packages with children); a poetry anthology (demonstrate some of the ways you help children transact with poetry); and so on. You may also wish to invite family members to demonstrate their own ways of working with their children.

6:40   *Reading.* Invite parents to explore the demonstrated strategies by reading, to or with their children, their chosen books from the display.

6:55   *Follow-Up.* Come back together and talk about interesting things the children did or said while reading, for example, "good errors," questions, or comments. Children can participate in this conversation, or you can arrange a separate area of the classroom for them to further respond to the reading through art.

7:05   *Cookies and Conversation.* Provide time for families to interact informally. On the first night, you may wish to ask them to fill out a questionnaire (see Figure 4–2) that will help you learn about their children and how to best meet their needs. Say goodnight at 7:30.

INQUIRE INTO LITERATURE EXPLORATIONS

This chapter has examined ways of using literature to help children develop knowledge and understandings, literacy processes and skills, and dispositions for continued learning. If you have questions, wonderings, or tensions about teaching and learning in these areas, you may wish to inquire into them (see Chapter 3). Your inquiries may focus on individual children, groups, or the whole class. Here are some examples of teacher inquiry questions:

- What reading dispositions do my students show? How do my teaching practices influence these dispositions?
- What do my students learn through books?

1. What sorts of home-school connection activities do you prefer?
   ____ visiting the classroom during the school day
   ____ evening activities and workshops
   ____ take-home activity packs
   ____ family-oriented homework (biographies, collecting family stories)
   ____ personal notes or e-mails to and from the teacher
   ____ phone calls to and from the teacher
   ____ other _____

2. What knowledge, guidance, or experiences would you like to offer to the classroom?
   ____ work with children on projects (help them write, read, find information)
   ____ listen to children read
   ____ bring in a story to read
   ____ tell a story (personal, family, community, folktale)
   ____ share a hobby or a pastime such as cooking, painting, sculpting, gardening, fishing, sewing, or woodworking
   ____ share work-related knowledge (carpentry, secretarial, retail, and so on)
   ____ share cultural knowledge (traditional stories, ways of living, beliefs)
   ____ share language knowledge
   ____ prefer to observe only
   ____ other _____

3. Does anything make it difficult for you to participate in home-school connection activities?
   ____ dates and times of school activities
   ____ conflicts with work
   ____ not comfortable speaking the language(s) spoken in the school
   ____ younger children at home (or others who may need care)
   ____ not enough information (about the activities, dates, times)
   ____ other _____

4. What sorts of reading and writing does your child do at home?
   ____ draws pictures and/or writes (or pretends to write)
   ____ reads mail, catalogs
   ____ helps with grocery lists, coupons, shopping, recipes
   ____ shares in reading of newspaper, magazines
   ____ goes to the library
   ____ reads storybooks (or pretends to do so)
   ____ uses computer
   ____ other _____

5. What reading and writing do you do at home? _____
   _____

FIGURE 4–2 *Family Questionnaire*

- How do my students construct world knowledge as they interact with books? How do they construct literacy knowledge?
- What is the nature of student participation in read-aloud sessions? What is my role?
- What kinds of language do children use as they discuss books/retell/reenact/browse and so on? How do children support one another as they engage in these activities?
- What knowledge of book handling do children demonstrate in the class library/retelling center/class theatre/browsing area?
- What kinds of literature and literature engagements seem most meaningful to my children? How does literature study in my classroom connect with children's home language and cultural knowledge?
- How is my philosophy of literacy development reflected in my teaching?

5 | TAKE-HOME LITERATURE PACKS

"Fun! Fun! Fun! We can't wait for the next tote."
"When the whole family became involved it seemed so natural."
"It gives me new ideas on activities to do with my child."
"I don't know who had more fun, Leandra or her dad."

Such are the sentiments of a group of kindergarten families in the midst of a take-home literature program (O'Connor 2000). Take-home literature packs are sets of books accompanied by sets of extending ideas and materials. They are sent home with children on a rotating or checkout basis, often serving as homework. A typical pack includes two to five books that are related by a theme (color, pets, rain, sports) and six to eight activities from which families may choose. Families are invited to read at least two of the books and engage in at least two of the activities over the course of a week. Activities include simple games, ideas for play, writing and drawing suggestions, and art and craft ideas. All of the materials needed to do the activities are included in the packs.

Take-home packs lead to many literacy-related benefits. For families, they offer myriad ways of exploring and interacting with books. The activities are more inviting than worksheets or memorization tasks, and they respect families' ability to choose the activities that seem right for their children. Also, as family members spend quality time with their children, they develop new ideas for helping them learn to read and write. For children, the packs offer a fun experience that is a medium for developing both literacy and world knowledge. Children enjoy the intimacy of sharing books with one or two other people and benefit from the collaboration that is part of most of the activities. For you, the packs provide a forum for connecting with families, learning from them, and sharing your expertise. Look for a sense of team to develop as you work with families and children toward a shared goal of developing children's literacies.

DEVELOPING THE PACKS

The major task in getting the program going is to develop the packs. This involves collecting books and materials and putting them into paper bags, backpacks, or homemade sacks (16 × 16) for transporting. The packs I suggest (located at the end of this chapter) could be used just as they are, but you may wish to do a little tailoring to make them fit your children and their curriculum. If an activity seems a bit complex, simplify it. If you have some of your own activity ideas, add them. If you are unable to obtain all of the materials for an activity, rework it. If you do not have all the books you need, make substitutions or leave some out. I have suggested four to five books for most of the packs, but two to three or even one would work. Try to include high-quality literature that adults will need to read aloud as well as some easy reads for children. The packs will work best if you adapt them to connect with your children and their curriculum and if you are well-equipped with the necessary materials.

As you put together the packs, choose inexpensive, easily replaceable items. Even the most careful of hands may damage or lose items. To the extent possible, have replacement items on reserve. Also, items should be easy to index. When packs are returned, you won't want to count to see whether a set of twenty items is still complete. Put forty items in the pack, and if some are lost, no problem. It is important for you to be consciously aware that "some teachers of poor students don't let them take materials home, out of fear that the materials will never be returned. Yet these same students tend to be very proud of taking materials home and are generally exceedingly careful to return them" (ASCD Advisory Panel on Improving Student Achievement 1995, 9). Effective teaching involves becoming consciously aware of our biases and, of course, holding equally high expectations for all of our students.

INVOLVING FAMILIES

If possible, arrange a workshop for families to participate in developing the packs. Family members can help gather materials, put packs together, and more important, help brainstorm ways of connecting the activities with home cultures and languages. Ask what they enjoy doing with their children and how this might be turned into a pack activity. Ask what they want their children to know, how they learn best, and what ideas or techniques may be of interest to their children. Substantive contributions from families can help you meet the NAEYC's recommendation that your curriculum "support children's home culture and language while also developing all children's abilities to participate in the shared culture of the program and community" (Bredekamp and Copple 1997, 20).

ACQUIRING THE MATERIALS

You probably already have some of the materials required for the packs. Others you can make. However, expendable items such as crayons, markers, and paints will need to be purchased. Consider the following options:

- Send home a wish list of needed materials. Include items that need to be purchased (a box of crayons, a watercolor paint set, a set of plastic insects, a book) as well as those that families may already have (buttons, fabric scraps, paper to be recycled, coupons).
- Consult your principal or director about funds for the project. Provide a one-page rationale along with an estimated budget. Discuss approaching the district office for funds.
- Team with other teachers, and request funds from your parent-teacher association.
- Write a proposal for a grant. State and national organizations offer grants for teacher research and curricular innovations. Consult *Language Arts*, *The Reading Teacher*, or the awards and grants pages at either <www.ncte.org> (National Council of Teachers of English) or <www.reading.org> (International Reading Association). Many state organizations have websites or journals with award and grant information as well. Your school district may also offer grants.

SCHEDULING

Develop a schedule that allows for choice. If you have twenty-eight students and twenty-eight packs, consider sending packs home for only twenty weeks, to leave room for choice. If you have twenty-eight students and fourteen packs, consider dividing the class into two, and starting group A one week and group B the next. Instead of going the full twenty-eight weeks, consider going twenty. This would allow each student to do ten packs. Yvonne O'Connor (2000), a kindergarten teacher, sends her packs home on Tuesdays and receives them back on Mondays. This gives her a day to make sure the materials are in order before sending them out again.

To organize for choice, send home a description of each pack, asking families and children to rank-order their preferences (see Figure 5–1).

When the rank orderings are returned, write the rank numbers for each child on a grid (see Figure 5–2). Then, when children check out packs, they can look first for their 1 ratings, then their 2s, and so on. To keep track of which packs a child has checked out, children or you can highlight the appropriate box.

Dear Families,

For the next four months, your child will be bringing home a different literature pack every Tuesday. (Please return on Mondays.) Each pack contains one to five books and several activities from which to choose. This is your child's homework. We would like for you and your child to choose the packs you would most like to do. Please rank-order the following twenty-five choices, and we will do our best to accommodate your wishes.

> 1 = We would love to do this pack.
> 2 = We will be very happy to do this pack.
> 3 = We will do this pack if our first choices aren't available.
> 4 = This pack is not so interesting to us.

___ *Alphabet:* Play around with and learn the letters and the sounds of the alphabet.

___ *Animals:* Learn all kinds of interesting things about wild animals.

___ *Bats:* Learn about the only flying mammal.

___ *Bedtime:* Read special bedtime stories together.

___ *Color:* Learn about colors and play around with artistic techniques.

___ *Counting and Numbers:* Practice and have fun with counting and numbers.

___ *Days:* Play around with and learn the days of the week.

___ *Family:* Engage in a family study.

___ *Growing Things:* Learn about the importance of living things and how they grow.

___ *I Can!:* Celebrate the many things that children can do.

___ *Language:* Explore words in other languages.

___ *Lap Reading:* Cuddle up together with some good books and quiet activities.

___ *Maps:* Explore all kinds of maps, including treasure maps.

___ *Online:* Engage in fun online activities at the library or on a home computer.

___ *Pets:* Are you pet lovers? Explore the joys of caring for and playing with pets.

___ *Poetry:* Read simple, child-friendly poetry together. Write some poetry of your own.

___ *Rain:* Learn about the wonders of rain.

___ *Recipes:* Like to cook? Read a children's book and make one of the story recipes.

___ *Shapes:* Explore shapes and how artists use them.

___ *Social Issues:* Discuss some of the tough issues facing children today.

___ *Sports and Movement:* Play around with sports and movement.

___ *Tales:* Enjoy some old folktales.

___ *Unique Me:* Explore how unique and special you are.

___ *Words:* Have fun as you explore what a word is and play around with words.

___ *Wordless Picture Books:* Use your creativity to "read" a set of wordless books.

FIGURE 5–1   *Note to Families*

Place student rankings (1–4) in the grid. Have students mark the appropriate box with a high-lighter when the pack is checked out.

Choice Ratings for Packs

Student Names																										
Alphabet																										
Animals																										
Bats																										
Bedtime																										
Color																										
Counting/Numbers																										
Days																										
Family																										
Growing Things																										
I Can!																										
Language																										
Lap Reading																										
Maps																										
Online																										
Pets																										
Poetry																										
Rain																										
Recipes																										
Shapes																										
Social Issues																										
Sports/Movement																										
Tales																										
Unique Me																										
Words																										
Wordless Books																										

FIGURE 5–2   *Students' Choice Ratings for Packs*

INQUIRE INTO HOME LITERATURE EXPERIENCES

Inquiry into families' experiences with literature packs can foster home-school relations and help you fine-tune the materials, the activities, and the organization of the program. Following are some ideas for organizing such an inquiry.

One option is to use home-school journals to dialogue with families and track their progress with the packs. Yvonne O'Connor (2000) includes a question or issue to which families respond in the journals. For example, "Have your child share a favorite family activity and write about it in the journal" (37); "Record in the journal your thoughts about the activities" (46); "Record your frog adventures in the journal. Also tell what you thought about this activity" (38). Yvonne uses the journals as part of an inquiry process in which she seeks answers to several questions:

1. What are families doing already to develop their children's literacy?
2. What benefits do families see in using the packs with their children?
3. How do family members' expectations about their children's literacy learning change as a result of the program?
4. What kinds of growth do the families see in children's learning?
5. What suggestions do families have for future packs?

Another option to gain insight into family members' perspectives on the program is to use surveys or interviews. Find out how children and their families feel about the program; what they like about the packs; what is working well; what they might like to change; what they would like more of; what else you could include; and what they are learning about the children. Consider placing a laminated tip sheet in each pack to help them take full advantage of the program. See Figure 5–3 for an example.

Finally, work samples could be collected to learn about the activities families are choosing and the ideas they bring to the experiences. Often, we hear that children are doing things at home that they are not doing at school. These samples could help you identify and understand the settings and situations in which children are most apt to demonstrate their knowledge.

Try the following when using the packs:

- Involve as many family members as possible. Children learn best when they talk, think, read, write, and learn *with others.*
- Allow time for exploring materials. Children may need time to play around with the materials before using them for our intended purposes.
- Teach as you read. Take a "picture walk" before you read. Encourage your child to describe what is on each page and predict what the story will be about.

  After you finish the book, discuss what you read. Ask what your child learned from the book; talk about what happened at the beginning, the middle, and the end; ask questions about characters, the problems and the issues they encountered, and how they were solved. Discuss parts you liked and didn't like, parts that made you feel happy and sad, and so on.

  Occasionally point to the words as you read. Discuss interesting words. For example, if your child notices a zebra in a picture, show him or her where the word *zebra* is, and point out the *z.* If you are reading a rhyming book, talk about the rhyming words.
- Teach as your child reads. Encourage your child to look through the pictures before reading. Be an audience to your child's reading, even if he or she is a beginner. Beginning readers can be expected to label pictures, tell stories using both pictures and what is remembered from previous readings, and/or pretend to read the words.

  If your child gets stuck on a word, help with strategies to figure it out. Suggest reading to the end of the sentence, then ask: "What would make sense? What would sound right? Can the first letters help? Shall we sound it out? Can the pictures help?" Helping with strategies rather than telling words supports children's independence.

  If your child makes errors that make sense, do not correct. Substituting *steps* for *stairs* or *mom* for *mother* shows that the child is learning to make sense of print. If the errors do not make sense, suggest rereading the sentence or the paragraph and talk about the meaning. If your child seems frustrated, the piece may be too difficult. Gently offer to take over.
- Teach as your child writes. Encourage your child to do as much of the writing as possible. Children learn to write by writing. Beginners may use scribble marks or random strings of letters. Eventually, they discover that letters are connected with sounds. Early spellings may be only one or two letters: (*p* or *pg* for pig, *gf* for *grapefruit*). Affirm the legitimacy of children's early writing by treating it as real and asking questions about its meanings.

  Let children come up with their own spellings. Or, encourage them to orally stretch words, writing the sounds they hear. When we correct or supply all spellings, children do not develop independence. However, depending on the purpose, it is okay to sometimes supply spellings. Help your child write the sounds he or she hears in words. Say words slowly, stretching them out. Children eventually learn to stretch their own words. Also, help your child learn to use resources in the environment to spell. For example, if the cover of a book contains the needed word, refer him or her to that resource rather than telling the spelling.
- Teach as you write. Stretch and spell words aloud as you write. Let your child see what you are doing as you write and hear your thinking processes.

FIGURE 5–3 *Tips for Families*

Alphabet

Choose at least two books and two activities.

Books

Eating the Alphabet, by Lois Ehlert
Fruits and vegetables from A to Z.

The Butterfly Alphabet, by Kjell Sandved
Letters of the alphabet take shape on butterfly wings.

From Acorn to Zoo, by Satoshi Kitamura
A highly imaginative alphabet book!

Alphabet City, by Stephen Johnson
Find letters of the alphabet that are hidden in scenes from the city.

Many Nations: An Alphabet of Native America, by Joseph Bruchac
A book representing diverse Native American cultures.

Materials

magnetic letters
assortment of blank booklets
small chalkboard
chalk
paintbrush
dark construction paper
colored pencils

Activities

1. Take a walk around the house or neighborhood looking for shapes of the alphabet. For example, a bowl might look like an *o* or a hose might look like an *s*. Use the chalkboard and chalk to record your findings.
2. Using the magnetic letters on a cookie sheet or the refrigerator, name the letters, put them in alphabetical order, spell names of family members, and spell as many words as you can (O'Connor 2000).
3. Create an ABC book. Write one letter per page, and then draw pictures to illustrate. Older children can write a word or a sentence for each page. Consider choosing a theme for the book (animals, things I like, things that are important to our family).
4. Get a cup of water and take turns painting letters on the chalkboard. Name (or think of words that begin with) the letters.
5. Place a piece of dark construction paper by a sunny window. On it, spell some words with the magnetic letters or arrange the letters in alphabetical order. Let them rest for a few hours, then remove them and observe how the sun has bleached the paper.

6. Place the magnetic letters in a sock. Take turns reaching in and naming letters by feeling them before pulling them out. More experienced children may think of a word beginning with the letter.
7. Play "I spy" something that rhymes with/begins like/ends like _____.

Animals

Choose at least two books to read and/or talk through, and do at least two activities.

Books

All About Deer, by Jim Arnosky
This child-friendly book introduces simple concepts about deer.

All About Owls, by Jim Arnosky
This child-friendly book introduces simple concepts about owls.

Black Bear Cub, by Alan Lind
A mother bear teaches her cubs about the forest.

Chipmunk at Hollow Tree Lane, by Victoria Sherrow
A simple, fact-based narrative describes a chipmunk preparing for winter.

Flying Squirrel at Acorn Place, by Barbara Gaines Winkelman
A simple, fact-based narrative gives insight into the life of a squirrel.

Materials

assortment of blank booklets

colored pencils
paper

Activities

1. Write an acrostic poem using the name of an animal you read about. For example, write *DEER* for the title and then write *D-E-E-R* vertically down the page. Then, write four words or sentences about deer that start with those letters.
2. Move your bodies like the animals on the covers of the books, then name as many animals as you can and act out their movements.
3. Closely examine and discuss the pictures in one of the books. Write and illustrate your own book of facts about an animal of your choosing. Try writing one fact per page.
4. Draw a picture of an animal you read about. Discuss what you learned about this animal.
5. Draw an animal you read about and label as many parts as you can.
6. Play "I'm thinking of" an animal that eats nuts/has a fluffy tail and so on.

Bats

Choose at least two books to read and/or talk through, and do at least two activities.

Books

Stellaluna, by Janell Cannon
Little Stellaluna, who accidently tumbles into a bird's nest, is raised by a bird family until she is reunited with her mother.

Bats, by Gail Gibbons
An informative introduction to bats.

Bats: Creatures of the Night, by Joyce Milton
Learn all about bats from this appealing, child-friendly book.

Zipping, Zapping, Zooming Bats, by Ann Earle
Learn about bats and how to make a bat house.

Materials

paper   half-sheets of paper
pencils   note cards
crayons   tape
assortment of blank booklets

Activities

1. Read more about bats at <www.batcon.org> or <http://intergate.cccoe.k12.ca.us/bats/>.
2. Make a book of bat facts. Try including one interesting fact per page.
3. Write an acrostic poem about bats: Write B-A-T-S or another bat-related term at the top of the page for the title and then vertically down the page. Write a word or a sentence that starts with each letter. The trick is to be sure that you write something that describes the title/topic.
4. Create a poster to teach others about bats. We will hang it at school.
5. Discuss what happened at the beginning, the middle, and the end of *Stellaluna*. Use the half-sheets of paper to draw a retelling of the story that includes the beginning, the middle and the end. (You may need more than three sheets.) Tape the pages together and retell the story.
6. Draw a bat and label as many parts as you can.
7. Use the note cards to write eight interesting fact questions about bats. Write the answers on the other side and quiz each other and other family members.

Bedtime

Choose at least two books and do one activity with each.

Books

Hush!, by Minfong Ho
A Thai lullaby.

My Parents Think I'm Sleeping, by Jack Prelutsky
A collection of poems about things that happen when kids can't sleep.

Tell Me Something Happy Before I Go to Sleep, by Joyce Dunbar and Debi Gliori
Willa can't sleep at first, but her big brother helps.

A Mouse Told His Mother, by Bethany Roberts
It's bedtime when a mouse tells his mother he is going on a trip. She tells him it is bedtime. He tells her he is going to the moon. She tells him to take his toothbrush, and so the story goes.

Bedtime for Frances, by Russell Hoban
It's bedtime for Frances, but she needs some milk first . . . and then a piggyback ride . . . and then her teddy bear . . . and so this story goes.

Activities

1. Read the books to your child just before bedtime. If your child has a favorite stuffed animal or toy, invite it to join you. Discuss parts of the book that you liked/found funny/could relate to and so on.
2. Invite your child to read (or tell about the pictures) to a sibling or a stuffed animal. Observe as they enjoy the book together.

Color

Choose at least two books and two activities.

Books

Hailstones and Halibut Bones, by Mary O'Neill
A collection of poems about color.

My Many Colored Days, by Dr. Seuss
Dr. Seuss connects colors with moods.

Brown Bear, Brown Bear, What Do You See?, by Bill Martin Jr.
A predictable book full of animals and colors.

Materials

watercolor paint set
paper
plastic fruit
crayons

Activities

1. Read *Brown Bear, Brown Bear, What Do You See?* and then invite your child to read it to you. Newer readers will pick up the pattern and "read" a version very much like the text. More experienced readers can be encouraged to point to the words, matching them one-for-one with what is said aloud.

2. Help your child choose a favorite poem from *Hailstones and Halibut Bones*. Read it a few times and then create illustrations using the watercolor set.

3. Read *My Many Colored Days* and invite your child to engage in the movements and show the moods of the characters. Discuss the colors you feel like right now/in the morning/while playing with friends/while eating ice cream and so on. Use the watercolors to paint a feeling or a mood you have had. Or, use the crayons to make your own *My Many Colored Days* book (Nikolai 1999).

4. Make patterns with the plastic fruits (apple-orange-apple-orange; yellow-green-purple, yellow-green-purple; and so on).

5. Choose a piece of plastic fruit and paint a picture of it.

6. Arrange the plastic fruits in a bowl and paint a picture of them.

7. Mix the paint colors. What colors can you make?

8. Experiment with shades. Choose a crayon and color with light, medium, and strong pressure. Discuss the results.

Counting and Numbers

Choose at least two books and two activities.

Books

More Than One, by Miriam Schlein
A thoughtfully written book about numbers.

The Icky Bug Counting Book, by Jerry Palotta
Count your way through a swarm of insects.

Over in the Meadow, illustrated by David Carter
An old counting rhyme.

Anno's Counting Book, by Mitsumasa Anno
A book full of things to see, count, and discuss.

Materials

5 paper cups labeled *1st, 2nd, 3rd, 4th, 5th*	number cards
	number-word cards
plastic insects	stamp pad
assortment of blank booklets	rubber stamps
	markers
blank (calendar) grids	popsicle sticks

Activities

1. Use one of the grids to create a calendar for next month. Help your child write in the numbers. Use the blank space at the top of the page for an illustration.
2. Make a counting book of your own (1–10). Write in the numbers and number words first, and then use the markers or rubber stamps to illustrate. Consider a theme for your book (insects, animals, household items). Read the book to each other.
3. Use the popsicle sticks to make various shapes. Start with two sticks, then three, then four, and so on. Discuss the shapes you are making and the number of sides they have.
4. Play a guessing game. Hide a plastic insect under one of the cups and invite your child to guess which cup it is under—the first, the second, the third, the fourth, or the fifth (Croft 1990).
5. Place the number cards (1–10) in order.
6. Place the number-word cards (1–10) in order.
7. Count the plastic insects by twos, fives, and tens. Play with them any way you wish. Make up a counting or number game.
8. Choose a day to observe how your family uses numbers. Write down eight ways in which your family used numbers on that day.

Days

Read both books and choose at least two activities.

Books

Today Is Monday, pictures by Eric Carle
An illustrated retelling of an old song.

The Very Hungry Caterpillar, by Eric Carle
A caterpillar eats its way through the days of the week.

Materials

days of the week cards	green sock and felt pieces
assortment of blank booklets	(1 apple, 2 pears, 3 plums,
	4 strawberries, 5 oranges,
paper	cake, ice cream cone, pickle,
colored pencils	cheese, salami, lollipop,
blank calendar page (photocopied)	cherry pie, sausage,
	cupcake, watermelon)

Activities

1. Put the days of the week cards in order (O'Connor 2000).
2. Make your own book about the days of the week.
3. Use the calendar to plan next week's dinner menu with your child.
4. Make a fun pretend menu and plan what you would like to eat each day and what animal you would like to invite.
5. Use the sock and felt pieces to retell *The Very Hungry Caterpillar*. Start with the sock rolled into a ball to represent the egg, then open it to represent the caterpillar. (Be sure the butterfly is hidden inside.) As the caterpillar eats, place the foods inside, and pull out the butterfly at the end. Take turns reading and manipulating props.
6. Choose a book. Read it and then have your child read it to you. Help with words as necessary.
7. Ask each family member which day of the week he or she likes the best. Write down the responses and categorize them. Which day do most prefer? Do they prefer weekends or weekdays?

Family

Choose at least two books and two activities.

Books

Celebrating Families, Rosemarie Hausherr
A photo-essay representing the diversity of American families.

Jingle Dancer, by Cynthia Leitich Smith
A contemporary Muscogee (Creek) girl participates in a family tradition by dancing in a powwow.

Allison, by Allan Say
Allison, who was adopted, discovers that she looks different from her parents. Read how she learns to accept her discovery.

How My Family Lives in America, by Susan Kuklin
Sanu, Eric, and April are learning the traditions of their families.

Peter's Chair, by Ezra Jack Keats
Peter's life changes when his sister is born.

When I Am Old with You, by Angela Johnson
A young boy imagines a future with his grandaddy.

The Patchwork Quilt, by Valerie Flournoy
A family makes a special quilt.

The Keeping Quilt, by Patricia Polacco
A cherished family quilt is passed on through the generations.

Materials

large, white paper	fabric crayons
finger paint	tape measure
assortment of blank booklets	yarn
markers	tape
6 × 6 patches of muslin	

Activities

1. Invite your child to write the last name(s) of your family in the center of a piece of paper. Together, draw pictures of things that are important to your family. Write a caption for each picture.

2. Help your child cover his or her hand with finger paint and make a handprint on a piece of paper. Collect a handprint from each family member and label with each person's name. Ask what your child notices about the prints.

3. Tell your child a story from your childhood and invite him or her to draw a picture of what happened in the story.

4. Construct a family tree together. List the names and the birth and death years of as many family members as you can. Put in a special place for safekeeping.

5. Construct a family storybook. Write down and illustrate one story from each person living in your home. You may wish to do the writing on this activity and invite your child to read it with you. Put in a special place for safekeeping.

6. Read *The Patchwork Quilt* or *The Keeping Quilt* and invite each family member to use the fabric crayons to decorate a patch for a family quilt. Hand stitch or tape together.

7. Cut a piece of yarn to represent the age of each family member. (A three-year-old gets a three-inch piece.) Use a piece of the tape to label each string with a name. Discuss the results, using vocabulary such as *length, age, longer, older*, and *younger*.

Growing Things

Choose at least two books and two activities.

Books

Miss Rumphius, by Barbara Cooney
When little Alice Rumphius grows up, she wants to travel to faraway places and live by the sea, like her grandfather. Her grandfather tells her that she must also find a way to make the world more beautiful. Find out how Alice accomplishes this charge.

The Reason for a Flower, by Ruth Heller
Find out all the reasons that flowers are important.

Gathering the Sun: An Alphabet Book in Spanish and English, by Alma Flor Ada

A bilingual book of short poems that celebrate the wonder of harvest time.

The Carrot Seed, by Ruth Krauss
A boy plants a carrot seed, but almost everyone is certain it won't grow.

Red Leaf, Yellow Leaf, by Lois Ehlert
Learn how a seed grows into a tree.

Materials

flower seeds	assortment of
bean seeds	blank booklets
baggy of soil	crayons
plastic cups	pencils
note cards	paper

Activities

1. Use the baggy of soil and a cup to plant three to four of the flower seeds. Discuss their progress each day. Draw a picture after one week, two weeks, and three weeks.
2. Wrap two to three bean seeds in a wet square of paper towel and place them in one of the cups. Keep the towel moist. Transplant when the seeds sprout (Chenfield 1985). Draw what you observe after one week, two weeks, and three weeks.
3. Read *The Carrot Seed* and invite your child to retell it. Observe whether the retelling includes the characters, the place, the problem, and the resolution.
4. Take a nature walk. Encourage your child to closely observe and describe a particular object (tree, flower, puddle). Ask, "What does it look/feel/sound like?" Go inside and draw and label what you observed.
5. Read *Miss Rumphius* and do something this week to make the world more beautiful. Write your action on a note card and report back to the class.
6. Make a *Growing Things* book of your own. Be as creative as you like: you could write a story, or draw pictures and label them, or draw the sequence of something that grows.

I Can!

Read both books and choose at least two activities.

Books

How Kids Grow, by Jean Marzollo
Read about the many things that kids can do.

Have You Seen My Cat?, by Eric Carle
Here is a book that kids can read.

Materials

paper	crayons
pencils	assortment of blank booklets

Activities

1. Tell your child a story about when he or she was younger. Invite him or her to draw a picture about the story.
2. Tell your child a story about when he or she was younger. Then, while you write the story, invite your child to illustrate it. Read together what you have written. Place this document in a special place for safekeeping.
3. Help your child create an *I Can!* book. Begin each page with "I can . . ." When the book is finished, read it to each other.
4. Fold a piece of paper in half. On one side, invite your child to draw a picture of him- or herself doing something when he or she was younger, and on the other, a picture of how he or she looks doing the activity now. Discuss the changes.
5. Help your child write his or her own version of *Have You Seen My Cat?* Substitute whatever you like for the word *cat*. Read the book to each other.
6. Reread *Have You Seen My Cat?* and then invite your child to read it independently. Acknowledge that he or she is a reader.
7. Encourage your child to draw a picture of anything and then write something about it. Acknowledge that your child is a writer.

Language

Choose at least two books and two activities.

Books

Aekyung's Dream, by Min Paek
A Korean immigrant adjusts to life in the United States. Written in Korean and English.

Margaret and Margarita, Margarita y Margaret, by Lynn Reiser
Margaret speaks English and Margarita speaks Spanish. When they meet in the park and play together, they both learn a new language.

I Hate English!, by Ellen Levine
Mei Mei, an immigrant to the United States from Hong Kong, learns to communicate in two languages.

Giving Thanks, by Chief Jake Swamp
A Native American good morning message written in English, with a Mohawk version at the end.

Three Friends, Tres Amigos, by Maria Cristina Brusca and Tona Wilson
Learn to count in Spanish and English. Learn other words, too.

What Is Your Language?, by Debra Leventhal
Learn to say "yes" and "no" in many languages.

Materials

assortment of blank booklets	2 books and 2 cassette tapes
white paper	(1 in English and 1 in
colored pencils	another language)
note cards	tape recorder

Activities

1. Use the books and/or your own knowledge of languages to write a book in two languages. Consider a number book, a book of words, a color book, a yes/no book, or an ABC book.
2. Using *two* of the first three books listed for this pack, discuss the feelings that the characters had about language. Draw a picture of a character from each book and list the feelings under each drawing. Compare how the characters felt.
3. Say aloud two to three of the new words you have learned and try to use them all week. Write on a note card which words you chose and how you were able to use them.
4. If you speak a language other than English, find an interesting piece of print in your home written in that language and share it with your child. Reading to children in their first language supports their reading in other languages.
5. If you speak a language other than English, write some words or sentences with your child. Invite your child to read them with you and draw pictures to remember their meanings.
6. Listen to a story in two languages. Follow along with each book while listening to the cassettes.

Lap Reading

Cuddle up together and read both books. Choose at least two of the activities.

Books

Snow, by Uri Shulevitz
This is a great book for lap reading because the pictures contain first one, then two, and eventually, many tiny, fun to find snowflakes.

The Legend of the Indian Paintbrush, by Tomie dePaola
A Texas legend about a boy who becomes an artist.

Materials

white tempera paint	white paper
watercolors	half-sheets of paper
markers	tape
light gray paper	

Activities

1. Paint snow any way you like.
2. Play around with and discuss colors as you paint.
3. Use the watercolors to paint a scene from outside.
4. Choose one of the books. Discuss what happened at the beginning, the middle, and the end. Use the half-sheets of paper to illustrate each part. (You may need more than three sheets.) Tape together and retell the story.
5. Ask your child what he or she thought of the books and which parts he or she liked. Create a poster for one of the books that might make the other children in the class want to read it. Bring it to school.
6. Point out and discuss some of the words in one book. Help your child choose three words he or she would like to remember. Write them down and practice spelling them.

Maps

Choose at least two books and two activities.

Books

Me on the Map, by Joan Sweeney
A fun introduction to maps.

Tough Boris, by Mem Fox
Boris von der Borch seems to be a hardened old pirate—or is he?

As the Crow Flies: A First Book of Maps, by Gail Hartman
Learn about the maps of animals and people.

Materials

state map	crayons
city map	red pen
paper	blocks
pencils	

Activities

1. Locate our town on the state map. Locate any other towns you know. Locate your street on the city map. Use the red pen to place your initials right where your house is located.
2. Draw a map of your bedroom, home, yard, or street. Label as many items as you can.
3. Use the blocks to build a map. Include roads, mountains, streams, lakes, houses, barns, stores, castles, and/or skyscrapers.
4. Read *Tough Boris* aloud together several times, as expressively as you can!
5. Design a treasure map for Tough Boris.

6. Design a treasure map to use around your own home. Find a treasure to hide somewhere and play together as treasure seekers.

Online

Read at least one book and do at least one activity.

Books

The Paperboy, by Dav Pilkey
While the neighborhood sleeps, a paperboy makes his deliveries.

Town Mouse, Country Mouse, by Jan Brett
In this old fable, two mice exchange homes and learn something important in the process.

Arthur's Computer Disaster, by Marc Brown
Find out what happens when Arthur gets hooked on a computer game.

Materials

paper	tape
crayons	pencils
safety scissors	

Activities

Read one of the books and then go to that author's website. If you do not have a home computer, the public librarian can help.

<www.pilkey.com>
Go to Dav's Page O' Fun and have fun with an activity of your choice.

<www.janbrett.com>
Go to the activity pages and find something interesting to do.

<www.pbs.org/wgbh/arthur>
Go to the parent's corner and choose an activity.

Pets

Choose at least two books and two activities.

Books

McDuff Moves In, by Rosemary Wells
An unwanted dog is adopted by a loving family.

Harry's House, by Angela Shelf Medearis
A young girl and her mother build a house for their dog.

Top Cat, by Lois Ehlert
Top Cat doesn't have much to do until a box arrives from the humane society.

Mrs. Katz and Tush, by Patricia Polacco
Young Larnel gives Mrs. Katz an abandoned cat, and as a result, some lifelong friendships develop.

Materials

toy dogs and cats	note cards
paper plates	popsicle sticks
safety scissors	blocks
elastic bands	crayons
tape	paper

Activities

1. Use the toy pets and the blocks to create a little pet kennel with cages. Discuss ways of holding, feeding, watering, petting, and playing with pets. Make up names for the pets and label the cages.
2. Use the blocks to build a special house for one of the toy pets. Pretend to care for it.
3. Use the toy pets to re-create a scene in one of the stories.
4. Use the paper plates and elastic bands to create pet masks. Spend some time playing as pets and pet owners.
5. Choose a story. Use the paper and popsicle sticks to create story character puppets. Replay a scene.
6. Play a memory game. Make a list of all the pets you can think of (dog, cat, bird). Write each name on two note cards. Turn the cards over and use your memories to find matches.
7. Choose a book. Make a poster that might convince the other children in the class to read it. Bring to school.

Poetry

Read as many poems as you like. Choose at least two activities.

Books

The Great Frog Race and Other Poems, by Kristine O'Connell George
A collection of poetry for children.

Imagine That!, selected by Jack Prelutsky
Poems of never-was.

Doodle Dandies, by J. Patrick Lewis
Poems that take shape.

Pass It On, edited by Wade Hudson
African American poetry for children.

School Supplies: A Book of Poems, selected by Lee Bennett Hopkins
A varied collection of poetry for children.

Materials

paper   pencils   crayons

Activities

1. Read any poem. Ask your child: "What do you think about the poem? How does it make you feel? What pictures come to mind? How does the poem connect with something in your life?" Share your thoughts and feelings about the poem, too.

2. Choose a poem you like; copy it; keep it to read over and over.

3. Write a poem together. Help your child understand that poems do not need to rhyme.

4. Make a list of words that rhyme. Write a couplet (two lines that rhyme) together.

5. Write a haiku poem together. This is not easy, so go ahead and take the lead. Haiku poems have three lines, with five, seven, and five syllables, and they usually describe a scene from nature. (See "Meadow," "Morning Grasses," and "Winter Swing" in Kristine O'Connell George's book for examples.)

6. Choose a few poems to read to your child while he or she closes his or her eyes. When you are finished reading, ask your child to describe what he or she saw.

7. Choose a poem to read several times. Ask your child to draw a picture about the poem before looking at the illustrator's pictures.

Rain

Choose at least two books and two activities.

Books

Come On, Rain!, by Karen Hesse
The city heat is intense, but finally, it rains!

Bringing the Rain to Kapiti Plain, by Verna Aardema
Ki-Pat changes the weather.

The Legend of the Bluebonnet, by Tomie dePaola
An old Texas tale is retold.

Materials

assortment of blank   note cards
   booklets   crayons
paper in shades of blue, gray, and white   pencils

Activities

1. Make a list of words that describe a rainy day. Choose one of the blank booklets. Write one word per page, and make a picture for each. Reread your book to each other several times.

2. Use your list of rainy day words from activity 1 to play a memory game. Write each word on two note cards, turn the cards over on the floor, and then use your memories to find the matches.

3. Take a "sky walk," noting what you see above you (Croft 1990). What do the clouds look like? What colors do you see? Are the clouds puffy? Light? Dark? Do they appear to be moving? Go inside and illustrate what you saw.

4. Choose two of the stories. Discuss how they are similar and different. Fold a piece of paper into thirds. Write the titles of the two books in the two outside columns, and write "Both" in the middle. Write or draw about the similarities and differences.

5. Choose one of the main characters and draw his or her face at a certain time in the story.

6. Look at the pictures in each book and discuss the different settings. Talk about why rain was important for the characters in each book.

Recipes

Choose at least two books and two activities.

Books

Pigs in the Pantry, by Amy Axelrod
Mr. Pig and the piglets set out to make chili, but they don't know how to follow a recipe.

The Gingerbread Man, by Jim Aylesworth
When the oven is opened, the gingerbread man pops out. So begins a great chase.

Oh, No, Toto!, by Katrin Hyman Tchana and Louise Tchana Pami
Little Toto Gourmand goes to the market with his Mami to get some meat and yams. Read about his adventure, which ends with Egussi soup.

Thunder Cake, by Patricia Polacco
In helping her grandmother bake a cake, a child overcomes her fear of thunder.

The Apple Pie Tree, by Zoe Hall
Two sisters watch an apple tree through the seasons.

Materials

4 × 4 pieces of fabric
yarn
rubber bands
assortment of blank booklets
magazines

food coupons and
   advertisements
note cards
pencils
glue stick

Activities

1. Choose a recipe from one of the books (chili, cookies, cake, pie, soup). Help your child make a list of any ingredients you don't have already. When you go to the store, help your child find the items on the list. Follow the recipe together, and enjoy.

2. Choose a recipe from a recipe book you have already. Bake or cook with your child, paying special attention to reading the recipe together.

3. Make a spice braid (Chenfield 1985). Braid three strands of yarn. Tie both ends. Place one teaspoon of a spice (nutmeg, cinnamon, cloves, mace, vanilla beans, allspice) on as many fabric squares as you like; bring up edges; fasten with rubber band. Fasten pouches to braid. Tie knot at one end of braid and hang. Write down the recipe you created and pass it on to a friend.

4. Invite your child to write a recipe for anything. Don't worry about getting everything right. Just enjoy your child's creativity and save the recipe for future entertainment. (You can skip making this recipe . . . or be brave and make it!)

5. Play as chefs and waiters. Use empty food containers, trays, plastic silverware, aprons, and toy (or real) food. Write recipes, food orders, and menus.

6. Sort through the magazines, the ads, and the coupons to make a book of food names your child can read. Also use empty food packages from your home.

Shapes

Choose at least two books and two activities.

Books

The Snowy Day, by Ezra Jack Keats
A young boy experiences the wonders of a snowy day.

The Big Orange Splot, by Daniel Pinkwater
When his house gets a big orange splot on the roof, Mr. Plumbean gets a creative idea.

Alexander and the Wind-Up Mouse, by Leo Lionni
A delightful little story about two mice and a special friendship.

Snowballs, by Lois Ehlert
Snow people are decorated in all kinds of ways.

Materials

construction paper shapes
plastic shapes
glue stick
glue
white paper

popsicle sticks
6-inch blue squares of
   construction paper
colored pencils
safety scissors

Activities

1. Use the paper shapes to form animals, buildings, people, or designs. After playing for a while, use the glue stick and white paper to make your creations permanent.
2. Sort the plastic shapes by color, size, number of sides, and so on (O'Connor 2000).
3. Think of a shape (star, heart, animal, face, square). Draw the shape very small, then just a little bigger, and so on. Talk about how objects can be made to look near or far depending on how big they are.
4. Choose a book. Discuss how the illustrator uses shapes. For example, notice the circles, lines, ovals, snowflakes, and snow angel in *The Snowy Day* or the shapes used to decorate the houses in *The Big Orange Splot*. Ask your child to trace them with his or her finger and name and describe them. Some are not so easy! For example, a circle is round, but what is a hill or a snowflake?
5. Use the white paper and popsicle sticks to make puppets to retell one of the stories. Talk about the shapes you put on the faces.
6. Place the plastic shapes in a sock. Before pulling out a piece, reach in, feel, and name the shape.
7. Fold a 6-inch blue square diagonally; cut along fold. Use terms such as *square*, *triangle*, and *diagonal*. Cut another square diagonally; make different shapes using the four pieces.

Social Issues

Choose at least two books and two activities.

Books

Amazing Grace, by Mary Hoffman
Grace is African American and a girl. Does this mean she won't be Peter Pan in the class play? Read to find out!

Boundless Grace, by Mary Hoffman
Grace's father, who lives in Africa, wants Grace to come and visit—and meet his new family.

The Lion's Whiskers, by Ann Grifalconi
In this Ethiopian folktale, Fanaye marries a widower with a young son. The new mother-son relationship is strained at first, but Fanaye finds the key to making it work.

Happy Birthday, Martin Luther King, by Jean Marzollo
A biography of Martin Luther King.

The Table Where Rich People Sit, by Bird Baylor
A young girl learns the meaning of rich.

Aunt Chip and the Triple Creek Dam Affair, by Patricia Polacco
A fun story about the dangers of too much television.

Materials

paper   crayons   pencils

Activities

1. Discuss the issues encountered by the main characters of the books and discuss how they were worked through.
2. Choose a book. Draw a picture of a main character at a particular point in time. Discuss how the character felt at this time.
3. Find three interesting words in one of the books you read. Write them down and discuss their meanings.
4. Draw all of the characters from one of the stories. Use your picture to retell what each person did in the story.
5. Choose a book. Ask your child to think of something he or she would like to say to a character, and ask how the character might respond. Write three to four lines of dialogue, then role-play or read it like a script.
6. Choose a book. Ask your child to draw and describe what he or she learned from the book.

Sports and Movement

Choose at least two books and two activities.

Books

Sports, by Gallimard Jeunesse and Pierre-Marie Valat
An introductory overview of a variety of sports.

America's Champion Swimmer: Gertrude Eberle, by David Adler
Gertrude, born in 1906, was the first woman to swim the English Channel.

A Picture Book of Jesse Owens, by David Adler
A biography of Jesse Owens, Olympic champion in track and field.

Beautiful Warrior, by Emily Arnold McCully
The legend of Nun's kung fu.

From Head to Toe, by Eric Carle
Animals move in all kinds of ways!

Materials

pipe cleaners   paper
ball   crayons
scarves (or crepe paper) bubbles

Activities

1. Take a brisk walk together. Discuss the importance of exercise.
2. Play with movement. Sit completely still, thinking about your body parts that can move. Move one part. Move two parts. Keep going until all parts are moving (Chenfield 1985).

3. Read *Head to Toe*, and engage in movement like the animals.
4. Use three to four pipe cleaners to make a human figure. Experiment with and name different motions and shapes (Chenfield 1985). Keep your creation!
5. Play catch with the ball, talking about your actions. For example, "Let's bounce it/roll it/toss it/pitch it/pass it."
6. Swirl and whirl the scarves, imitating each other's movements.
7. Draw a picture of yourselves or each family member doing a favorite sport or movement activity.
8. Play a favorite song or listen to a song on the radio and do aerobics or exercises to it.
9. Play around with bubbles. Listen to your child's use of language.

Tales

Choose at least two books and two activities.

Books

The Three Little Pigs, by Paul Galdone
Three pigs go head-to-head with a crafty wolf.

The Tale of the Mandarin Ducks, by Katherine Paterson
A Japanese kitchen maid releases a beautiful mandarin duck that has been caged by a greedy lord.

The Rough-Face Girl, by Rafe Martin
An Algonquin Indian tale in which goodness prevails.

The Secret Footprints, by Julia Alvarez
An enchanting legend (with Dominican roots) about the *ciguapas*, whose toes point behind them.

Mufaro's Beautiful Daughters, by John Steptoe
Goodness prevails in this story inspired by an African folktale.

Materials

felt board (12 × 12 piece of cardboard covered with felt)
7 felt pieces for *The Three Little Pigs* (3 pigs, 3 houses, 1 wolf)
half-sheets of paper
tempera paint
tape
pencils

Activities

1. Examine the illustrations in *The Tale of the Mandarin Ducks*. They were inspired by *ukiyo-e*, a Japanese art technique. This wood-block technique (we'll use vegetables) allows prints to be reproduced. Cut a design onto a potato or a carrot. Dip into the paint and make prints (Sebesta 1992).

2. Discuss the similarities between *Mufaro's Beautiful Daughters* and *The Rough-Face Girl*. Are these like any other tales you may have heard or read?
3. Use the felt pieces to retell *The Three Little Pigs*.
4. Choose a book. Draw a picture of a character's face at a certain point in time.
5. Go to the library to find more folktales or use a home computer to visit <www.pitt.edu/~dash/grimm.html>. This site contains links to folktale and fairy tale websites.
6. Use the half-sheets of paper to draw the beginning, the middle, and the ending of a story. (You may need more than three pieces.) Tape together and retell to a family member.

Unique Me

Choose at least two books and two activities.

Books

Two Eyes, a Nose, and a Mouth, by Roberta Intrater
A thoughtful study of the similarities and differences of faces.

I Like Me!, by Nancy Carlson
A book about feeling good and taking care of yourself.

Yoko, by Rosemary Wells
Yoko's classmates make fun of her lunch. Find out how the problem is resolved.

Tico and the Golden Wings, by Leo Lionni
A book about similarities and differences.

All the Colors of the Earth, by Sheila Hamanaka
A celebration of the beauty of all children.

Shades of Black: A Celebration of Our Children, by Sandra Pinkney
A book affirming the beauty of diversity.

Materials

multicultural crayons	paper
paintbrushes	colored pencils
enamel paints	felt bird with feathers
buttons	pencils
acrylic paints	stationery
assortment of	envelopes
blank booklets	mirror

Activities

1. Make a list together of feelings (happy, embarrassed, worried). Help your child write those that he or she has experienced, and draw a face to go with each.

2. Choose an envelope and a piece of stationery to write a note to a friend or a family member. Tell the person why he or she is unique. You just need an address and a stamp.

3. Use the mirror to create portraits of yourselves. Discuss skin, hair, and eye colors; hair textures; eye shapes; and other features (Derman-Sparks 1989).

4. Use the enamel paints and a small paintbrush to create a unique button (Chenfield 1985). Sew it onto an item of your child's clothing.

5. Create an *I Like Me!* book like the one in the pack. Read the book to each other several times.

6. Reread *Tico*, and then use the felt bird and feathers to retell the story together.

7. Reread *Yoko*, and discuss your favorite foods. Plan to cook one of your child's favorites within the next week. Invite your child to help with the cooking and with reading any recipes or food packages you use.

8. Find an object that you don't mind painting (lid, cotton ball, piece of sponge). Cover one side with acrylic paint. Make prints. Bring to school and we'll see if the children can guess what you used. (Each child's choice will be unique.)

Words

Read the book and choose at least two activities.

Book

Toot and Puddle, by Hollie Hobbie
Toot and Puddle are good friends and as different as can be. Follow the adventures of each as they move through the months of the year.

Materials

paper	large note cards
markers	small chalkboard
small note cards	chalk

Activities

1. Use your bodies to spell some of the two-letter words you find in the book (*to, me, in, do, is*). Find another family member or friend and spell some of the three-letter words (*the, all, you, and*) (Chenfield 1985).

2. Help your child choose any word from the book. Have him or her spell it for you as you write it in large block letters. Encourage your child to trace the letters with a finger while saying them aloud and then decorate the paper. When the piece is finished, have your child close his or her eyes and try to spell it without looking. If you wish, repeat with a few more words.

3. Just for fun, invite your child to choose any word and write it five times, using worst to best penmanship (Chenfield 1985). This should be good for some laughs!

4. Play a memory game. Use the small note cards to collect two to four words from each family member. Write each word on two cards. Turn all cards over and then use your memory to match them.

5. Walk around your house looking for words on appliances, food packages, mail, and so on. Read the words together and record them on the chalkboard.

6. Use a large note card to create a postcard for a friend. You just need a stamp and an address.

Wordless Picture Books

Choose at least two books and two activities.

Books

Will's Mammoth, by Rafe Martin
Will's parents believe that there are no more mammoths, but Will believes differently.

Niki's Walk, by Jane Tanner
Niki takes a neighborhood walk, passing by shops, a construction site, a river reserve, and more. Each page contains some sort of environmental print.

Deep in the Forest, by Brinton Turkle
A bear sneaks into a family's cottage, tasting the porridge, trying out the chairs, and playing on the beds.

Do You Want to Be My Friend?, by Eric Carle
A little mouse follows a tail, looking for a friend. Many animals are encountered along the way.

Free Fall, by David Weisner
Travel with a young boy through a fantastic dream.

Materials

sticky notes	assortment of blank booklets
pencils	note cards
crayons	premade story cards

Activities

1. "Read" to your child.
2. Listen to your child "read."
3. Use the sticky notes to write a sentence or a label for each page. Adults can do the writing for this one. Read the book together

several times, and send the writing back to school for sharing with the class.

4. Create your own wordless picture book.
5. Use the note cards to draw four pictures of something happening in sequence. Mix them up and put them back in order, telling their story.
6. Put the story cards in order.
7. Get your child a library card. Ask the librarian where to find the wordless picture books.

6 | STORYTELLING

When I was little, I made two wishes.
The first was that I would live to see the
year 2000. The second was for a crooked
tooth. One of my teachers—I don't know
if she was from the Sunday school or the
grammar school—had a crooked front
tooth. I must have liked her, because I
wanted a crooked tooth, too. I guess I
made that wish before my permanent
teeth came in. Must have been ninety
years ago. Anyway, both of my wishes
came true. I'm alive, and I've got a
crooked tooth [smiles].

—Juanita (age 96)

Stories enrich our lives. For me, Juanita's story summons images of a little Quaker girl growing up on an Indiana farm—a girl in boots and skirts and lacy hair ribbons—who goes to a white wooden building for meeting (worship) and to a red brick building for school. Young Juanita is all eyes, and one of the many things she notices about the world around her is her kind teacher's crooked tooth. Ninety years later, she tells her story.

THE FUNCTIONS OF STORY

Juanita is my grandmother and our shared stories serve many functions in both of our lives. They connect us socially as we convene on her farm two or three times a year. Usually, we sit in her familiar living room and, among other things, tell stories. I love our stories because they provide a forum for sharing laughter, passing on family history, catching up on things, and continuing to know each other better. I learn about the world as it is seen through her eyes; she learns about it as it is seen through mine. Connecting with my grandmother through story enriches both of our lives in many ways. As you will see in the following sections, stories serve many important functions in the lives of children, too.

Mark: [Sitting before his peers on the storytelling stool] I went to Washington, D.C., with my family. We saw Washington Monument and the Lincoln Memorial and the White House. Plus, my brothers and my sister and I walked up the Capitol steps.

William: Was the president there?

Mark: No, he wasn't there. He was at Mississippi.

William: He was probably on a business trip.

Jay: Yeah, visiting the king.

Lexy: Mississippi doesn't have kings!

Storytelling provides a rich context for children to construct knowledge about the world. In order for Mark to transform his lived experience into a medium for others to understand, he must take it through a process of transmediation. Transmediation involves moving ideas from one content plane (in Mark's case, his experience) to another (his oral language). Because no two content planes can carry exactly the same meaning, transmediation requires a mental reconfiguration of existing ideas, thereby contributing to the development of new perspectives (Short, Harste, and Burke 1996). Any time a child talks about something he or she has lived, written, drawn, or thought, new perspectives are formed.

Mark: It was really weird because they didn't have no George Washington stuff.

Christian: Well, think about that big pointy thing you saw. What was it called?

Mark: Washington Monument [The room becomes momentarily silent, as the other children wait for Mark's response] . . . *Ohhh!*

Storytelling also fosters learning by providing a context for children to get feedback on their thinking and ideas. For this brief period of the day, the curriculum is built around Mark's experience; his story provides a frame of reference for building on what he knows. Is Christian "covering" the curriculum at this point? In a traditional sense, no. This material does not show up in her school's written curriculum. But, she knows that storying is a way for children to expand their knowledge of the world and that world knowledge supports all areas of the curriculum.

Mark is not the only child who benefits from this experience. Because stories create a common experience among children, they provide a framework for jointly constructing knowledge:

Tina: He [Washington's statue] was stone?

Jake: No. That's the *Lincoln* stone.

Max: Lincoln's dead. That's why it's called the memorial.

Jake: What's memorial?

Hailey: It's when a whole bunch of people get together and it's kind of like church, but people died.

Christian: So, *memorial* is like *memory.*

Valuing storytelling as you value other language events in your classroom opens doors that allow children to construct all kinds of knowledge. Through this formal storytelling session, Mark provides the context and his peers provide the questions that lead the whole group to new understandings.

But, we don't have to formalize children's stories in order for them to be facilitative of their learning. As children work on projects or engage in informal discussions throughout the day, they use personal stories to build new understandings and connect with new content. For example, when a literature circle in Christian's classroom was studying things that grow, Cory told about how he had fed his dog as it was growing, concluding with ". . . I brung the whole dogfood bag and then she ate and then she turned into a big dog." Hailey, who had just gotten a new kitten, told about the cute things it had been doing and about how she was feeding and watering it. Bethany, who had drawn a series of progressively larger pictures of her mother, said, "My mom was a little girl, then she growed." Stuart wrapped up the conversation with, "We change a lot. Sometimes we are little. Maybe we might get big. Why? Because we eat." These children were using their personal stories to connect with the content they were studying, and in the process, they were building new knowledge.

Before we move on, let's think about one more thing. As you are teaching, do you ever ask, "Do you have any questions?" only to find several children with stories to tell, rather than questions to ask? I used to say, "Wait, is this a story or a question?" Because I believe that children learn through storying, I have had good reason to reconsider such a response. "[The] point is to raise the question of whether a storying mode need conflict with the information passing goals of whole-group instruction situations" (Lindfors 1991, 423). If I ask for questions but children are ready to respond with stories, is one more important than the other?

Children Encounter a Diversity of Perspectives

Another benefit of stories is that they are enmeshed in a diversity of perspectives. Stories give us insight into multiple ways of living, thinking, being, and acting, helping us develop a multicultural perspective. "Because we have often learned that there is only one 'right answer,' we have also developed only one way of seeing things. A multicultural perspective demands just the opposite." It demands that we "learn to approach reality from a variety of perspectives" (Nieto 1999, 25). The stories children bring to school come with this variety.

For example, in Christian Bush's classroom one day, all of the children told stories about their families. Lexy shared the story of her birth:

"When I was little, I had to have a bath because I just came out of my mom's tummy. My Aunt Becky had to do it because my dad didn't want to because I was too yucky and I was screaming." Including Lexy's, how many perspectives could we explore through this story? Cayla told of her summer trips to Lebanon: "Every summer, I go to Lebanon with my mom and my brother and my sister. My dad can't go because he has work. I have a house with my grandma and I go skating with my cousin and aunts." Cayla is the only first-generation American child in her classroom. What perspectives could she offer?

On another occasion, Christian's students interviewed a grandparent, asking, "What do you remember about your grandparents? Where were they from? What stories did they tell you?" When the children brought in their interview notes, Christian read them aloud. The variety of responses opened doors to conversations ranging from issues of slavery, to what it must have been like to travel by horse as a midwife, to the travails of walking across the United States on wagon tracks. And the stories were rich in perspective: "They're from Russia. They escaped the Red Army by crossing the river when it froze." "My grandparents worked in the Holocaust as a kid. They had to sleep in a tent for a lot of days. And you think it's hard taking the garbage out and cleaning the house." "My grandma lived in Palestine. She went to an English school. She lived with her grandmother. She was very religious and told her religious stories." "They didn't have computers back in those days."

"Every story told or written is a reflection of the storyteller, whose words, word order, and emphases give rise to infinite variety" (Miller 2000, 667). The variety of perspectives brought by children is probably more diverse than you could bring on your own, and when families become a part of classroom storytelling, perspective sharing is even further extended.

However, the stories children bring to school are not always easy to hear. Along with happy and inspiring stories may come stories of drug abuse, physical and emotional abuse, murder, suicide, racism, hate, and prejudice. Young children, who are often unfamiliar with school discourses, may not know which stories are most appropriately told to the class, to other children, or to a teacher, a counselor, or a principal. Because of the social and emotional complexity of such hard stories, even you may have difficulty deciding what to do with them.

Just keep in mind that there is more than one way to deal sensitively and appropriately with children's stories. As with other aspects of teaching, you make your decisions on a case-by-case basis. The important thing is that your children see school as a place where hard stories *can* be told and discussed. When they arise in Christian's classroom, she gently helps children decide whom the story is for (who the appropriate audience is), unless, of course, it is a story that a principal or a parent or even Protective Services *needs* to know. She also makes an effort to provide ground for her children to critically reflect on hard stories—

ones she feels they can emotionally handle and understand. As examples, when William's grandparents experienced an act of hate, the class discussed it and talked about the action taken to resolve it. Books such as *Amazing Grace* and *The Story of Ruby Bridges* are regularly read and discussed. And, any time a hard issue arises in the classroom or on the playground, a discussion, rather than a punishment, is protocol. Christian believes that hard stories are valuable tools for teaching and learning: "If we want children to learn from the mistakes of others, they can't be hidden away from them. We just have to approach them on a level that they understand."

Children Develop a Sense of Story

Another good reason for storytelling is that it helps children develop a sense of story (Applebee 1978; Cullinan and Galda 1998). Basic components of a story typically include characters, a setting, a problem, plot episodes, and a resolution. Having a sense of story enhances children's writing, and they "profit more from reading experiences if they are able to recognize a story and to identify its basic components" (Brown and Briggs 1992, 143). A sense of sequence is desirable as well. "We want children to be able to tell (or follow the telling of) a 'story,' a series of related events, either real or imagined, in an orderly time sequence" (Lindfors 1991, 356). This enhances both life and learning.

Having a sense of story and a sense of sequence does not mean that children must conform to a particular way of storying or to a chronological time sequence. Different cultural groups have different ways of telling and listening to stories. What we do want is for children to be able to present a coherent and interesting message to their particular audiences. Effective telling, in general, includes thoughtfully selecting what to tell, staying on track, keeping the sequence clear, and using variety in the delivery (Lindfors 1991). This applies to both oral and written stories.

LETTING STORIES LIVE IN THE CLASSROOM

"I rode a two-wheeler all by myself . . ."
"I saw a dog with just three legs . . ."
"Chamika and I built a snow fort . . ."
"Our bus got in an accident . . ."

Children are full of stories and are eager to find an audience for them. They need and want to tell stories and, as we have seen, stories serve numerous functions in their learning and their lives. It makes sense, then, to make room for stories in the classroom. But, when children hasten to you first thing in the morning with their bundles of words and armloads of new experiences, do you sometimes find it hard to listen? It's likely that as you are welcoming children, you are also doing other things—collecting permission slips, searching for a missing journal, unclogging the tip of a glue bottle, and making arrangements with the child who will be leaving at noon. Then, at group or work time, when you would like to listen to stories, do you find yourself hurrying tellers along so that other children won't get fidgety? Time is limiting, but if we want children to bring their lives into the classroom, and to use their stories to inform their learning, we must give them time to talk (Kaser and Short 1997).

Formal Storytelling Sessions

One way to give stories a life in the classroom is to organize formal storytelling sessions. (Earlier, we saw Mark, Lexy, and Cayla engaged in formal storytelling.) These sessions do not require memorization or extended practice. Children simply decide upon a story, rehearse it briefly, and share it with the class.

Model. To begin the formal storytelling process, model the telling of your own stories. Here is one that Christian told her children: "When my grandma was twelve or thirteen, she was in charge of the cows. Her job was to go out and get all the cows and bring them back to the barn. Her brother's job was to get the wagon and take it back to the barn. One day, her brother sneaked off because he wanted to be [whispers spiritedly] *with his girlfriend* [the children laugh]! So, he didn't do his job and Grandma had to bring the wagon back in. But, she didn't do her job . . . so the cows started to wander and they had to go running down the road after those cows. This story happened about seventy or seventy-two years ago. Now, I've told my daughter Brittani the story and when she gets older, she'll tell it. That's how stories are passed down."

Identify children's stories. Invite students to formally share their own stories. To help them generate ideas, remind them of stories you've heard them tell; ask them to recall any special, funny, interesting, or scary experiences they've had; remind them of favorite books or stories from the oral tradition that might be fun to retell. Consider involving families. Send home a note requesting help with "locating" stories for children. Children could tell stories they've heard about themselves when they were young; stories about parents or grandparents; bedtime stories; or folktales. Christian's students' families help their children collect stories by taking notes, helping them write their own notes, and/or collecting photographs or artifacts to enhance the telling.

Develop a schedule. Schedule storytelling time into your day, with adequate time for follow-up conversation. One option is to arrange for one or two children to tell a story each day. In Ben Mardell's (1999) classroom, this allows time for him to consult with his preschoolers before they share their stories with the class. Ben asks his children about the characters, the settings, and the plots of their stories, and as they rehearse, he clarifies any questions he has. He also makes suggestions regarding content and presentation style.

With her first graders, Christian Bush either assigns children to collect a story for homework or organizes class time for developing stories in writing. She then gives the children time to practice, independently or with peers, while she consults with students who request her help. Finally, she chooses a day for formal telling and the children share throughout the day. (You could take a whole week.) Although the stories may take only one or two minutes to tell, the valuable conversations that follow can take much longer.

Kathy Meakins keeps formal storytelling in her preschool classroom very informal. Children develop stories at play time and tell them at circle time. Children are encouraged to participate, but only if they choose to do so.

> **Kathy:** Are you making stories to read to us?
> **Children:** Yes!
> **Julia:** Not me. I'm too . . . I'm too scared to go up there.
> **Kathy:** You're too scared to read stories? I didn't know that. I'll be up there. I'll help you if you want to try.

Consult with individuals. Consult individually with children who are hesitant to tell stories. Suggest alternatives, such as sharing with just one person, drawing a story to show, writing a story to read, or dictating a story for an adult to read. Children, for personal, social, and cultural reasons, are likely to have varied orientations toward performing publicly (Lindfors 1991). Being alert to their orientations, and consciously seeking them out, will help you individualize your storytelling instruction.

Record stories permanently. Audiotape or videotape the children's stories. Make the tapes available in the listening or viewing center during play or center time. Each time we listen to and delight in children's stories we affirm the importance of their own voices in their learning and in the lives of the people around them.

Family Storytelling

Another way to bring story into the classroom is to arrange for family members to do the telling. Use greeting cards or a carefully crafted letter to send out a special invitation. Or, if you meet with families regularly, you could develop this project together. Either way, suggest multiple possibilities to help family members get started. Ask whether they have childhood stories or special traditions to share or if they might share an experience they had in elementary school. Ask whether they have a new baby, puppy, or kitten they might like to introduce and tell a story about. Do they have interesting objects in their homes, such as old photos, quilts, heirlooms, or letters? Do they have collections of shells, rocks, books, bears, recipes, art, or music? Interesting objects are often connected with interesting stories.

Ensure that storytelling is nonthreatening to guests by providing a variety of forums for sharing. Sharing need not occur with the whole class, but this is a possibility. Other possibilities include talking to small groups, doing a demonstration, displaying a set of objects or artifacts, or inviting the children to ask questions about a particular topic.

Class Anthologies

Collect a story from each child to form a class anthology. You may wish to take dictation, even for children who are beginning to write readable text. While overusing dictation prevents children from deeply exploring their hypotheses about written language, occasionally doing so can be desirable. In this case, children's stories become permanent and can be read over and over. Because they are written conventionally, you can use them for small-group reading instruction; because they are child-authored, they will be of high interest. Class anthologies show value for the connections between home and school and allow children to use their own experiences as frames of reference for learning.

Story Museums

To build a story museum, clear off some shelves or a large table. Invite children to bring in, display, and tell the story of an object from home. Possibilities include handmade crafts, art, favorite books, recipes, poems, photographs, tools, or special objects from their earlier childhood. Invite children to write a description or a label for each object in the display. Children could play as tour guides, curators, museum visitors, and catalogers.

On a similar note, family treasure hunts (Bruce 1997) involve children in consulting with family members to learn the story behind an object of importance to the family. Children interview the owner to contextualize the piece. If possible, they then bring the object to school; if not, they bring a drawing or a photograph of it. Family treasure hunts help children discover the capacity of a treasure to shed light on their heritages, communities, countries, and world (Bruce 1997).

Family Recipe Books

Invite children—with help from families—to collect a special recipe from home and to share the story behind it (Winston 1997). For example, some recipes have been passed down from grandparents or have come from another country. Some are special because they are used every Sunday or every year for a picnic. Bind all of the recipes and stories together into a book. Invite family members to come in and cook with the children, or follow the recipes yourselves. If possible, send a book home with each child.

Story Boxes

Story boxes are collections of items, sometimes suggestively related, that can be used to play around with story. In an empty shoe box or laundry detergent box, place the following:

1. one bouncing ball, one empty cup
2. ten wooden blocks, one beaded necklace, one ring, and a few pieces of multicolored fabric
3. one wolf, three pigs, a hand broom, a stick, and a brick
4. ten shells, two small paper bags, a piece of blue fabric, and a piece of tan fabric
5. miniature toy animals and several pipe cleaners
6. paper, pencils, a stapler, scissors, popsicle sticks, glue, and crayons
7. miniature cars, a length of rope, and a piece of fabric
8. three puppets (any will do)

Make the boxes available at play or center time. Encourage children to use the items to spontaneously create stories. Demonstrate a few stories of your own to inspire children's interest and communicate how you would like the materials to be used. Once they get the idea, invite children to create their own story boxes for classroom use.

Oral Histories

Another way to bring story into the classroom is to teach children to collect oral histories. Oral histories are "people's stories about events in their lives or the life of their community" (Stasz 2000, 561). Oral historians collect information primarily through interviewing and then organize it in a way that helps them understand and preserve it. You could start an oral history project by requesting that families help their children choose an individual to interview. It might be easiest to interview a grandparent or an older relative—someone with whom they feel comfortable. If you have the opportunity to meet with families about the project, brainstorm lists of questions with them. The following list provides examples of the kinds of questions that oral historians ask:

1. What has been the most important world event in your lifetime?
2. What is your earliest memory?
3. Where did you grow up? Tell me about your childhood home(s) and neighborhood(s).
4. What languages were spoken in your childhood home and neighborhood?
5. Tell me about your elementary school(s). What teachers do you remember? What children do you remember? How did you get to school?
6. What did you play when you were a child? With whom did you play?
7. How did you celebrate holidays or other special days as a child?

8. What stories do you remember hearing about yourself when you were little?
9. What stories has your family passed on to you?
10. What do you remember about your grandparents? What stories did they tell you?

Use this list as a beginning. Your children are most likely to become invested in the project—and to understand what they're doing and why—if they develop their own questions. As you brainstorm questions together, discuss the kinds that will get a yes or no response versus the kinds that will get an elaborated response. Notice that most of the questions on the list begin with "How," "What," or "Tell me about."

Consider bringing some of the interviewees into the classroom. They need not all come on one day or even in the same week. The children in Christian's classroom, who all asked the same four questions, made phone calls, sent e-mails, or met personally with their interviewees. If you send home written questions, the interviewee or any family member can help do the reading and even jot down the responses. Or, children could sketch a response.

If you try out some of these techniques on your own before using them in the classroom, you will have a powerful set of experiences for modeling. Choose a person who is important in your own life, whose stories you would like to know and remember. Conduct an interview. Get a feel for what it's like to take notes. Get a feel for what it's like to summarize the information. Then, share it with your children to demonstrate the processes they will encounter.

Once your children have collected their stories, discuss ways of transforming them into a written document for sharing. They could write in the first person or write a time line. Christian's children wrote biographies. Many answered one question per page or wrote one interesting thing they had learned on each page. The pieces were brief but rich in history and intrigue (spelling and punctuation are edited):

Evan wrote: So many important events, but [a] sad one was when President Kennedy was shot. The whole world was sad. She [grandmother] grew up in Avon, Ohio, on a farm. They had lots of animals. They had a rooster that chased the kids—like a watchdog. She went to a Catholic school and the nuns were teachers. We had prayer in our school. There wasn't a lot of toys but she played a lot of hopscotch and there was one swing set. Her grandparents were from Germany.

Bethany wrote: World War II [was a significant event in Grandfather's life] because he was nine years old and because it was a long war and they had to have stamps for food and gas and everything. He grew up on a farm in Owosso with lots of animals and lots of fields. He had seven brothers and eight sisters to help with the work and play with. It was a one-room school with twenty students in kindergarten through eighth grade. They [his grandparents] died before he was born. His mother and father came to the United States of America from Germany on a ship to Ellis Island in New York, in 1903. They were sixteen and twenty years old. Then, they moved to Michigan.

Max wrote: The most important world event in my Grandma Dailey's lifetime was the moon landing. My Grandma Dailey grew up on a farm in Armada, Michigan. They had sheep and cows. My Grandma went to country school. All the kids in kindergarten through eighth grade were in the same classroom. All together, there were twenty kids.

Many children found it difficult to write all they wanted to say, so they expressed part of their stories through drawing. Figure 6–1 shows one page of Cory's detailed written/drawn biography of a great grandparent.

The reasons for conducting oral history are many: children learn about themselves, their histories, and the life of their community; they see themselves in the curriculum; and they have an opportunity to talk, write, and read about things that are meaningful to them (Stasz 2000).

Stories Inspired by Books

The following text sets are likely to inspire children to tell, write, and draw stories of their own. Many connect logically with the projects described previously.

Spunky Kid Set

It Takes a Village, by Jane Cowen-Fletcher
Yemi's plan is to watch her little brother, Kokou, at the market, but he wanders away.

Oh, No, Toto!, by Katrin Hyman Tchana and Louise Tchana Pami
Little Toto goes to the market with his Mami and gets into all kinds of trouble. He tips over the puffpuffs, tumbles into the palm oil, and eats Mami Peter's koki and cassava stick.

No, David!, by David Shannon
Little David tips over the fish bowl, writes on the wall, plays with his food, and runs naked down the street. His mother's admonishments are always a bit too late.

Lilly's Purple Plastic Purse, by Kevin Henkes
Lilly loved her school and her teacher . . . until she brought in her purple plastic purse, that is, and just could not wait to show it.

Too Many Tamales, by Gary Soto
Maria tries on her mother's ring as she helps make tamales, but it turns up missing. Where could it be?

FIGURE 6–1 *Cory's Biography*

My Grandpa was in the World War 2.

After hearing these stories, your students will be eager to tell their own stories about the spunky things kids do. Invite the children to tell, write, and draw their stories. Look for patterns in the stories and create a class book organized by story themes.

Retelling Set

Goldilocks and the Three Bears, by James Marshall
The traditional tale retold.

Ming Lo Moves the Mountain, by Arnold Lobel
Ming Lo doesn't like the mountain near his house but he can't figure out how to move it. Read with your children to find out how a wise man helps.

Lon Po Po, by Ed Young
A Red Riding Hood story from China.

The True Story of the 3 Little Pigs!, by John Scieska
This traditional tale is told from the perspective of the wolf.

Gingerbread Baby, by Jan Brett
A gingerbread baby jumps out of the oven and is chased all over town.

Invite your children to dramatize these fun-to-retell stories as you read them aloud. Consider making puppets or costumes. Or, place the books in a center and invite children to create props for retelling.

Memoir Set

When I Was Little: A Four-Year-Old's Memoir of Her Youth, by Jamie Lee Curtis
Now that she is grown up, a four-year-old girl describes her early days.

When Frank Was Four, by Alison Lester
A playful scrapbook of pictures about the early lives of seven children.

The Upside Down Boy, by Juan Felipe Herrera
The author recounts his migrant family's move to the city so that he could attend school for the first time.

When I Was Young in the Mountains, by Cynthia Rylant
A childhood memoir from Appalachia.

Invite your students to talk about their own memories and share them with the class. They could draw or write one memory per page and then arrange the pages in order. Or, they could develop a time line, having family members help record one event from each year. Another possibility is to invite children to interview and write a memoir of an older family member.

Family Set

Papa Tells Chita a Story, by Elizabeth Fitzgerald Howe
A young girl joins in the telling of her papa's tales from the Spanish-American war.

Tell Me a Story, Mama, by Angela Johnson
A mother and young daughter share memories from the mother's childhood.

Isla, by Arthur Dorros
Through story, Rosalba visits the Carribean island where her grandmother grew up.

The Chalk Doll, by Charlotte Pomerantz
A young girl is tucked into bed as her mother tells memories of her childhood in Jamaica.

Invite your children to talk with family members about their special memories. (Send a note home.) Afterward, provide time at school for retelling.

Story and Object Set

Aunt Flossie's Hats (and Crab Cakes Later), by Elizabeth Fitzgerald Howe

Sarah and Susan's Great Aunt Flossie has many hats, each with a story of its own.

Home Place, by Crescent Dragonwagon
The remains of an old house give hint to the stories of the lives of the people who lived in it.

The Lemon Drop Jar, by Christine Widman
A young girl visits her Great Aunt Emma, who shares a special family story about a treasured lemon drop jar.

After reading the stories, invite children to bring in an artifact from home (or their yard) that is connected with a story of their own. Or, they could collect an item from a family member. Sometimes, items (fragments of dishes or old toys found in yards) may not be connected with known stories, but they suggest things about the lives of those who used them. Reflect on the significance of all items. Send a note to parents explaining the project. Provide time for sharing and discussion.

INQUIRE INTO STORYTELLING

As you reflect on storytelling in your classroom, do you find yourself wondering or marveling or wanting to know more? If so, choose to inquire:

- How do my children learn through story? What do they learn?
- What am I learning about my children's lives through the stories they tell?
- What do my children tell stories about? Are patterns evident across children?
- What are my children learning about language and literacy through the stories we tell?
- How does the language children use to tell stories change over time (Landis 1999)?
- What sequencing patterns are evident in children's stories? Do the children tell stories in a linear sequence? Is the pattern more cyclical? Is it recursive?
- Are there differences between the stories told by boys and those told by girls? Are there cultural or class differences? Are there differences in the ways in which boys, girls, or different groups of children tell stories? What is the nature of all of these differences?
- How are stories received? Do my children and I privilege some kinds of stories over others?
- Do certain stories or ways of telling stories carry more authority in our classroom?

Figure 6–2 shows an example of a form for collecting storytelling data. It can be adapted to meet your goals. Consider using such a form for conferencing with children and families.

Here is what I have learned about _____'s . . .

Life and experiences outside of school:

Family:

Interests:

Ways of using language (including stories) to shape understandings:

Ways of speaking in front of an audience (eye contact, expressiveness, audibility, gesture, and facial expressions):

Ways of telling and sequencing stories:

Other observations:

FIGURE 6–2   *Form for Observing Storytelling and Other Language Events*

7 | LITERATURE CIRCLES

Christian: What went well in your literature circles today?
    Archie: We told good stories.
      Jake: Everybody was listening.
     Tina: Everyone was being serious.
    Adam: I liked when they told us a serious question.

Literature circles have the potential to create a love for literature and an intelligence about books that will last a lifetime. Participating in literature circles contributes to children's developing knowledge by providing a structure for children to read and mull over books together and, as Christian's children put it, to tell good stories, to listen, and to be serious about learning. Typically, literature circles involve children in reading or listening to books tied to their curriculum or personal interests, responding individually through multiple sign systems, and engaging in follow-up discussions (see Figure 7–1). Very young children may take one or two days to complete this process; older children may take up to two weeks. As we will see in the following sections, the benefits of participating in this activity are well worth the time and effort.

CHILDREN DEVELOP KNOWLEDGE

A major benefit of literature circles is that they provide a structure for children to learn from books. In the literature circle setting, young children typically listen to a book, explore it by drawing, writing, sculpting, painting, playing, dramatizing, or composing, and then discuss it with peers. The listening—often coupled with discussion—provides an initial exposure to the book, an initial opportunity to enjoy the content and begin to make personal connections. The follow-up explorations, because they require processing thoughts and information through multiple sign systems, take children's understandings to a deeper level.

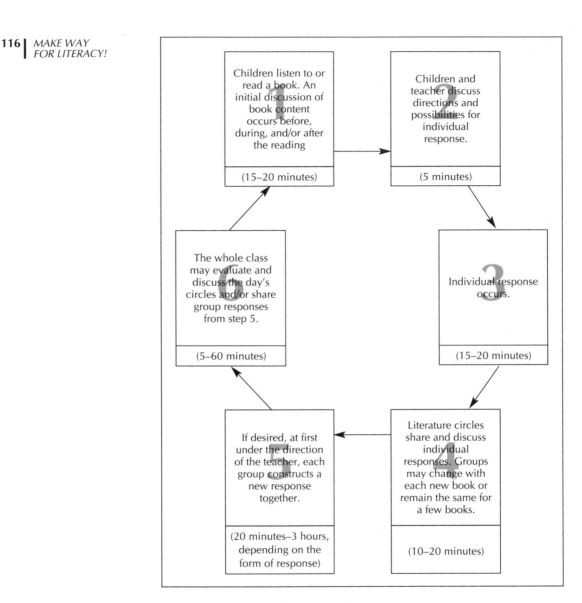

FIGURE 7–1   *Literature Circle Flow Chart*

Because each system has a unique meaning potential, each enables children to connect with a book and explore it in a new way. For example, creating a piece of art enables a child to explore a different kind of meaning than composing a written response. Sculpting allows a child to explore a book in a different way than dramatizing. "Because each sign system has a different potential for meaning [Eisner 1994], students [who transform their thinking from one to another] do not transfer the same meaning, but create new ideas, and so their understandings of a

book become more complex" (Short, Kauffman, and Kahn 2000, 160).
Listening and responding to books through multiple sign systems provides a structure for children to build their world knowledge.

CHILDREN SHARE KNOWLEDGE

Literature circles also provide important opportunities for children to share and jointly construct knowledge. Conferring around a shared topic makes the conditions just right for seeing how others interpret and respond to text. The joint focus provides a structure for building understandings together. Consider the following exchange, in which four children are constructing a web to retell a story:

Jake: The problem was the animals kept eating the food.
Hailey: And the snow melted.
Archie: What is the resolution?
Hailey: She kept on building and she put it in the fridge. [Hailey writes as Jake provides spellings.] What's the setting?
Jake: Where it takes place. On the snow.
Bethany: [Pointing out the word *Snowman* on the book cover] Copy this.
Jake: It doesn't take place on the snow*man*!
Bethany: [Covers *man*] Snow.

The children's mutual focus on constructing the web provides a structure for sharing knowledge about story content, story elements, words, and ways of retelling. As is typical of children working together, the social signs these children use to communicate serve to mediate their learning (Thomas and Rinehart 1990; Vygotsky 1978). In other words, the questioning, the answering, and the pointing to and covering of print mediate knowledge construction. Sociocultural theory teaches that the signs first used to mediate action in social contexts are eventually internalized and used as tools for thinking; the interpersonal becomes intrapersonal (Vygotsky 1978). Therefore, we could say that Christian's children's social use of language and gesture (to accomplish the goals of literature circles) helps them develop tools for independent thinking and learning.

While the potential for joint construction of knowledge is significant, it is wise to keep an eye on the actual conversations that occur. If children do not achieve a certain level of mutual understanding—a shared understanding upon which to build a conversation—they may be limited in what they can construct together. Merely sitting in a circle to discuss a book does not guarantee that rich interactions will occur. Kidwatching (described a bit later) can help you make literature circles work for all children.

Kiara: My auntie has a daughter named Pamela and she's my friend.

 Max: I thought she was your cousin.

Kiara: She's my friend, too.

 Max: *Cousin* and *friend* are not the same. You're making it up, aren't you?

Another benefit of literature circles is that they provide a meaningful context for exploring the vocabulary encountered in books. The context, provided by both the book and the surrounding conversation, helps children learn words as concepts rather than just words. "Just defining or demonstrating words does not markedly increase vocabulary unless children actually use the words introduced. When words are used in daily conversation and activities, they are far more likely to become a part of children's vocabulary" (Neuman, Copple, and Bredekamp 2000, 63). Literature circles provide a natural arena for exploring new vocabulary through reading, conversation, and writing.

Literature circles also provide a valuable tool for second language development. When second language learners discuss a piece of literature with native language speakers they have a rich context for hearing how others use language to describe potentially similar reactions. The mutual focus provides substantive ground not only for building new language knowledge but also for building concepts related to book content (Watts-Taffe and Truscott 2000). Research shows that there is some question regarding the extent to which young children who are learning a second language benefit from listening to books in that language (Garcia 2000). If possible, arrange for children to listen to stories in their native language or both languages. If you can offer English only, provide lots of contextual support: read very expressively, use gestures and facial expressions, point to pictures, use props to illustrate words and events not found in pictures, and provide opportunities for children to discuss the book in their native language with parents, volunteers, or other children in the school.

CHILDREN CRITICALLY EXAMINE TEXT

Another benefit of literature circles lies in their potential to spur thoughtful critique. When children read quality literature together, they often have something to say; they want to share their opinions, ideas, thoughts, or feelings, and literature circles provide a structure for doing so. However, in-depth critique requires knowledge and experience, and you may find that early on, it does not emerge without your support. Children may stick with what's easy (what they like, how they feel) or with limited modes of response (always talking about pictures, always reflecting on what they liked best).

You can help your children learn to critique by modeling your own critical thinking about texts and engaging with them in discussions about their views. As you teach, it is important to attend to both local and beyond-text issues. Local critique is characterized by a focus on the craft of authors and illustrators.

Children engage in local critique by reflecting on illustrations, content, and style.

Illustrations

- what they think of illustrations; whether they are interesting, aesthetically pleasing, well-arranged, reader-friendly
- how the illustrations help readers understand the author's work; how they take the author's ideas a step further; how they help convey moods and feelings; how they help readers get to know the characters and the setting
- how the illustrator uses color, texture, space, shapes, shadows, lines, and so on

Content and Style

- how language is used; whether the language sounds natural
- with fiction, whether the author tells a good story; whether the problem-resolution sequence is interesting and could really happen; whether the characters seem real; the way the theme or lesson is revealed
- with nonfiction, whether it is easy to understand the author's words; whether ideas and concepts are presented in a way that makes sense; whether good examples are provided
- how the author's use of literary language (imagery, alliteration, rhyme, and so on) contributes to meaning and sound

Local critique compels children to reflect on diverse components of a text, thereby helping them see it in a new way. By drawing readers into thinking deeply about illustrations, language, and meanings, it enhances not only their appreciation but also their understanding.

Beyond-text critique focuses on broader social and cultural issues—those that are directly addressed or raised by the author as well as those that may be implicit in the ways in which the author's message is presented. Beyond-text critique is important because it helps children learn to "create alternative images of what can be or is possible" in this world (Yenika-Agbaw 1997, 450). For example, children who read *The Story of Ruby Bridges* (Coles 1995) learn that Ruby was one of the first African American children to attend a desegregated school. From critical discussions and explorations surrounding this book, they may come to an understanding of the power that a society has to change and also of the difficulties associated with change. Children who critically read and discuss *The Day the Earth Was Silent* (McGuffee 1996), a story about children who take their call for world peace all the way to the

United Nations, may come to appreciate the potential for children to make a difference in the world and also to understand the barriers they may face. It is likely that much of the curriculum-related literature you are already using would be appropriate for beyond-text critique.

To support beyond-text critique, engage with your students in reading "against and around the text" (Yenika-Agbaw 1997, 450). This means consciously posing critical questions together and thinking about texts from multiple perspectives:

- What is this book about? Why do you think the author wrote this piece?
- What do we know about the author? Do you think that being in a wheelchair/a woman/Native American makes a difference in what this author has to say?
- Do the words and illustrations provide a real picture (authentic representation) of a child's life/what a child experiences/how people live/how people treat others/what children do when they are upset/what people look like and so on? What are other ways to represent these things?
- Are boys/girls/men/women/people of color/people from parallel cultures presented realistically or in stereotypical roles?

ORGANIZING LITERATURE CIRCLES

Now that we have explored the learning potential inherent in literature circles, let's look at how you might organize them in your classroom. We will begin by exploring Christian Bush's practices for getting literature circles started in her first-grade classroom.

Ensure a Sense of Community

To prepare for literature circles, Christian spends the first month of the school year helping her children build and adjust to the literacy practices in their new classroom. If literature circles are going to be a success, the children must feel safe in taking the risks associated with publicly sharing writings, drawings, and ideas, and they must know the discourses for doing so.

Christian helps her children feel safe by fostering a classroom culture in which children are seen as competent to write and to talk about literature. From day one, she responds to children claiming they can't write or can't draw with, "Well, show me what you *can* do, so I can help you grow." As these hesitant children get their ideas on paper, Christian helps them understand that literacy develops over time; children do not write or draw like adults, nor does she expect them to do so. When children say they don't have ideas for writing, Christian helps them to find a connection with the text. She asks, "What does this book/page/

picture make you think about? Have you seen or heard something like this before?" When children write or say something that is treated as out of whack by the other children, Christian responds with, "Wait. Everyone sees things differently. Let's listen so we can see in a new way." Christian's focus is on developing a classroom culture in which learners will take risks with writing and drawing and will actively, sensitively listen to what others have to say.

To help her children understand the procedures, or discourses, associated with literature circles, Christian begins the school year by inviting them to listen to books, record their impressions, and share them with the whole class. Christian models the procedure by writing and sharing her own responses. Sometimes, the possibilities for response are open-ended. For example, children may record through drawing or writing what they have learned from a text, a personal connection, or something they found interesting. At other times, Christian asks the children to focus on a particular idea: how they feel about a character's actions, what they would have done in a similar situation, or what they think of the problem-resolution sequence. Christian's goal during the first month of school is to help her children learn the discourses for listening, responding to, and sharing ideas about literature.

Provide Demonstrations

When her children understand the discourses for responding to literature and then sharing those responses, Christian invites a small group to demonstrate the literature circle process:

> Christian is sitting on the floor—heads together—with a small group of children. The rest of the class is sitting in a wider circle, surrounding the group.

> **Christian:** Okay . . . we have a circle within a circle. Why?
> **William:** It looks like a tire.
> **Christian:** But it's not going to look like this always. We are going to have a bunch of small circles when we do this. We are in a literature circle.

Rather than selecting for this demonstration only children who are likely to put on a good show, Christian has selected a group that is heterogeneous in many ways. She wants the class to see a variety of responses and to see her way of showing respect and support for different ways of responding. Thus, some of the children in the group are already writing readable text, while others are just beginning to do so; some are drawing with great detail, while others are still developing this competency; some of the children are talkative, while others speak infrequently; some have demonstrated an eagerness to discuss literature, while others seem to prefer different kinds of experiences. This variety helps Christian demonstrate that there is more than one acceptable way to respond.

To prepare for the demonstration, all of the children in the class have listened to *Rain*, by Donald Crews, and have responded by writing a text-to-self connection (Keene and Zimmermann 1997). Christian is the first to share.

Christian: I wrote in my journal about a weather experience I've had. [Reads her response about splashing in mud puddles as a child before getting on the bus to school] Who has something to say about what I wrote?

Jacob: It's good.

Christian: That makes me feel good inside. Thank you, Jason.

Amelia: I like it.

Christian: Thank you, Amanda. [Pauses; briefly looks at each child in the group] Now, I see that nobody else has anything else to say. Now, Evan, you read.
[Evan reads his response.]

Amelia: That was a good story.

Bethany: That was a really great one.

In this first circle, most of the talk is light, complimentary, and characterized by an "individualistic structure" (McCormack 1997): the speaker shares and the audience responds without making a conversation-building connection. This does not seem like the stuff of a great conversation, but Christian is not concerned. Her experience has taught her that children need to learn the discourses for interacting in a literature circle before they can dig in deeply.

Don't be surprised if your children's early conversations seem light in weight, too. However, as you provide demonstrations, and later, as you move from circle to circle, do keep a sharp eye out for the teachable moment. "When a topic surfaces that holds a common interest and has the potential for altering perceptions, [encourage children to] shift the discussion from sharing to dialogue" (Peterson 1997, 43). Ensure them that it is okay to abandon formality and to say what they want to say. For children to become critical readers and thinkers who consider varying perspectives, they must move from sharing personal connections to jointly focusing on issues (Short, Kauffman, and Kahn 2000).

Kidwatch

Christian: What went well today?

Jeremy: The stories were not fake.

Jay: The stories weren't long.

Kiara: Everybody wasn't laughing when I was telling my story.

Mitchell: I liked how one of the people in my group was being nice.

Christian's intention is for the structures demonstrated early in the year to provide a scaffold for structuring future conversations. She wants the children to remember that each child must share, each must actively listen, and a conversation may ensue around any child's response. Although the children run their own circles after a day or two of demonstrations, Christian does not leave them to their own processes after this point. She spends the year kidwatching, primarily by collecting anecdotal notes and writing samples, to help her reflect on her teaching as well as on the children's progress. Her schedule for the first few months involves visiting one or two circles each meeting day. In her class of twenty-seven this year, she typically has five circles running simultaneously.

Her data help her reflect on the ways in which children are interacting and constructing knowledge. For example, through kidwatching, Christian learned that Jerome was saying very little during literature circles. Instead of sharing his ideas he often looked down with an uncomfortable expression on his face. Christian's notes reminded her that she would need to touch base with him. As they talked, Christian learned that Jerome was uncomfortable because he could not read what he had written. Most of the other first graders couldn't read *their* writing either, but this seemed to bother Jerome more than it did the others. After several mini-conferences to address this issue, during which Christian helped Jerome reread what he had written and encouraged him to tell rather than read what he wanted to say, Jerome was able to participate more effectively.

Along with individual children, Christian supports group processes. Each meeting day, she talks with the whole class about how things are going. She asks, "What went well?" and "What do we need to work on?" Depending on the issues that arise, she may address the following:

- ways of responding to others' thoughts and ideas
- ways of questioning
- what it means to actively listen
- what children are doing to help their groups have a meaningful conversation
- what children are doing to improve how well their groups work

As you can see, Christian's procedures for getting literature circles started are aimed at helping children feel safe and at helping them learn how to reflect, share, and listen. Early on, she demonstrates, models, and provides lots of support. As the children gain experience and independence, she is able to change her support from a focus on discourses and group processes to a more substantive focus on book content.

Choosing the Literature

Christian's students are sitting in literature circles, discussing their written responses to *Hattie and the Fox* (Fox 1987):

Samantha: I think Hattie should warn the animals like this: "There is a fox in the bushes!"

Tina: Hattie could say, "Are you listening? I see something!"

Jacob: She can tell them, "I am warning you!"

Zeke: What warning? Like, "Leave him alone!" Or, what?

Jacob: Yeah.

When you feel like your children are ready to try out literature circles, take some time to look for books that may open doors to thoughtful conversation. What kinds of books might raise interesting questions and provoke intrigue in the eyes of your children? Which books connect with their interests and prior knowledge? Which connect with your curriculum? Thoughtful discussions emerge when children encounter believable characters, familiar circumstances, compelling content, and unusual twists (Johnson and Giorgis 2000). Using these criteria to select books will help your children become engaged with the literature and ensure that they are able to build rich conversations.

Following are some book possibilities for getting started. All of the suggested books can be read in one sitting, but longer books, even short chapter books, could be read over the course of several days. The books represent a variety of topics and genres; their commonality is in their potential to stimulate conversation.

Amazing Grace, by Mary Hoffman
An African American girl auditions for the role of Peter Pan in the class play.

The Story of Ruby Bridges, by Robert Coles
The story of one of the first African American children to attend a desegregated elementary school.

The Big Orange Splot, by Daniel Pinkwater
Mr. Plumbean expresses his individuality through the painting of his house and begins a neighborhood trend.

The Relatives Came, by Cynthia Rylant
A brood of relatives gets together for a family reunion.

Chrysanthemum, by Kevin Henkes
Chrysanthemum loves her name . . . until the other kids make fun of it.

Lilly's Purple Plastic Purse, by Kevin Henkes
Lilly loves her school and her teacher . . . until she brings her purple plastic purse to school and cannot wait to show it.

It's Pumpkin Time, by Zoe Hall
All summer long, a young boy and girl prepare for their favorite holiday.

When Winter Comes, *When Spring Comes*, *When Autumn Comes*, and *When Summer Comes*, by Robert Maass
Read one of these books, or use all four as a text set. Each contains simple text and color photographs portraying seasonal activities and events.

The First Strawberries: A Cherokee Story, by Joseph Bruchac
A Cherokee legend explaining how strawberries came to be.

The Secret Footprints, by Julia Alvarez
An enchanting legend (with Dominican roots) about the *cigua-pas*, whose toes point behind them.

Something Beautiful, by Sharon Dennis Wyeth
A young African American girl looks for, and discovers, beauty in her city neighborhood.

Babushka Baba Yaga, by Patricia Polacco
A warm little community learns a life lesson from the loving old Baba Yaga.

No, David! and *David Goes to School*, by David Shannon
These books make a fun text set. In both, little David stirs up all kinds of challenges for the adults in his life.

The Empty Pot, by Demi
A Chinese emperor must choose, from all of the children in the land, his successor to the throne.

The Salamander Room, by Anne Mazer
A boy imagines an environment for his pet salamander that is most like its natural environment.

Reading the Books

Several formats are available for reading literature circle texts. For example, you could read one book to the whole class. This works especially well with kindergartners and beginning first graders, many of whom are not yet reading text independently. Another option for very young children is to give them wordless picture books to explore independently or in small groups.

For children who are more familiar with literature circles, you could offer a choice of five books to be read by small groups. Collect five different books or six copies each of five different books and introduce each book to the whole class. Then lay out the books and invite children to place a nametag on their first choice. When six tags have accumulated on a book, that choice is closed. Older children may read the books independently, in pairs, or as a group. Parents, grandparents, and/or older students may help read the books to younger children. In Christian's class, by December, two of the first graders were able to read the books to their groups.

You could also create text sets for small groups to explore. Collect five text sets, each with seven to ten different books focusing on a common topic, theme, author, or illustrator. Briefly introduce each set to the whole class. Then display the five sets and invite children to place a nametag on their top choice. When six tags have accumulated on a set, that choice is closed. Each child then chooses from the set a book to read independently. Or, children may read a few of the books aloud together.

Possibilities for Individual Reflection

After a book has been read, children independently construct a visual or written response, which will later be shared with the circle. Or, if children are reading longer or more complex pieces, you may wish to arrange for responses and meeting times partway through the book. Two possibilities for response are child-chosen responses and teacher-directed responses.

When working with child-chosen responses, children choose what to write and/or draw. Any impression, question, or idea is permissible. Note: You may find that child-chosen responses work better later. Some initial direction helps children understand the repertoire of choices available to them. To foster independence, you may wish to start a poster of response ideas with your children (Figure 7–2).

When working with teacher-directed responses, children respond visually or in writing to particular questions or issues that you pose. Some examples:

- What are you thinking or feeling now that you've read this text?
- What surprised you or piqued your interest in a special way?
- What connections can you make to your life? Did the piece help you learn more or change your ideas about something you already knew?
- Which characters did you like? How do you feel about the way they handled events in the story? Which characters did you dislike? Why?
- How did a character change over time?
- What did you learn from the text? How does it compare to what you knew already? Did you learn something that you can use in your life?
- What questions do you have?
- Why do you think the author wrote this text?
- What are the roles of girls and boys/men and women/people of color? Whose words and actions are valued? To whom do people listen? Are there stereotypes?
- What actions might we take now that we've read this book?
- What did you like/not like about what you've read? What was your favorite part? Why?
- What do you think about the illustrations? How did they help you understand or appreciate the story?
- Record important/confusing/surprising words.
- Record or mark (with a bookmark, a tab marker, or a sticky note) interesting or important quotes, sections, or pictures.

Getting the Circles Going

When individual responses are complete, children bring them to circles for sharing. To help groups run smoothly, you may wish to designate a

Write about, sketch, draw, paint, or sculpt . . .

- an interesting event
- a favorite part of the book
- a feeling you had while reading
- something that surprised you
- something that confused you
- a personal connection
- a question
- a wondering
- a character/a character at a particular point in time
- what the main character or personality did; what you would do in a similar situation
- changes in a character
- the setting
- a map of the changing settings
- the problem-resolution sequence
- an alternative to the resolution
- a main idea; or a main idea with supporting details
- a diagram, a picture, or a model that shows what you have learned
- something you noticed about the illustrations

FIGURE 7–2   *Response Ideas*

group leader or let children choose a leader for the day. Keep a record sheet (Figure 7–3) to ensure that all children have experiences as the leader. Group leaders may be responsible for collecting any necessary materials; beginning the conversation by sharing their ideas first; ensuring that all voices are heard; recording information; and reporting back to the whole class, when this is a goal.

To ensure that children can hear one another, it is important that circles be spread throughout the room. When the children are settled, invite them to take their time to share their thoughts. Early on, you may find that some groups finish in five minutes or less but have not had the kind of in-depth conversation for which you were hoping. Have a plan in place to help these children further reflect or to construct a group response (see following section).

Possibilities for Group Reflections

After the children have discussed their individual responses, each group may jointly construct a response for sharing with the whole class. At first, you may wish to suggest ways of responding, but start a possibility chart on the wall so that children can eventually become independ-

Children's Names	Literature Circle Leader

FIGURE 7–3 *Literature Circle Leaders*

ent. Follow-up may occur every time literature circles meet or every so often. Following are some possibilities for group reflections:

- One Interesting Thing: Each group shares one interesting thing it discussed.
- A Question: Each group responds to a question. For example:
    What did you talk about? (requires synthesis of information)
    What have you learned? (requires abstracting information)
    How did your group feel about the piece? (taps into the affective domain)
    You talked about why you think the author wrote this text. What ideas did you generate? (requires critical thinking)
- Exploration Through Multiple Sign Systems:
    write a book in the style of the author or the illustrator or address a similar topic
    write a book review
    create a set of puppets to be used for retelling
    develop a web, a map, or a time line for retelling
    create a piece of art (mural, painting, drawing, sculpture) to visually represent some part of the text
    compose a skit based on a scene or an event from the book
    compose a script for a readers theatre performance
    gather and display objects representing some element of the story
    build a block structure to represent some part of the story or to represent something the group has learned
    compose a poem, a song, or a piece of music related to the book
    sculpt a scene from the book
    create a labeled diagram to explain some concept from the book
    draw a picture that synthesizes part of the book

INQUIRE INTO LITERATURE CIRCLES

Christian: What didn't go well in your literature circles today?
  Dana: Somebody at my group didn't get a turn.
Jeremy: Somebody in my group laughed at my story.
 Amelia: Some people was talking and I had to stop a lot and I didn't like it.
   Jake: People, like, were looking around.

Having children follow the procedures for a literature circle is one thing, but having them use literature circles to deeply explore what they have read is another. As in any classroom, it is likely that your children will need support aimed at fostering the processes and kinds of discussion that lead to deep and critical thinking. Inquiry can help you identify your children's needs and learn to provide such support. Following are examples of the kinds of inquiry questions you might ask, and Figure 7–4 provides an example of a data collection form. The form is designed for one child but could be adapted for group or whole-class use.

- What are my students learning about the world/about topics of inquiry in our classroom as a result of their participation in literature circles?
- What are they learning about language and literacy?
- How are they learning about the world/topics of inquiry in our classroom/language and literacy?
- What seems to promote substantive conversation? What are the barriers?
- What do children talk about as they engage in literature circles?
- How do they support one another in developing understandings of concepts?
- What is the experience of children for whom literature circles seem to not be working?

Literature circles provide a wonderful medium for children to connect with and learn from books, to develop their language, and to learn to read and think critically. Let literature circles be a central part of life in your classrooms—and watch your children use books to explore, dream, and discover.

Kidwatching Literature Circles

Child's Name: _____

Teacher Observations During Individual Preparation/Circle Discussions	Child's Self-Evaluation of Learning/Participation	Ideas for Instruction
(record language and actions here)	(record child's reflections on learning)	(determine goals together)

Examples of questions:

1. What do you learn through literature circles? *Prompt child to address content as well as literacy-related skills and strategies.*

2. What kinds of things do you and others talk about in literature circles?

3. What makes literature circles work well?

4. What could you do to improve the way literature circles work?

5. Who is good at literature circles? Why is this person good?

6. _____?

7. _____?

FIGURE 7–4 *Form for Kidwatching Literature Circles*

8 | READERS THEATRE

Children: *Harry and the Dirty Dog*, by Gene Zion.
Narrator 1: Harry was a white dog with black spots.
Narrator 2: He played with some other dogs and became dirty.
Narrator 3: He slid down a coal chute and became even dirtier. In fact, he changed. Now he was a black dog with white spots.
Harry: [Playing and sliding and getting dirty]
Little Girl: By the way, has anyone seen Harry?

Enter a classroom during a readers theatre performance and you are likely to see a small group of children confidently reading aloud a text—one they have chosen themselves, analyzed extensively, and transformed into a script. The audience is likely to be engrossed by the performance, laughing, empathizing with characters, or simply being amazed by what their peers have accomplished.

WHAT IS READERS THEATRE?

Readers theatre is a forum for interpreting and orally presenting a written text. Typically, children choose a piece of literature, and if it is not already in the form of a script, they transform it into one. Then they rehearse the script extensively and read it for an audience. Performances usually involve few physical actions, props, sets, or costumes. The audience relies on the oral interpretation of the cast as well as on their own imaginations (Pickering 1975). For children, the benefits of participating in a readers theatre are many, as we will see.

Children Develop Appreciation for Literature and Drama

Readers theatre provides a forum for children to deeply engage in and develop appreciation for literature and drama. As children read, interpret, and rehearse texts, they transform themselves into colorful worlds where wolves blow down houses, friendly dragons walk city streets, animals can talk, and children solve big problems. What child would not love to play around in such a world? When these worlds are shared with an appreciative audience, the experience is even further enhanced; there is laughter, silliness, drama, and intensity, with children as the creators. If a goal for your literature program is to help children develop positive dispositions for reading, then readers theatre makes good sense.

Children Are Motivated to Read and Write

As children play around in their theatrical text worlds, internal motivations for quality writing and reading run high. Children want to perform well because it is fun and because it feels good to bring pleasure to an audience. With these goals in mind, they work hard to understand characters and events, to tailor scripts to their liking, and to rehearse until they sound just right. Developing such internal motivation for literate activity is important because it inspires long-term literacy commitments, enhances strategy development, and increases time spent in literate activities (Sweet and Guthrie 1996).

Language Is Integrated

Another positive aspect of readers theatre is that it is an integrated language event that refines children's ability to read, write, listen, and speak effectively (Sloyer 1982; Tierney, Readence, and Dishner 1990; Watts-Taffe and Truscott 2000). Composing processes develop as children collaboratively write scripts, exploring together the choices that authors make to create texts that are just right for conveying their intended meanings (Tierney, Readence, and Dishner 1990).

Reading fluency and expressiveness develop as children engage in repeated readings (rehearsals) (Martinez, Roser, and Strecker 1998/ 1999). From the first rehearsal to the time of the performance, there is almost always an exciting and marked improvement. Readers theatre also helps children develop their language and vocabulary. Through rehearsals, discussions, and writing, children are immersed in actual use of language and are "surrounded by situations which provide crucial, and often subtle, connotative meaning" (Busching 1981, 333).

Second language learners especially benefit from the contextualized use of language (Pross 1986) and from hearing language as they follow along with text. The expressive readings can help these children develop a sense of character; follow story actions and events; and develop their language proficiency. Theatre activities help put meanings and structures into place for all language users by maintaining a focus on meaning and keeping language whole.

All Children Can Participate Successfully

A final benefit of readers theatre is that with a little thoughtful planning, all children are able to participate successfully. You can ensure success for every child by reading aloud to the class the pieces to be used for scripts. Thoroughly discuss these pieces and consider arranging for children to do a little drawing or writing to help internalize the content. Then, spend some extra time with children who may not have grasped the essential meanings and important elements. Children who have a good understanding of the piece will find it easier to script and dramatize it. You can also arrange for parts of scripts to be written at different levels to meet children's varied reading needs. Either take dictation or require that children write their own speaking parts. Allow all children adequate time for practice. Finally, as children move into small groups to rehearse, continue to kidwatch, finding ways to support children who need extra help.

PROCEDURES FOR IMPLEMENTING A READERS THEATRE

To introduce your children to readers theatre, read a play or a script with them. Aaron Shepard's readers theatre page (<www.aaronshep.com>) includes scripts that may be copied for classroom use. As you explore scripts, help children attend to both content and format. First, let them enjoy the piece as a whole, then help them sort out its format: what names in margins mean, how dialogue is used, what a narrator does, and so on. Having a good feel for the format of scripts informs children's process of constructing their own.

Selecting Materials

As children move into constructing scripts, allow them to take part in deciding which texts to use. By allowing students to choose their instructional material, we convey the idea that their interests and opinions matter, and we support them in using meaningful frames of reference for constructing new knowledge. It is likely that your first efforts at scriptwriting will be at the whole-class level. For initial demonstrations, choose books that are class favorites. When smaller groups begin to construct their own scripts, offer several choices, and invite children to form their groups by choosing the book they would most like to explore.

Both fiction and nonfiction are appropriate for readers theatre. If fiction is your genre choice, choose stories with tight plots, clear endings, suspense, interesting characters, and appealing themes (Tierney, Readence, and Dishner 1990). This draws performers into the world of their characters and leads to an exciting performance for the audience. If you use nonfiction, choose biographies, autobiographies, or other pieces written about interesting personalities with interesting things to say. Nonfiction pieces should connect with curricular concepts your class is exploring.

Recommended Books for Readers Theatre

The Fat Cat, by Jack Kent
A Danish folktale about a cat who eats everyone and everything he sees.

The Flying Dragon Room, by Audrey Wood
With a special set of tools, Patrick creates something out-of-this-world.

Goldilocks and the Three Bears, by James Marshall
The traditional tale told in a very humorous way.

The Great Kapok Tree, by Lynne Cherry
A menagerie of animals living in a Kapok tree urges a man to leave it standing.

The Greatest Treasure, by Demi
A Chinese folktale teaches some old proverbs.

It's Mine!, by Leo Lionni
A fable in which three frogs learn a valuable lesson.

Meet Danitra Brown, by Nikki Grimes
A collection of poems about a wonderful friend, Danitra Brown.

Mirandy and Brother Wind, by Patricia McKissack
Mirandy sets out to catch the wind.

My Many Colored Days, by Dr. Suess
Dr. Seuss pairs emotions with color.

Owl Babies, by Martin Waddell
Three owl babies awake to find their mother missing from the trunk of their tree.

Prince William, by Gloria Rand
After a tanker spills oil into the waters of Prince William Sound, a girl rescues a seal pup.

Rain Talk, by Mary Serfozo
Listen to the onomatopoeic talk of the raindrops.

Tacky the Penguin, by Helen Lester
A tale about individuality.

The Three Billy Goats Gruff, by Paul Galdone
Three clever billy goats outsmart the troll who lives under the bridge.

The Three Little Pigs, by Paul Galdone
Three little pigs go head-to-head with a crafty wolf.

Walter the Baker, by Eric Carle
The duke and the duchess love Walter's baking . . . until there is
a mishap that almost costs him his job.

Germs! Germs! Germs!, by Bobbi Katz
Germs talk about what they can do.

Babushka Baba Yaga, by Patricia Polacco
A warm little community learns a life lesson from the loving
Baba Yaga.

Teaching Scriptwriting

To help children understand the scripting process, engage with them in
shared scriptwriting. If you teach older children, they may eventually be
able to construct scripts on their own. Christian Bush's first graders
were able to do so by February, with some teacher support. We found
it helpful to have at least one strong reader per group. Following are
some tips for teaching scriptwriting.

Use short, familiar pieces that are full of dialogue. Spend quality
time on initial readings and discussions of the text. A good understanding of content facilitates the scripting process. If possible, use a big
book so the children can see how to make the transfer from book to
script. For first- and second-grade children, final scripts work well if
they take only two to five minutes to read.

If appropriate, children may choose a favorite scene to perform,
rather than working through a whole piece. If this option is used, the
scene should convey a whole message so that you can emphasize the
importance of getting across key events and ideas.

Engage with the children in a discussion of characterization, settings, problem, plot episodes, and resolution, helping them see why all
are necessary to a meaningful presentation. Story maps can be helpful
in pulling out key information, providing a visual representation of
what to include, and helping children organize their thinking (Cooper
2000; Cronin, Meadows, and Sinatra 1990).

Then, using a piece of poster paper, invite the children to help you
list the speakers and to determine whether a narrator is needed. Help
children understand that narration serves a special function; it can take
the audience "into the air, through mouse holes, and into the minds of
the characters. Characters can swim in the ocean, leap from parapets, and
change bodily form" (Busching 1981, 335). Then, refer to the map and/or
the big book to decide who should talk first. Write speaker names in the
margin. Talk about whether it would make sense to copy the dialogue or
to change the language into your own words. Help your students see why
they don't need to include language such as "he said" and "she said."

Let children know that book ideas can be changed, added, dismissed,
and put into their own language. Children are allowed creative expression
as long as they are able to maintain the basic theme, character descriptions, and the sequence of events. Determine whether actions or sound ef-

fects would be helpful in conveying the message. If so, show children how to use brackets. Bracketed words indicate action as opposed to dialogue.

As you demonstrate scriptwriting, continually reread what has been written. Help children develop a sense for revision by asking, "Does this make sense?" and "Does it sound right?"

Encourage continual evaluation of whether the audience will understand what is happening. Ask, "How will you let the audience know what this character is thinking or doing?" and "Will this make sense to the audience?" Through this process, children learn to communicate effectively and think from the perspective of those who will be listening.

Throughout the year, you may wish to construct all of your scripts with the whole class and then divide children into groups to rehearse and perform the same piece. Or, you may wish to follow these procedures with small groups and construct four or five different scripts. Older children may eventually write their own scripts. As an alternative to traditional scriptwriting, children may simply highlight their speaking parts on a photocopy of the text they are going to perform. Another option is for children to expressively read a piece as it is, including both the narration and the dialogue. Preschool and kindergarten children can dramatize their roles as you read.

Rehearsing

Once a script is ready, allow for several rehearsals. Encourage children to show their characters' personalities by using their voices and expression. Do not encourage children to memorize lines. This causes anxiety and unnatural stage habits and is not very helpful in advancing development (Busching 1981). Rehearsals should be aimed at playing around in the text world and at making reading expressive and fluent.

Encourage children to try out varying roles, but let them choose their own roles for the actual performances. Some may need help easing in to performances and some may be most comfortable reading their lines chorally. It is important that all children feel capable of doing their parts well and do not feel excluded because of what they may not be able to do well in the eyes of other children. Be careful that theatre does not become something that limits some children's aspirations (Kohl 1988, 2).

If students have written their own scripts, early rehearsals are likely to reveal some areas that need fixing up. Allow them to decide how much editing and revising is appropriate. Don't worry about getting it perfect. They should be encouraged to use their own fix-up ideas—with encouragement and support from you—and should be acknowledged for recognizing the needs of their audience.

The Production

When the time comes for the performance, value process over product. More important than the actual performance is what children do and learn along the way. If a script is not just right, go ahead with it anyway. If somebody gets stuck on a word or loses his or her place, provide the necessary support. In prevention of getting stuck, children should be able to easily read the scripts and should have had many opportunities to practice. Still, young learners can be unpredictable, especially as they try new things. If children stop for any reason during the performance, simply provide the necessary help, and then remind the audience what was happening before the cut.

Consider the following ideas for arranging an engaging production.

Stage. Set up a formal stage area in a well-lit area of the room. Dim the audience lights to bring the focus to the players. Provide a plain backdrop. Children may stand or sit on high stools or sturdy boxes.

Seating. Arrange semicircle seating for the audience.

Scripts. Scripts should stay open easily and be easy for small hands to hold. Music stands can be helpful. Use an easy-to-read font. Avoid situations in which pages must be turned as a performer is reading. Individual parts can be highlighted.

Props and actions. Although it may be tempting to incorporate props and actions, remember that children need to focus on the script. We don't want readers to break "the dramatic spell" by awkwardly trying to do some kind of action at the same time as holding and reading a script (Busching 1981, 336).

Staging. Teach children to place themselves strategically. For example, in *The Three Billy Goats Gruff*, the troll could sit far left, with each of the three billy goats moving in for their speaking parts. Show children how to convey movement by walking in place, but keep in mind that movement should be minimal so that readers can focus on expressiveness and on keeping their place in the script.

Sound effects. Children who are not part of the actual performance can make sound effects. For example, a shoe could be used to indicate clip-clopping over a troll's bridge.

Introduction. Arrange for the narrator to introduce the performance with the title, the author, and the performers' names.

Costumes. Costumes are not necessary but may be used. Simple costumes can help the reader get into character, lend a special air of formality, and provide a helpful visual for the audience. For example, in *Little Red Riding Hood*, Little Red could wear a simple cloak, the grandmother a bonnet, and the wolf a furry piece of fabric draped around the shoulders. Another costuming option is to collect a set of large, plain T-shirts to be used as cloaks. Or, bargain pieces of fabric can be turned into cloaks by cutting a hole for the head, hemming the edges, and saving a thin strip for a belt. If costumes get in the way of reading, they should not be used.

Meeting audience needs. Allow time for discussions about meeting audience needs. The following tips for kids may be helpful:

1. When you are reading, keep the script down from your face. Speak so that the audience can hear you, but don't use a yelling voice. Read slowly, even if you can read fast.
2. When it is not your turn, follow the lines of the script along with the reader. It may help to use your finger. Stand or sit very still; audience attention should always be on the reader.
3. If the audience laughs, pause until it is quiet. Try to stay in character. Keep your focus on the next line to be read.
4. If a reader gets stuck for more than three seconds, someone should provide help.
5. If you lose your place, ask someone to help.

Closing. To indicate that a performance is over, readers close their scripts, hold them by their sides, and bow together.

Cast parties. Have cast parties. The goal of the cast party "is to create a sense of community through theater, one that just might spill over to the rest of the time the class spends together and even to life beyond the school" (Kohl 1988, 6).

Video recordings. Videotape the performances and provide a copy for families to view. Video recordings are a way for children to watch themselves and for the parents to discover their children's literacy in a different way.

Studying the Art

Studying the art of drama can enhance children's enjoyment of readers theatre activities as well as their development of literacy. You may want to explore the following topics with your students.

Use of voice. Encourage children to talk in the voices of characters. They can try louder or softer voices; speak quickly or slowly; or adjust their tone or pitch. Ask, "What does a worried voice sound like? How does an excited voice sound?" and so on.

Use of facial expressions. Study facial expressions with children. For example: "Look at the picture in the book. What do you see in the character's face? How does a face show love? How does it show fear?" Have mirrors available.

Use of gesture. Study dramatic uses of gesture: "Look at the picture in the book. What do you see in the way the body is positioned? How does a body show sadness? How does it show joy? What do we do to show that we are confused? What does *sneaky* or *clever* look like? What techniques can one character use to indicate that another is large? Small? Far away? Out of sight? Intimidating?"

Dramatic creativity. To stimulate creativity, help children warm up with some improvisations:

1. Pet a mouse; a cat; a dog; a horse; an elephant; a dinosaur.
2. Climb a tree; climb over a fence; climb over a couch; crawl under a bed; crawl into a box.
3. Pass an imaginary object around in a circle (Cecil and Lauritzen 1994).
4. Take on the roles of the characters in scripts, but extend words and actions into new situations (Kohl 1988).
5. Decide the who, the what, and the where for a scene, and act it out in any manner (Pross 1986).

INQUIRE INTO READERS THEATRE

Because readers theatre involves interpreting, reading, writing, listening, and speaking, it offers many possibilities for observing and reflecting on children's learning. Following are examples of questions you might ask as you inquire into the processes of individual children, groups, or the whole class:

- What do scripting processes look like in early childhood classrooms?
- How do children decide what to include in a script?
- What scripting problems arise as children write? How are they solved?
- How do children's fluency and expression change over the course of a project?
- How do children explore character roles?
- How do children decide which roles to take?
- What is the experience of children for whom readers theatre seems to not work well?
- How do children use language as they construct scripts? Booth (1991) contends that they may use it for "planning, speculating, predicting, listening, organizing, mapping, storytelling, sequencing, narrating, interviewing, questioning, asking for information, persuading, reporting, giving details, tape recording, elaborating, reasoning, criticizing, evaluating" (92). It could be interesting to explore any one of these areas.

Readers theatre can play a constructive role in your language arts program. It actively engages children in literature and drama, stimulates intrinsic motivation for reading and writing, and facilitates the construction of literacy knowledge. The process is authentic, and the product is tangible evidence of a job well done.

9 | POETRY

In the summer
under the wind
children are playing and jumping.

— Lexy

Stepping into a poem is like stepping into another world; it takes us to
a different time and place, showing us a new perspective on life. Children love poetry for what it makes them think and how it makes them
feel. Poetry surprises, raises questions, puzzles, tickles, transcends,
challenges, and stimulates. We know that very young children can
enjoy listening to and reading poetry, but can they write it, too? You bet
they can! As poet-author Georgia Heard states, "Some of the best poems
I've read have come from . . . young writers" (1989, 99). In this chapter
we draw from the work of Christian Bush's first graders to help us examine the extraordinary benefits of bringing poetry into the classroom.

POETRY INSPIRES NEW WAYS OF SEEING

Christian: Close your eyes. [Reads the poem "Falling Star," by Kristine
O'Connell George (1997)] What did you see?

Hailey: A little star floating across the air. He stops where there's
daisies, and finally, he lays down.

Dana: A little star rushing through the sky.

Roxanne: It can be a wishing star if you wanted to wish and it might
make your wish come true.

Poetry inspires new ways of seeing. With their falling stars that "won't go
to bed" and weeping willows that weep "piles of tears" (George 1997),
poets create images and ideas of a special sort. Through their words and
rhythms, they create new little twists on life, making the ordinary seem
extraordinary and the everyday unusual (Graves 1992; Cullinan and
Galda 1998).

Christian works hard to support her children's seeing because she believes it helps them connect with poetry and want to read more. She asks,

"What did you picture in your mind when I read that poem? What did you hear? What was unusual? What was new to you? What are the piles of tears that weeping willows weep?" Because she wants poetry's magic to gently touch her children, she accepts all responses as valid. "Everyone sees poetry differently," she tells them. "No two responses will be the same."

When her children write poetry, they create for themselves new ways of seeing. The act of writing evokes special insights for children that they may not otherwise have considered:

Zeke: I have a question. What do rocks smell like? I've seen them but never smelled.

Stuart: They smell like a little mini-skunk. Pretend a skunk is right there. That's what they smell like.

Christian teaches her children to write about things they know but to consciously consider them from new perspectives. As they write, she asks them to reconsider, remember, and think again: "Think back to what you saw. What was around you? What did you hear? What did you smell? What were your feelings?" The children's charge is to display for their readers the images, the feelings, the smells, the sounds, the sensations, or the tastes that they as authors have in their own minds . . . and to add their own twists if they wish. The results can be quite striking:

Autumn

The trees are still the leaves are
falling.

—Dana

The Fish

I smelled fish in the air
and piranhas were near
and the bobber was down.

—Jake

When children are given a supportive environment for exploration, poetry reading and writing can be a way of seeing anew for them, a way of looking at the world—and expressing their experiences—through fresh, new lenses.

POETRY IS A MEDIUM FOR CONTEMPLATION

I saw a girl
with no one to play with
so
I played with her

—Bethany

Poetry is also a medium for children to contemplate the social and emotional issues of their lives. "Children need to encounter poetry which deals with powerful emotional issues, since poetry condenses feelings into words and enables life to be contemplated, examined, and reflected upon" (Grainger 1999, 296). Christian and her children read poetry addressing all kinds of issues—friendship, kid power, diversity, loneliness, fear, empathy, and honesty. Such weighty topics often open doors to rich conversations, which provide a medium for building new understandings together. And, because poetry has touched these children emotionally, it is no surprise that their own writing serves as a tool for exploring emotional issues, too:

> When I looked around I
> saw a man that had
> no house
> no furniture
> and he was always cold
> he almost froze
>
> —Amber

Poetry is an important medium for contemplation, a medium for "coming to know in a different language" (Luce-Kapler 1999, 299). Children are capable of being on both the receiving and the creative ends of such contemplation.

POETRY DEVELOPS INSIGHT INTO LANGUAGE

> Do you have hair?
> Then you don't care.
> Do you care
> or do I care?
>
> —Zeke

Children delight in the sounds of language. They "love rhythm, rhyme, alliteration, assonance, and all the devices poets use to make the words feel good to say" (Bagert 1992, 16). Given the freedom to read, write, talk, and move, children will create a "verbal playground" (Grainger 1999, 296) in which language is enjoyed in its own right—as it ought to be! As children chant and move to poetry, they develop a sense for sounds, rhymes, and rhythms. As they read and reread poems, they "become familiar with the voice of poetry" (Heard 1989, 3). As they write, they develop insights into the complex meanings and structures of language. Imagine the reasoning that Bailey had to go through to develop the following acrostic poem:

Beautiful she is
Artist she is
I have a cat
Like [the] world I live in
Eat my sugar all up
Yes, you can be my friend

As Bailey wrote, she experimented with several different sentence structures and different word choices. Hunched over her desk, she wrote and erased, read and reread, eventually creating a piece that sounded just as she wanted it to. In her classroom, the verbal playground includes poetry as one important piece of equipment for nurturing language growth.

POETRY PROMOTES PRINT KNOWLEDGE

A final benefit of poetry is that it fosters children's development of print knowledge. One way this happens is through repeated and choral readings. Much of the poetry written for children is short, catchy, and fun to read again and again. This is a good thing, because repeated reading helps children become familiar with the language of poems, making poems easy (predictable) to read on their own. Predictability helps children experiment with matching their voices with written words and helps them associate written symbols with the sounds they hear in words (Neuman, Copple, and Bredekamp 2000). Repeated reading also exposes children to many new words, and a familiarity with words makes reading easier. For example, which of the following words is easier for you to read: *Andrzej* or *Andrew*? If you speak Polish, perhaps both are easy! "Students recognize words in print more readily if they have heard those words spoken or read aloud" (Cullinan and Galda 1998, 127).

Exploring poetic elements, such as alliteration, repetition, and rhyme, is another way children develop knowledge about print. But, let me rush to say that the idea in teaching poetry is *not* to break poems into parts in order to teach children about these elements. The idea is to read poetry and love poetry, and when children are intrigued by it, to discuss how the poet uses language to create aesthetically pleasing effects.

For example, Kristine O'Connell George (1997) begins "Weeping Willow" with "I waited all summer for my weeping willow to weep." After reading and inviting children to respond aesthetically to this poem, you might discuss with them the effect that the alliteration has on the poem's meaning and on the way it is read. Talk about what it feels like to enunciate all the *w*s. Ask whether the repeated *w* sound makes them slow down a little, as if they are waiting and waiting. Ask whether the alliteration gives a pleasing sound quality to the line. Do you see how you can help children develop print knowledge through poetry without decontextualizing its letters and sounds?

Rhyme is another element that is common in poetry—and, again, children need not be pushed to analyze spellings or make out rhyme schemes in order to learn about rhyming words. Trust that something in their human ears will draw them to rhyme and make them want to play around with it in ways that make sense to them. Playing around with both alliteration and rhyme gives children experience with manipulating and segmenting speech sounds, skills they regularly use in writing and reading.

Repetition is another poetic device that children can understand and appreciate. Inviting children to read repetitive lines with you and think about why poets use them helps them enjoy the poet's artistry and develop their print knowledge. For example, after reading together several times, you might ask children why they think Christina Rosetti uses repetition in "The Swallow": "Fly away, fly away, over the sea . . ." (dePaola 1988b) or how repetition enhances Georgia Heard's "Eagle Flight": "Eagle gliding in the sky / circling, circling way up high—" (1992).

Repeated reading and exploring poetic devices help children enjoy poetry and, at the same time, develop knowledge about print. To teach print concepts through poetry does not require that we break poems into meaningless parts. We teach poetry with the overall goal of helping children enjoy it, connect with it, and appreciate the poet's artistry. It just happens that a nice by-product is the advancement of children's print knowledge.

MAKING POETRY A PART OF LIFE

We have seen that poetry reading and writing have the potential to expand children's perspectives on the world and to advance their language and literacy. "If we want children to see poetry as an exciting and powerful vehicle for them to use to experiment with their own words, perceptions, and ideas, they must be continually surrounded by a wide range of poetic stimuli" (Cecil and Lauritzen 1994, 60–61). To make poetry a part of life in your classroom, consider the following ideas.

Daily readings. Start each morning with a poem. Whether your first group meeting of the day is for greetings, sharing journals, telling stories, or tracking the weather, you can add poetry to the experience. Consider connecting your daily poetry readings to the topics of your content area inquiries.

Weekly poetry. Spend twenty to thirty minutes exploring poetry one day of every week. This time can be used for listening, reading, writing, browsing, interpreting, performing, and dramatizing.

Breaks. Take breaks with poetry. Lively poems with an energetic rhythm get children moving and using their voices; the activity and change of pace will refresh and revitalize. Soothing poems can help children relax. Invite them to take a deep breath, stretch a little, and then say the lines softly and expressively. Allow time for a drink of water and a little conversation before moving on.

Spontaneous readings. Place large-print poems on classroom walls. Refer to them at any time of day. Hang them low enough for children to use a pointer to read them during play or center time.

Poetry center. Establish a poetry center that includes anthologies and collections of poetry, child-written poems, audiotaped poems with accompanying text, paper, pencils, and materials for illustrating. Also make available a selection of very short poems for children who wish to experiment with memorizing and performing.

Poetry notebooks. Arrange for children to keep special notebooks for copying favorite poems and/or for writing their own poetry.

Poetry readings. Organize a formal poetry reading for families or for another class in the school. In preparation, ask your students how they might like to share their poetry expertise. Some may wish to illustrate or sculpt interpretations of poems. These could be placed in a browsing gallery. Others may wish to read aloud a professionally published poem or one they have written themselves. Often, children commit poems to memory, making recitation a possibility. Children who read aloud will need plenty of time to practice and find a suitable style for reading. Kohl (1999) recommends trying out the reading of a poem with different emotions—joy, frustration, silliness, determination, boredom, peskiness, and so on. Bagert (1992) suggests making facial expressions to facilitate expressive reading. Try it yourself, he recommends: Make a sad face, and say, "I am not very happy." "You will find that voice, body, and timing tend to follow your expression" (19). Then, keeping that sad face, try to say, "I am very happy." It doesn't feel right!

When the time comes for the reading, prepare a browsing gallery, arrange seats in a semicircle, set up a podium, and lower the lights. Children may make hors d'oeuvres for a follow-up celebration. Consider having one performance in the fall and one in the spring, to highlight changes and growth. If possible, make a videotape so that children can reflect on their development.

Special publications. Help each of your children write and publish a poem to become part of a class anthology. Provide materials for creating an accompanying piece of art. Having children do illustrations for each other gives writers feedback on their use of imagery and helps illustrators listen deeply to the words of the poet. Bind the poems and illustrations together and make the anthology available in the class library.

Big books. Copy your children's favorite poems on large, sturdy paper to create a big book of poetry. Use the book as a tool for teaching phonics and print concepts.

Teacher's favorites. Make your own book of favorite poems to share with your children. They will appreciate reading a book that is special to you.

Author studies. Collect several books and pieces of poetry by the same author. Discuss the author's characteristic style, format, topic choices, and uses of language. Teach children to gather their own text sets, and invite them to write in the style of their favorite authors.

Connections with families. Prepare a newsletter to inform families of your classroom poetry activity. Explain how reading and writing poetry helps children develop literacy. Include a polished poem written by each of your students; a poem you have written with the group; and/or a few poems by published authors. Also, go to your local library and scope out anthologies that might be appropriate for children. Include a bibliography, letting families know about these books and indicating their availability at the library.

READING POETRY WITH YOUNG CHILDREN

In today's classrooms, reading poetry is a joyful experience. The days of overanalyzing are over, and for this there is good reason. Children need to feel a comfortable and personal connection with poetry before it can become a means of developing new insights into their lives and worlds. This suggests the importance of creating a climate in which (1) poetry is accessible and connected to children's lives and (2) the study of poetry occurs in a developmentally sensitive way. Let's consider how you can meet these goals.

Choosing the Literature

Many collections of short, fun poems are available for classroom use. Mary Ann Hoberman, Jack Prelutsky, and Shel Silverstein write clever, humorous verse that is easy to understand and appealing to many children. However, children appreciate all kinds of poetry and the more broad your collection, the more likely that all of your children will connect with it. As you select poetry, keep in mind that children prefer poems that are contemporary, understandable, written in narrative form, and related to their own experiences, as well as poems that contain rhyme, sound, and rhythm (Cullinan and Galda 1998). Also keep in mind that limiting your reading to rhymed verse may cause children to want their own written poems to fit this mold, which is difficult for many young writers to achieve.

To develop your collection, go to the library and browse through poetry written for all ages. The list of recommended books at the end of this chapter may provide a helpful starting point. Look for short, readable poems that might capture your children's interests. But don't worry about using only simple poems. Some poems just need a few readings and a few conversations before their potential meanings are unveiled. As you browse, ask yourself which poems might be relevant for particular children. Which connect with a project your class may be pursuing? Which make you wonder how your children will respond? Which do you like? Also ensure that children have opportunities to read poems written by other children. We want them to know that writing poetry is something that children can do and do well (Routman 2000). If you don't have any child-written poems, borrow some from this chapter or go to a website containing children's poetry. I like these: <www.yahooligans.com/School_Bell/Language_Arts/Poetry/> and <www.poetryzone.ndirect.co.uk/poems.htm>.

Attending to Personal Connections

As you read poetry with children, share the personal connections you make and encourage them to make their own. Simple questions and invitations will help:

- What does the title make you think about?
- Can you think of something the author may have seen or experienced that made him or her want to write this poem? Have you experienced something similar?
- What pictures/smells/tastes/sounds/sensations come to mind as you listen to this poem? What emotions do you feel?
- Does the poem change your way of thinking about or seeing something?

As with any literature, children experience poetry in unique ways. If two children see something differently or feel differently about a poem, highlight and appreciate the diversity. Personal interpretations are what bring meaning and pleasure to reading, and they offer the best material for conversation.

Developing Tastes and Preferences

An important part of connecting with poetry is developing tastes and preferences. Help children develop and articulate their tastes by encouraging open-ended discussions:

- What do you think about this poem/type of poem/poet's writing?
- How does this poem/type of poem/author's work make you feel?
- What words does the author use to make you feel this way?
- What is it that you like/don't like about this author's poems/this genre?

To become skilled, rounded readers, children need to examine and talk about their personal tastes in poetry and listen to the impressions of others. "Intelligent readership depends upon . . . informed judgments and tastes" (Kohl 1999, 3).

Attending to the Author's Craft

> Learning to listen to other people's voices provides me with the opportunity to expand my own. (Kohl 1999, 31)

When children have made some personal connections with poetry, we can begin to help them explore the author's craft. Exploring craft fosters aesthetic appreciation, helps children use poetry as a lens for contemplation, and helps them develop a sense of what poetry is and can be. To explore craft, young children can be encouraged to attend to sounds, meanings, and format.

Sounds and meanings

> An Easter Egg
> It's going to hatch
> with a chick inside
> eating scrambled eggs.
>
> —Jay

Poets use language in the most intriguing of ways. They focus on both sounds and meanings to create pieces that are at once musical and insightful. To help children enjoy sounds and meanings, explore the following:

- What makes this poem fun to say?
- Why does this poem make us want to move and dance?
- Why do you think the poet chose this language?
- Let's hum this poem together.
- Close your eyes and think about the picture the poet creates with words. Open your eyes and talk with a friend or the group about the pictures.
- How does the poet appeal to our senses?
- Why do you think the poet chose this language?
- What face should I make when I say these words (Bagert 1992, 19)?

Notice that the questions are not aimed at drawing correct answers, but rather at enhancing the ways in which children listen for sounds and meanings. It takes time for children to develop a vocabulary for responding to poetry. For now, let them express their ideas in their wonderfully childlike ways as you respond with adult terminology.

Format

Christian: Look at how this poem is set up. Does it look like a sentence?

Tina: No. It looks like one of those three-word things.

Christian: Like those haiku poems?

Tina: Yeah.

Poetry is a unique genre in that its visual layout contributes much to its sounds and meanings. Poets use spaces and line breaks to speed us up, slow us down, change our intonation, create a rhythm, keep us on a thought, or shift our focus (Kohl 1999). As you discuss formats with children, show them how you read through the selection once or twice to get an overall picture of what it looks like. An initial examination helps readers get their bearings and become familiar with the language and structure of the piece (Kohl 1999). On a second or third reading, explore the following:

- What looks like writing you've seen before? What breaks this pattern (Kohl 1999)?
- What about the format stands out? What are the phrases or sentences like?
- How are spaces and line breaks used?
- Let's listen to what the poem sounds like without line breaks.
- Why do you think the poet chose this format?

When children write their own poetry, help them think about where to place line breaks. In writing rhymed verse, children can be encouraged to break lines where the words rhyme; in list poems, lines often break each time a new item is added. Free verse has no prescriptions about how to end a line, but Janeczko (1999) suggests the following:

- Keep together words that seem to belong together.
- Emphasize words or phrases by putting them at the end of a line.
- Emphasize words and phrases by giving them their own line.

In formatting their poetry, poets may also use shapes to represent their meanings. For example, in "A Dizzy Little Duzzle," Prelutsky's (1996) words swirl around the page, indeed making the reader dizzy. In J. Patrick Lewis' "Lashondra Scores!" (1998), the words are placed in an arc, representing the path of a basketball.

Writing Poetry with Young Children

I saw in the summer some cows
and I smelled some
apples.

—Zeke

Because children experience love, friendship, fear, and unkindness; because they eat crispy apples and walk through freshly fallen snow; because they swing high on swings and relish in the smoothness of finger paint, they have ideas for writing poetry. The best ideas come from real-life emotions and experiences. But, if you've taught poetry, you know that good ideas for writing don't simply jump onto paper. While ideas undoubtedly fill children's worlds, they may not be recognized without some support and practice.

You can help children develop their ideas by supporting their aware-ness of their own material—things that are important to them, move them, and engage their senses. What are your students' experiences? Do any students resolutely like or dislike certain foods; have special or unique relationships with grandparents or siblings; or have an interest in playing soccer, dancing, or riding on the bus? Have any of your students told you about a time when they have had their feelings hurt or when their sense of justice has been challenged? Have any commented on the wonder of something? Help your students realize that any of these are potential topics for writing. Also, talk with them about where they think poets' ideas come from. Such discussions will raise children's con-sciousness about their own potential material.

It is also important to model your own poetry writing. It's hard to teach something well if you've never done it yourself. If you've never written poetry before, start now. If a five-year-old can do it, so can you. Don't worry if you don't love what you write at first. As Christian told Jeremy when he asked how poets "write so good," "It takes lots of prac-tice!" As you compose, show children how you draw from experiences that are meaningful to you. Tell them about real events in your life and show how you represent them through poetry. Once they—and you— have some experience with getting ideas on paper, show them how you

- play around with words, changing, removing, and adding them
- ask yourself, "Is this what I want to say?" and "Does this sound right?"
- think about whether you have portrayed a desired image
- think about whether you have provided a special insight or twist
- play around with spacing and line breaks

Free verse

> I am in summer
> I see around me is grass
> Above me is a big blue sky
>
> —Jeremy

Free verse is an important genre of poetry in early childhood class-rooms. Free verse poems are unrhymed and have no prescribed rhythm, format, or length. Children tend to not get stuck when they write free verse because they are freed to focus on what they want to say. Because free verse has few constraints in terms of form, reader expectations are high in terms of imagery, insight, and feeling. But the focus on meaning does not mean that sounds are unimportant. In fact, sounds, rhythms, and tones may emerge once meaning is conveyed, as in Jeremy's poem.

To help children get started, first help them identify their material. Once they have topics in mind, encourage them to write using their senses and emotions. Christian has found it helpful to invite children to close their eyes and think about the sights, feelings, smells, sounds, tastes, and emotions surrounding their topics. You may also find it helpful to allow children to draw as they write.

Rhymed verse

> In the spring
> I look around
> What did I see?
> I'll tell you
> What I found
> Flowers . . . daisies . . . roses.
>
> —Cayla

Rhymed verse is fun to listen to, move to, chant, and read chorally. While some children love to write rhymed verse, it can be frustrating for others and often results in contrived language:

> **Zeke:** *Habitat.* What rhymes with *habitat*?
> **Samantha:** Habitat. Cabitat. Abitat.
> **Jerome:** Try *nectar.* What rhymes with *nectar*?
> **Zeke:** Hey, I'm not in college.

This is not to say that children should never experiment with rhyme. In fact, they may be highly pleased with the lines they create, even though they often sound awkward to an adult ear, and playing with rhyme is a sure way to learn about language. It may be helpful to suggest that children who are interested in exploring rhymed verse begin with couplets (two lines of verse that rhyme) before moving on to longer, more complex pieces. Most important, help children understand that poetry does not have to rhyme.

List poems

> Crunchy and buttery
> Soft and salty, kind of
> Mushy on my tongue
> Feels plain, kind of
> Crumby
> Really crumby
> And really mushy
> And I call it like popcorn
>
> —Cory

> I saw raining popcorn
> and a jelly doughnut
> a chocolate candy bar
> and I smelled chocolate chip grass
> with sprinkles
> and felt two chocolate shakes in
>   my hand
> I call it candy land
>
> —Cory

List poems (a subset of free verse) name or describe things in a list format. Items in the list can be single words, phrases, or sentences. Cory drew on a list format to write his poems about food. John Agard uses a list format in "Don't Call Alligator Long-Mouth Till You Cross the River": "Call alligator long-mouth / call alligator saw-mouth . . ." (Harrison and Stuart-Clark 1999, 38). Arnold Shapiro uses a list format in "I Speak, I Say, I Talk": "Cats purr. / Lions roar . . ." (dePaola 1988b, 64).

Janeczko (1999) suggests inviting children to write a history of something using a list format. For example, a child might write about houses lived in, schools attended, new things tried, or how to do something such as make a pizza, be a best friend, or be a gerbil. Koch (1970) suggests beginning poems with "I wish," "If I were," or with a color ("Green is"). Another idea is to use the five senses to frame a list poem. For example, "Silly . . . sounds like . . . smells like . . . tastes like . . . looks like . . . feels like . . ." (Tompkins 2001).

A list format provides a "literacy scaffold" (Cecil and Lauritzen 1994)—a temporary framework for writing that may help children begin the process. Cecil and Lauritzen suggest the following techniques for using literacy scaffolds: first, provide the scaffold (in this case, the list format); then, read examples of children's work that use the scaffold; then, write a poem together using the scaffold; and finally, invite children to use the scaffold for their own compositions. (If you are tentative to write poetry, a scaffold may be helpful for you, too.)

Poems with special shapes

Christian: Look at the shape of this poem.
Children: It looks like an egg!

Shape poems draw on their visual appearance for meaning. For example, the lines in Kristine O'Connell George's (1997) poem "Egg" are presented in the shape of an egg. The words in Jack Prelutsky's (1996) "I Was Walking in a Circle" are presented—as you might guess—in a circle. After reading shape poems with children, discuss with them possibilities for their own writing. How might a poem about soccer or a star or a kitten be laid out? How does the layout enhance the meaning?

Acrostic poems

Grapes	**Snow**
Green	Silently falling
Red	None of it anymore
And	Oh, it's coming again!
Purple	White like paper
Eatable	—Christian Bush's first-grade class
Squishy	
—Amber	

An acrostic poem begins with a topic that also functions as a title. Each letter of the title becomes the first letter of a line of the poem. Lines can be either a word, as in "Grapes," or a phrase, as in "Snow." Beginners may find it challenging to fit their ideas into an acrostic format. For example, one morning, Maxwell started to develop an acrostic poem using his name. After struggling to come up with a sensible string of words, he changed his title to "MOM." Still struggling, he quickly jotted down the following and declared himself finished:

MOM

Monkey
Orange
Maxwell

Although acrostic poetry is challenging to write, go ahead and teach children about this form. Read and discuss examples and provide opportunities for them to explore acrostic forms in writing. Providing access to many genres of poetry allows for children to develop their tastes and preferences and allows for choice in writing.

Haiku

Bats

We were watching bats
with caring aunt and uncle
I had a great time

—Ivy

Haiku has its history in Japan, but it has become popular throughout the world. The haiku poet typically portrays a scene from nature, with the goal of stirring up images and emotions in the mind of the reader. Often, reference is made to a season. Haiku poems often contain three lines written in a five-seven-five syllable pattern (for a total of seventeen syllables). Sentence structure varies and placement of line breaks is flexible. Because of its predetermined structure, haiku is challenging for young children to write. When Christian taught haiku to her children, she did not discuss line breaks or syllable patterns. Instead, she focused on helping her children discover that haiku contains three lines and often portrays a scene in nature. After reading, Christian's children wrote haiku-like poems, without worrying about syllables or lines:

I hear birds tweeting
I smell air
I feel leaves
falling in the fall.

—Samantha

I hear the waves
I see the playground
I am up north

—Mitchell

Some books containing haiku are *The Great Frog Race and Other Poems* (George 1997), *Cool Melons—Turn to Frogs!: The Life and Poems of Issa* (Gollub 1998), and *Shadow Play: Night Haiku* (Harter 1994). Word Dance (<http://www.worddance.com/magazine/worksheet.html>) is a website containing a haiku writing worksheet and information about the form, the essence, and the style of haiku. Several examples of haiku written by children and adults are included.

INQUIRE INTO CHILDREN'S EXPERIENCES WITH POETRY

After exploring poetry with your children, what questions remain for you? Has poetry become a habitual and joyful experience in your classroom? Is it facilitating your children's growth as users of language? As lovers of language? As human beings? If you have questions that linger, you may wish to systematically inquire into the teaching and learning of poetry in your classroom. Following are examples of the types of questions you might ask:

- How do my students feel about poetry? What has contributed to this feeling?
- What do my students know about poetry? How do children develop as poets?
- How do my students use poetry as a tool for reflection and contemplation?
- What kinds of poetry topics and genres appeal to them?
- How is poetry a tool for my students' literacy development?

As you pursue poetry with children, take time to enjoy their responses and creations. Something in their characteristically uninhibited ways of expressing themselves comes to life in their poetry, making it sing, dance, and ring with honesty. I believe you will find, as many teachers do, that some of the best poetry comes from young children.

RECOMMENDED BOOKS

Adoff, A. 2000. *Touch the Poem*. New York: Blue Sky Press.

Bierhorst, J., ed. 1994. *On the Road of Stars: Native American Night Poems and Sleep Charms*. New York: Macmillan.

Bruchac, J. 1995. *The Earth Under Sky Bear's Feet*. New York: Philomel.

Bryan, A., ed. 1997. *Ashley Bryan's ABC of African American Poetry*. New York: Atheneum.

de Paola, T. 1988. *Tomie dePaola's Book of Poems*. New York: G.P. Putnam's Sons.

Florian, D. 1999. *Winter Eyes*. New York: William Morrow & Company.

———. 2000. *Mammalabilia*. Orlando, FL: Harcourt Brace & Company.

George, K. O. 1997. *The Great Frog Race*. New York: Houghton Mifflin.

———. 1998. *Old Elm Speaks: Tree Poems*. New York: Clarion.

Giovanni, N. 1996. *The Sun Is So Quiet*. New York: Holt Henry.

Gollub, M. 1998. *Cool Melons—Turn to Frogs! The Life and Poems of Issa.* New York: Lee & Low Books.

Greenfield, E. 1978. *Honey, I Love and Other Poems.* New York: Harper & Row.

Grimes, N. 1984. *Meet Danitra Brown.* New York: Lothrop, Lee & Shepard.

Harrison, M., and C. Stuart-Clark. 1999. *One Hundred Years of Poetry for Children.* Oxford, England: Oxford University Press.

Harter, P. 1994. *Shadow Play: Night Haiku.* New York: Simon & Schuster.

Heard, G. 1992. *Creatures of Earth, Sea, and Sky.* Honesdale, PA: Boyds Mills/Wordsong.

Hoberman, M. 1991. *Fathers, Mothers, Sisters, Brothers: A Collection of Family Poems.* Boston, MA: Little, Brown.

Hopkins, L.B. 1995. *Good Rhymes, Good Times.* New York: HarperCollins.

Hudson, W., ed. 1993. *Pass It On.* New York: Scholastic.

Hudson, W., and C. Hudson, eds. 1995. *How Sweet the Sound.* New York: Scholastic.

Hughes, L. 1994. *The Dreamkeeper and Other Poems.* New York: Alfred A. Knopf.

Johnston, T. 2000. *It's About Dogs.* Orlando, FL: Harcourt Brace.

Kennedy, X. J., and D. M. Kennedy, eds. 1992. *Talking Like the Rain: A Read-To-Me Book of Poems.* New York: Little, Brown.

Kennedy, X. J., and D. M. Kennedy. 1999. *Knock at a Star: A Child's Introduction to Poetry.* New York: Little, Brown.

Lewis, J. P. 1998. *Doodle Dandies.* New York: Simon & Schuster.

Lueders, E., and P. St. John, eds. 1976. *Zero Makes Me Hungry: A Collection of Poems for Today.* New York: Lothrop, Lee, and Shepard.

Mavor, S. 1997. *You and Me: Poems of Friendship.* New York: Orchard.

Mora, P. 1996. *Confetti.* New York: Lee & Low Books.

Mora, P. 1998. *This Big Sky.* New York: Scholastic.

O'Neill, M. 1961. *Hailstones and Halibut Bones.* New York: Doubleday.

Panzer, N. 1999. *Celebrate America in Poetry and Art.* New York: Hyperion.

Pomerantz, C. 1993. *If I Had a Paka: Poems in Eleven Languages.* New York: Greenwillow.

Prelutsky, J., ed. 1983. *The Random House Book of Poetry for Children.* New York: Random House.

———. 1985. *My Parents Think I'm Sleeping.* New York: Greenwillow.

———. 1996. *A Pizza the Size of the Sun.* New York: Greenwillow.

———, ed. 1998. *Imagine That!* New York: Alfred A. Knopf.

Silverstein, S. 1974. *Where the Sidewalk Ends.* New York: Harper & Row.

Steptoe, J. 1997. *In Daddy's Arms I Am Tall: African Americans Celebrating Fathers.* New York: Lee & Low Books.

10 | SOCIODRAMATIC PLAY AND LITERACY

Samantha is playing as principal when Amelia, a "student," approaches.

> **Amelia:** Can I come in the office?
> **Samantha:** No, you cannot come. I'm working.
> **Amelia:** Then, where do I get my bus pass? [Hands Samantha a note she has written before coming in to the office]
> **Samantha:** [Lifts her chin and peers at Amelia before reading the note aloud] "I am going to ride bus fifteen today." [She takes a note card from the basket on her desk and writes, "You can go."]

During the early childhood years, sociodramatic play is a natural medium for literacy development. Children playing sociodramatically—as principals, secretaries, teachers, students, maintenance workers, lunch workers, or librarians—frequently use written language to support and carry out their play themes. They write notes and bus passes; read calendars and lesson plans; fill out forms and report cards; and do projects and homework. As we will see in the following sections, these playful opportunities support children in developing knowledge in several areas.

KNOWLEDGE ABOUT LANGUAGE FUNCTIONS

Developing literacy is about more than learning to read and write; it is also about developing the sociocultural discourses needed to effectively use language in a variety of situations. In our society, language, both written and oral, serves numerous functions: we use it to accomplish the tasks of daily living, do our jobs, satisfy our curiosity, gain and share information, make connections with others, regulate behaviors, imagine, remember, and bring pleasure to our lives. Making use of these functions requires more than knowing how to read and write; it also requires a broader set of sociocultural understandings. For example, to

FIGURE 10–1   *Ivy's Weather Report. It will be fully sunny today. There is a chance that we will have clouds. 50 degrees is in sunny weather. Clouds, 40s. Let's all hope that all will [be] sunny today.*

provide a weather report, Ivy has to know what listeners care about (sunshine and temperature); she has to know how a weather report is worded (briefly and efficiently); and she has to know about the tone of the reporter (always upbeat and hopeful). Because children's uses of language in play reflect uses in the real world, play helps them develop sociocultural discourses.

Often, children's language in play seems more advanced than it does in real life. For example, during Samantha's morning as principal, she used written language to control the behaviors of others and used an authoritative, almost brusque style of talk very different from her otherwise soft-spoken classroom demeanor and from what she typically has license to do. Ivy's weather report allowed her to play around with adult workplace language. She wrote confidently and then read with expression. Why the confident performances in play? According to Vygotsky, "in play a child always behaves beyond his average age, above his daily behavior; in play it is as though he were a head taller than himself" (1978, 102). Bruner (1983) explains it this way: "To play implies a reduction in the seriousness of the consequences of errors and of setbacks. In a profound way, play is an activity that is without frustrating consequences . . . an activity that is for itself and not for others. It is, in consequence, a superb medium for exploration" (60–61). By its nature, play frees children to explore culturally patterned activities, which include language and literacy, that they may not have the authority or confidence to explore outside of play.

For second language learners, the rich visual and contextual cues that are characteristic of play are helpful in expressing and understanding language meanings. For example, imagine two French-speaking children, Aurelie and Pierre, playing in the doll corner with English-speaking Kate. Aurelie touches one of Pierre's dolls, raises her eyebrows, and asks, "Comment s'appelle t'elle?" Pierre replies, "Michel." Then, Aurelie touches Pierre's other doll and asks, "Comment s'appelle t'elle?" Pierre replies, "Marie." Finally, Aurelie touches Kate's doll and asks, "Comment s'appelle t'elle?" Because of the visual and contextual cues—the social situation, the dolls, the gestures, and the facial expressions—Kate knows the meaning of the question. Play provides a rich context for second language learners to make sense of and through language.

KNOWLEDGE OF FEATURES, FORMATS, AND GENRES

In the previous section, we saw that exploration of written language functions is important because it helps children develop the language and discourses of their sociocultural communities. Exploring functions is also important because it leads to exploration of written language features, formats, and genres. Together, these comprise the basics for making meaning from text. Let's consider Ellen's example from Figure 10–2. In writing a receipt, which had the function of providing a record of purchased items, Ellen naturally explored several important features: letter formation, common sight words (*did, you*), phonics patterns (*ea, ink, oy*), and the concept of word. Her functional use of print also led her to explore elements of format. Ellen appropriately chose a list format and included the names of the purchased items. Familiarity with format and genre aids writers in getting ideas on paper in an efficient way and in connecting effectively with an audience.

Experiencing functions, features, formats, and genres as they occur in real contexts makes learning make sense, much more so than when these elements are presented to children in isolated bits and pieces. Experiencing the whole helps children fit new concepts into their growing

FIGURE 10–2   *Ellen's Grocery List. Name. Address. What did you buy? Orange, Apple, Meat, Toy, Sink, Toy.*

understanding of the world. This does not mean that it is inappropriate to discuss, analyze, and teach pieces; it just means that as we teach the pieces, we must always keep the whole in sight.

CONTENT AREA KNOWLEDGE

Now that we have discussed the value of play in fostering language and literacy knowledge, let's think about its value in fostering content area understandings. Research and theory suggest that play fosters the mastery of new concepts (Johnson and Christie 2000). As children play, they think, question, discuss, reflect, problem solve, challenge, and put their minds together. For these reasons, many teachers set up play centers that relate directly to the content area concepts they are teaching. For example, Christian Bush arranges for her children to study snails in the science play center and to explore weather concepts through a weather station. Christine Eaton encourages her students to explore math concepts through a store center and social studies concepts through a travel agency. Jacquie Whitmore sets up a veterinarian center for children to explore responsible pet care as well as the science of animals. Providing children with opportunities to play out curricular concepts enables them to

- explore phenomena and develop an understanding of relationships
- develop a repertoire of useful information and facts
- practice skills in meaningful and authentic contexts
- transfer and apply skills to problem-solving situations
- develop dispositions that support learning and the use of knowledge and skills (Kieff and Casbergue 2000, 45)

For second language learners, play provides a particularly important medium for developing content knowledge. "Not surprisingly, many students who do not speak English fall behind in their studies early, because they are not taught content in their native language" (ASCD Advisory Panel on Improving Student Achievement 1995, 16). Providing opportunities for learners to play in their first language helps them connect with and build upon content area concepts. For example, playing as zoologists in a snail center prompts observing, describing, predicting, and hypothesizing—universal scientific discourses. These skills, necessary in conducting and understanding any kind of science, transfer from one language to the next. They are available to children in both languages. If you do not speak your students' first language, you could recruit other children in your class, older children, family members, or volunteers to act as first language play partners.

Since children learn about the world through play, it is worth the effort to ensure that they have opportunities to explore content area concepts through play. Setting up play centers that connect with chil-

dren's life experiences, as well as your curriculum, enables them to expand their literacies and knowledge of the world.

Sociodramatic | **161**
Play and Literacy |

A CONTEXT FOR CRITICAL REFLECTION

Christian: [After play one day] Is it okay for a boy to be a nurse?

Shannon: Yeah, but nurses are mostly girls . . .

Christian: Can you think of a job that normally you think of as a boy's
job that girls could do?

Pat: Usually girls are teachers and boys aren't.

Mark: There could be a girl police.

Tina: But usually there's boy police.

Pat: Because, when the world goes by, girls could be principals,
and teachers could be boys.

Hailey: There is a job that boys should just do.

Christian: Like what?

Hailey: Removing asbestos out of walls.

Christian: Why?

Hailey: I don't know. Because my dad does that, and plus, there's
only boys that do it.

This conversation occurred after Christian's children had been observed
creating a rather traditional "text" in their play. Many of the girls had
been developing domestic roles and quiet themes for themselves, while
the boys had been developing more powerful, aggressive roles and
themes. Christian's children illustrate that even when we encourage
children to choose how and what to play, they may play in ways that
replicate the social hierarchies they have observed in their worlds.
James Gee (1996) believes that schools replicate social hierarchies;
Christian's children's activity raises the question of whether school play
is any different. Although, as we have seen, play helps children explore
culturally patterned activities, it may not pave a smooth path for crossing all cultural borders.

As a teacher, is there a point at which you would intercede? Much
of the literature on play establishes that children's themes are what matter most. However, if play is part of children's "grooming" (Wink 1997)
for life, should we sometimes interrupt its text? To explore this question, you may wish to observe the ways in which your children interpret, reflect, and modify the culture as they play. Do girls take
leadership roles? Do they play as police officers, principals, bosses, and
directors? Do they do so when they are playing with boys? When an
ethnically diverse group of children is playing together, who takes
which roles? Whose stories are played out in your classroom?

If you have concerns about what you find, go ahead and take action. I am not recommending that you intervene in the play itself, by

redirecting children's activity, or that you attempt to change what children do, by assigning roles, for example. This may detract from the play and from the authority and confidence with which children explore. Instead, I am suggesting that you use play as a context for helping children reflect on their actions and ways of thinking about the world. Before, during, and/or after play,

- Ask critical questions: "Is it okay for a boy to be a nurse?" "I noticed that only boys were vets and lab technicians and that only girls were clients. Why does it turn out this way?"
- Encourage critical dialogue: Help children articulate their ideas and listen to those of others. "Dialogue in this context is a structured discussion with an extended focus and a critical purpose. It makes the objects of study the mutual property of teacher and students" (Shor 1999, xiv).
- Break stereotypes: As you help children develop background knowledge for play, and as you set up play centers, ensure that guest speakers, field trips, books, and play materials serve to break rather than enforce gender and class stereotypes. Discuss your efforts with children.

Critical reflection brings to children's conscious awareness issues that may only be implicit in their play. It helps children think thoughtfully about the texts of their play and thereby develop insight into the texts of their worlds.

A CONTEXT FOR EXPANDING LITERACIES

You can do much to support children's construction of knowledge through play. When possible, use play time as teaching time, rather than for working with small groups or engaging in other classroom tasks.

First, provide centers that are connected with your children's experiences. (Figure 10–3 provides a form that can help you do so.) Sociocultural relevancy is important. If children have visited a veterinarian's office, a mechanic shop, or an art gallery, they are most likely to know the discourses for interacting in these settings. Knowing the discourses enables children to interact effectively together and to explore materials in depth. Within the centers, allow children freedom to develop their own roles and themes. This enables them to build on what they know and develop new insights into the perspectives and life experiences of the people in their worlds. Or, you can provide curricular experiences (field trips, speakers, videos, literature) to help children develop their world knowledge, then "recast" (Van Hoorn et al. 1993) the curriculum through play.

Equip play areas with familiar reading and writing materials. Then, as your children develop their play themes, be on the lookout for other

Over the course of the year, we will be setting up a variety of imaginative play centers. To help plan meaningful centers, please place a check by the places your child has visited. We will try to design centers that are consistent with the experiences of the children. Place a star by the centers you feel your child would particularly enjoy.

___ Art Studio/Gallery/Museum	___ Laundromat/Dry Cleaner
___ Arts and Crafts Shop	___ Library/Bookstore
___ Bakery	___ Market (Fruit/Vegetable)
___ Bank	___ Mechanic/Automobile Service Shop
___ Barber Shop/Salon	___ Post Office
___ Campsite	___ Print/Copy Shop
___ Construction Site	___ Restaurant
___ Dance Studio	___ Space Museum/Observatory
___ Daycare Center/Preschool	___ Sporting Events
___ Dentist's/Doctor's Office	___ Store (Foods)
___ Farm	___ Store (Hardware)
___ Fast-Food Restaurant/Ice Cream Stand	___ Store (Shoes/Clothing)
___ Fire Station	___ Theatre/Auditorium
___ Garage Sale/Auction/Swap Meet	___ Travel Agency
___ Garden Shop/Florist	___ Veterinarian's Office/Humane Society
___ Gas Station	___ Video Rental/Music Shop
___ Hospital/Nursing Home	___ Wildlife Sanctuary/Aquarium/Zoo

Other Familiar Places: _____

_____

To help make the play centers especially meaningful, we would like to invite family members to come in and share their expertise on anything children might like to explore in their play. If you would be willing to come in and share some home- or work-related skill, craft, hobby, or interest, please name it here: _____.

Adapted from Owocki (1999).

FIGURE 10–3   *Places Your Child Knows*

materials they may need. Also, let them know that if they do not find the materials they need, they can request them from you. Before and after play, show children the literacy—and other—materials that are available, and demonstrate and discuss the ways in which they may be used.

Finally, model uses of written language as you play with children. For example, if they are playing as drivers, play along, pretending to read maps, traffic signs, and store signs. If they are playing as teachers, be a student who needs help with writing or reading. And, actively respond to children's uses of written language. Purposefully look for opportunities to affirm what they know and help them expand what they are doing.

Remember to document children's play time literacies (see Figure 10–4). Documentation provides information that enhances instruction and can be shared with families. You may wish to focus on particular children (those who struggle; those whose parents may question the value of play) or take several months to create a portrait of each child's play time literacies. Share your play time observations with families. Let them know about the functions, the features, the formats, and the genres of written language that their children are exploring as they play.

LITERACY-ENRICHED PLAY CENTERS

This section contains ideas for setting up and facilitating sixteen play centers. Once you and your students establish the physical environment of these centers, go ahead and take their lead as you teach. By choosing their own roles and themes, they will build knowledge that makes sense to them. If you want children to explore particular concepts through a center, plan to spend more time there observing, suggesting, and modeling. The ideas here are aimed at helping you get started. Go ahead and add, omit, pick, and choose, based on your children's interests, needs, and experiences.

Art Gallery

Building background knowledge
- Invite a curator, an exhibit designer, a tour guide, or an artist to come to your classroom and show occupational materials or provide a demonstration to be followed by a question-and-answer period.
- If students have family members who are artists, invite them to come in and provide a demonstration of an artistic technique.
- Tour an art gallery, a frame shop, or a museum. Help children read the print in the environment.
- Share literature focusing on art and artists from multiple cultural backgrounds.
- Encourage students to use the art gallery to explore and expand the art concepts they are learning at school.

During play time at school, _____ has been observed:

_____ Reading to support play themes.

Examples:

1. _____

2. _____

While reading, your child

____ holds material right side up   ____ makes up stories or meanings

____ turns pages left to right   ____ reads some of the print

____ labels pictures   ____ reads the print

_____ Writing to support play themes.

Examples:

1. _____

2. _____

While writing, your child

____ moves left to right, top to bottom   ____ uses some conventional spellings

____ uses invented symbols   ____ uses many conventional spellings

____ uses random strings of letters   ____ puts spaces between words

____ matches some letters to sounds   ____ experiments with/uses punctuation

_____ Sharing reading/writing ideas with peers.

Examples:

1. _____

2. _____

_____ Observing and participating in reading/writing suggested/demonstrated by others.

Examples:

1. _____

2. _____

FIGURE 10–4   *Documenting Children's Play Time Literacy*

_____ Exploring a variety of functions of written language:

___ advertisements	___ maps
___ bills	___ menus
___ calendars/schedules	___ music and songs
___ cash register/money/checks	___ newspapers
___ charts/diagrams	___ nonfiction books
___ coupons	___ notes/cards/invitations
___ food and other packages	___ price tags
___ forms	___ programs
___ instructions	___ receipts
___ labels	___ recipes
___ lists	___ scripts
___ logs/journals	___ signs
___ magazines	___ storybooks
___ manuals	

Other: _____

_____

Summary Statement of Literacy Understandings Demonstrated:

Ideas for Working with the Child:

Adapted from Owocki (1999).

FIGURE 10–4   *Continued*

Props and materials

Rope off (as in a gallery) a corner of the classroom, leaving plenty of wall space for hanging children's art. In the middle of the space, place a freestanding shelf; arrange children's sculptures on the shelves and use the backside for more pictures. Include a stand for patrons to pay for tickets and pick up brochures—either real from museums visited or created by students for play. Using an easel and a small table, arrange a separate but connected area for artists and frame makers to work. Provide the following materials:

- paper, crayons, chalk, pastels, pens, paints, pencils, and clay for artists (Craft shops offer multicultural clay to represent many skin colors; also, be sure to allow for mixing of paints, helping children achieve desired skin, hair, and other colors.)
- glue, tape, cardboard, and sturdy paper for frame making
- materials for making tickets, gallery maps, and brochures
- cash register and money
- note cards for naming the artist and the piece of art and/or for providing background information on the piece

Roles and perspectives

Before, during, and after play, explore the following with your children:

- Who contributes to the workings of an art gallery? What do exhibit designers/tour guides/patrons/artists/custodians/museum shop workers/cashiers/ticket takers do? What materials and tools do they use to do their jobs? What print materials do they use?
- How are you using the art gallery to explore the artistic techniques you are learning at other times of the day?

Bakery

Building background knowledge

- Tour a bakery. Help children read the print in the environment.
- Invite students' family members to demonstrate the mixing of a recipe. Arrange to bake it in the school oven.
- Bake breads, cakes, cookies, and muffins with your children. (Yeast bread is fun because the children get to knead it.) As you bake, be sure to read recipes together.
- Share literature related to baking. Examples include *Bread, Bread, Bread*, by Ann Morris (1993); *The Gingerbread Man*, by Jim Aylesworth (1998); and *The Apple Pie Tree*, by Zoe Hall (1996).

Props and materials

Set up a table for baking, a shelf to display baked goods, and a cashier's stand with a cash register and money. Also include these materials:

- cookie sheets, pie and cake pans, muffin tins, bowls, pots, spoons, rolling pins, cookie cutters

- plastic spice containers; empty food packages; containers labeled *flour, sugar, brown sugar, baking soda*, and *baking powder*
- homemade play dough to be used as pretend dough/baked goods (children can help make it); or varied shapes of plastic blocks to represent cakes and cookies; or plastic baked goods
- cake-decorating items to be used with play dough cakes and cookies—beads, buttons, marbles, and other small objects that can easily be washed
- recipe books, note cards for recipes, and materials for labeling and pricing objects
- aprons

Roles and perspectives

Before, during, and after play, explore the following with your children:

- What are the jobs in a bakery? What ingredients, equipment, and tools do bakers/cake decorators/cashiers need to do their work? What literacy materials do they use?
- What do people bake? How do people learn to bake?

Construction Site

Building background knowledge

- Tour a home-improvement retail store. Help children read the environmental print.
- View a home-improvement show or a video of a construction site.
- Invite architects, construction workers, road workers, excavators, plumbers, roofers, electricians, or home-improvement retail store workers (preferably family members of students) to provide brief demonstrations and/or show some occupational tools.

Props and materials

Provide an open floor space on a low-pile rug to reduce noise. Stock the space with

- hardhats and safety glasses; toy trucks and bulldozers
- blocks, stored in containers for quick pickup (Establish a safe height for building and provide a measuring stick so that children may independently check their work.)
- materials for constructing blueprints, plans, road signs, caution signs, and warning signs
- large boxes for painting, wiring, plumbing, roofing, flooring, and siding; paint, brushes, wire, plastic piping, glue, tile, pieces of plastic, scraps of linoleum, carpet remnants, fabric
- books and trade journals representing a wide variety of people and focusing on architecture and home improvement

Roles and perspectives

Before, during, and after play, explore the following with your children:

- How do buildings/roads/homes get built? Who contributes to this effort? What do architects/construction workers/road workers/excavators/plumbers/roofers/electricians do?
- What tools and materials do tradespeople need to do their jobs? What literacy materials do they use?
- How do people learn trades? What safety issues do tradespeople face? How do they protect themselves? How are master tradespeople important to our community?
- What roles are you taking in the construction center? Why do you prefer these roles?

Hospital/Doctor's Office

Building background knowledge

- Take a field trip to a hospital, a nursing home, or a doctor's office. Help children read the environmental print.
- Invite a hospital, nursing home, or doctor's office worker (preferably a family member of a student) to your classroom to describe a typical day at work or to show some occupational materials.
- Read literature focusing on health and the human body. Try *Germs! Germs! Germs!* by Bobbi Katz (1996), *What's Inside? My Body*, by Angela Royston (1991), and *The Human Body*, by Gallimard Jeunesse and Sylvaine Perols (1996).

Props and materials

Gather two or three beanbag chairs or rugs to serve as hospital or examination beds. Set up a small table for an office/reception area. Include the following items:

- a doctor's kit (or equipment to use for examinations); lab coats; patient gowns; bandages; dolls to serve as patients; trays and play food for feeding patients/residents
- nonfiction materials representing a variety of people working in various areas of the health profession and focusing on health and the human body
- a computer, a stapler, note cards, and sticky notes for office workers; pencils, crayons, and paper for making greeting cards, writing prescriptions, and recording patient information

Roles and perspectives

Before, during, and after play, explore the following with your children:

- Who works in a hospital/nursing home/doctor's office? What tools and materials do physicians/nurses/nutritionists/office workers/therapists use to do their jobs? What literacy materials do they use?

- Why do people go to the hospital/nursing home/doctor's office? How long do they stay? How do they feel? What do they do while there? What do family members do while someone is in the hospital or a nursing home? What feelings do they have?
- Where do people live when they are too old to take care of themselves? What kinds of feelings do you think these people have about leaving their homes and neighborhoods? Would you like to do something to show caring for these members of our community? What could we do?

Humane Society/Veterinarian's Office

Building background knowledge

- Tour or visit a humane society or a veterinarian's office. Collect some environmental print.
- Invite workers from these businesses (preferably family members of students) to provide a demonstration or show some occupational materials, to be followed up by a question-and-answer period.
- Share literature on pets and pet care.

Props and materials

Set up a corner of the room with small boxes and little blankets to serve as kennels; include a plastic container with water for fish. Include a table to serve as the front desk, as well as a smaller examining table toward the back. Also include

- stuffed cats and dogs; plastic fish
- doctor's kit; bandages; brushes; empty containers for bathing pets
- scrub shirts
- bowls for feeding and watering; empty pet food containers; buckets, rags, and scrub brushes for cleaning kennels/fish tank; leashes and collars (never to be placed around children's necks)
- materials for making signs, labeling kennels with pet names, keeping records of feedings, groomings, kennel cleanings, and exercise, making appointments, writing prescriptions, and writing receipts
- a small desk with a microscope, tweezers, eyedroppers, and worms (rice)
- literature on pets and pet care

Roles and perspectives

Before, during, and after play, explore the following with your children:

- Who works in a humane society/vet's office? What do office workers/ veterinarians/animal control workers do? What tools, equipment, and materials do they need to do their jobs? What literacy materials do they use?
- Many pets are abandoned or taken to a humane society by their owners. What actions could we take to support these pets? How could we promote more responsible pet ownership?

- How do people feel when their pets are sick or hurt? What do people do when they do not have enough money to take their pets to the vet? How could we support these people and their pets?

Kitchen

Building background knowledge

- Invite each child to bring in two pieces of print—empty containers or packages, a recipe book, a refrigerator magnet, a measuring spoon—from their kitchens at home. (A note home will facilitate this process.) At circle time, encourage children to show and tell about their materials. Given permission from families, stock the kitchen area with these materials.
- Invite family members to cook or bake with your children, highlighting all of the print that is necessary for accomplishing such a task.
- Take a field trip to one of your student's (or your) home. Make a list of all of the kitchen items containing print. Bake a batch of cookies or muffins, highlighting the use of print.

Props and materials

Set up an area of the room like a home kitchen. Consider including

- play stove, sink, cupboards, and refrigerator with magnets for holding print materials; kitchen table and chairs; play foods, pans, bowls, mixing spoons, measuring spoons, cups, plates, and silverware; mops, brooms, dustpans, buckets, sponges, and rags
- pads of paper and pencils; recipe books, recipe cards, food packages, and calendars, as well as materials for making these props (Using some real props from children's homes will ensure that they are representative of children's experiences.)
- dolls representing hair, facial, and skin features of various racial groups

Roles and perspectives

Before, during, and after play, explore the following with your children:

- Who are the members of a family? What do family members do in a kitchen? What literacy materials do they use to do these things?
- What roles are you taking in the kitchen center? How/why did you decide to play in this role? What stories/themes are you creating in this center? How is this like or not like what really happens in people's kitchens?
- What kinds of family events make use of a kitchen? Encourage children to use the kitchen area to plan and play out birthday parties, family celebrations, holiday/cultural celebrations, picnics; care for babies; and make special treats for loved ones.

Mechanic/Body Shop

Building background knowledge

- Tour a mechanic/body shop. Help children read the print in the environment.
- Invite a mechanic or a shop worker (preferably a family member of a student) to provide a demonstration and/or show some occupational materials. Follow up with a question-and-answer period.
- Share literature (representing a wide variety of people) about automobiles and mechanics.

Props and materials

Set up a workbench with stools and a storage shelf. Also include

- tools (without sharp edges); toolboxes, tool belts, hardhats, safety gloves, safety glasses
- pretend (empty) spray bottles labeled *oil*, *solvent*, and *cleaner*; rags for cleaning and wiping parts
- large toy cars, trucks, and buses for repairing (or paint a few cardboard boxes to look like cars, trucks, and buses)
- foam pieces, soft wood, wire, cord, springs, plastic piping, hosing, pieces from discarded radios and televisions, and other odds and ends; varied sizes of nuts and bolts
- materials for creating instructions, engine manuals, fix-it manuals, and advertisements
- children's books focusing on automobiles and building things; engine manuals; fix-it manuals

Roles and perspectives

Before, during, and after play, explore the following with your children:

- What do auto mechanics/tool and dye makers/machinists/material handlers/sheet metal workers/welders do? What kinds of things do they work on? What tools and materials do they need to do their jobs? What literacy materials do they use?
- How do people learn skilled trades? What safety issues do skilled tradespeople face? How do they protect themselves?
- How are skilled tradespeople important to our community? If mostly boys play in this center, ask your children why.

Office

Building background knowledge

- Talk with your children about the various kinds of offices they know about or have visited. Encourage them to choose their own theme for the office center. I have seen children create police, doctor's, sports, mall, poetry, home, and sales offices. The possibilities are endless.

- Record as many kinds of offices as your children can name. Keep a running list.
- Help your children interview family members about their office experiences. Give each child a note card to take home and record responses to questions such as What kinds of offices have we visited as a family? What kinds of offices do our family members have in their workplaces? and What do people do in these offices? Use the data to plan future play centers.

Props and materials

Set up a table with chairs and a variety of office materials:

- pens, pencils, sticky notes, note cards, paper, staplers, paper punches, paper clips
- a computer, telephones, a pretend copy machine
- rubber stamps, sticky stamps, envelopes
- folders and baskets for organizing materials

Roles and perspectives

Before, during, and after play, explore the following with your children:

- What kinds of offices have you visited/do you know about? What do office workers do? What kinds of literacy materials do they use?
- What kinds offices are you creating in your play? What roles are you taking?

Post Office

Building background knowledge

- Invite each child to bring in and share a piece of mail—a letter, card, advertisement, newspaper, catalog, and so on. Discuss various functions, formats, and genres of the mail; how the envelopes are addressed; and any other interesting elements the children notice.
- Write a letter with your class and mail it to someone outside the school who will write back. Model how to include a greeting, a body, and a closing and how to properly address an envelope.
- Invite a postal worker (preferably a family member of a student) to your classroom to provide a demonstration or share some occupational tools.
- Tour a post office. Help children read the environmental print.
- Read books such as *A Day with a Mail Carrier*, by Jan Kottke (2000), *Goodbye, Curtis*, by Kevin Henkes (1995), and *Postal Workers*, by Paulette Bourgeois (1999).

Props and materials

Place a mailbox anywhere in the room. Make available mailbags and mail hats. Set up a table with the following materials:

- pencils, paper, cards, envelopes, materials for making stationery; address books; maps
- scale, stamps, stamp pads, cash register, money; materials for wrapping packages
- newspapers, magazines, catalogs, advertisements, and other materials that come by mail

Roles and perspectives
Before, during, and after play, explore the following with your children:

- Who helps the mail get delivered? What do mail carriers/post office workers/truck drivers/pilots do? What equipment and materials do they use to do their jobs? What literacy materials do they use?
- What conventions are important to keep in mind as we write letters? (for example, greetings, closings, how to address envelopes, penmanship, conventional spellings)
- Where does mail go when it is picked up from a mailbox? How do postage stamps work?

School Office

Building background knowledge
- Take your children on a tour of the school's office or, if possible, arrange for a principal or a staff person to give the tour. Help children read the print in the environment.
- Invite your principal and secretary to come to your classroom and show some of the occupational materials, including literacy materials, they use to do their work.

Props and materials
Set up a front desk/reception area for a secretary and a separate but connected area for a principal's office. Include a place for students/parents/teachers to sit and/or work. Also include

- a pretend computer, telephone, telephone book, photocopy machine
- notepads, pencils, staplers, paper clips, tape, sticky notes
- materials for gathering and recording student information, planning student projects, making report cards, communicating with families, ordering materials, disseminating information, and organizing school policies, procedures, and events
- teacher mailboxes
- very simple teacher idea books and teacher magazines/journals
- copies of attendance and lunch count slips you use at your school and other materials kids see you using over and over
- children's books for designing literature-based lessons

Roles and perspectives
Before, during, and after play, explore the following with your children:

- What are the jobs in a school office? What do secretaries/principals/ student helpers do? What literacy materials do they need to do their work? What do students/family members/teachers/school guests/maintenance workers/lunch workers/librarians do when they go to a school office?
- In which roles do you like to play at the school office? Why?
- What kinds of stories and play themes are you creating in the school office?

Science Laboratory

Building background knowledge
Use this center to help reinforce and expand the science concepts your children are exploring. Whether they are studying insects, mammals, energy sources, magnets, liquids and solids, human development, or weather, invite your children to play as scientists who are conducting research on these things. "Sciencing centers should be safe, attractive areas with frequently changing activities that invite children to investigate and to extend their observations using tools and representations" (Kilmer and Hofman 1995).

- Invite a scientist (preferably a family member of a student) to your classroom to provide a brief demonstration or show some occupational materials. Leave time for questions and answers.
- Discuss the reasons for observation in science; discuss the process of testing hypotheses.

Props and materials
Set up a table with materials and specimens that will reinforce and expand the scientific concepts your children are exploring. Consider including the following:

- white coats, safety glasses, latex gloves
- plastic containers, trays, scales, rulers, tape measures, measuring cups and spoons, a timer, magnifying glasses, flashlights, and microscopes
- nonfiction reference books
- notebooks, pencils, and paper for labeling, recording, organizing, and sharing observations

Roles and perspectives
Before, during, and after play, explore the following with your children:

- What kinds of scientists are there? What do geologists/biologists/ chemists/archeologists/zoologists do? How do they make discoveries? What tools, equipment, and materials do they use? What literacy materials do they use?
- Why are scientists important to our community? How do scientists learn to do science? What safety issues do scientists face? How do they protect themselves?

- What roles are you choosing in the science center? Why? What are you doing in this center that is similar to what adult scientists do?

Space Station

Building background knowledge

- Visit a website containing information about outer space; print pieces of information that may be of interest to your students. Two good starting points are <www.yahooligans.com> (click on "Science and Nature") and <http://kids.msfc.nasa.gov/>. These sites contain news for kids; photographs and diagrams; projects and games; information on astronauts; and links to many other excellent sites.
- Share books about outer space with your students. Try *The Magic School Bus: Lost in the Solar System*, by Joanna Cole (1990), or *The Best Book of Spaceships*, by Ian Graham and Aan Graham (1998). The Let's-Read-and-Find-Out Science series has a number of good titles, including *The Planets in Our Solar System* (1999), *Floating in Space* (1998), and *What the Moon Is Like* (1986), by Franklyn Mansfield Branley, and *The Moon Seems to Change*, by Barbara Emberly (1987).
- Visit a planetarium, an observatory, or an astronomy museum. Read the environmental print.

Props and materials

Get a large box (washer, dryer, refrigerator) to serve as a spacecraft; cut holes to serve as doors and windows; invite children to decorate. Place a table next to the box to serve as mission control or as a center for telescopes/space scientists to work. Also include

- toy (or paper towel roll) telescopes; larger cylindrical objects to serve as larger scopes
- books, pamphlets, and other literature about outer space
- old keyboards and other technology with buttons and knobs to serve as a control board; helmets, coveralls, old headphones
- papers, pencils, rulers, and other materials to make charts, plans, maps, diagrams, and reports

Roles and perspectives

Before, during, and after play, explore the following with your children:

- What jobs do people involved with outer space have? What tools and equipment do engineers/astronauts/mission controllers/space scientists use to do their jobs? What literacy materials do they use? Who can learn to be a space scientist?
- Why is space science important to our community? Our world?

Theatre for Performing Arts

Building background knowledge

- Take your children to a performance at a local theatre, high school, or middle school.
- If your high school or a nearby school has an auditorium, arrange for your children to tour it. If possible, recruit a high school student to give the tour. Or, tour a community theatre. Help children read all the print in the environment.
- Visit a dance studio when children or adults are rehearsing or receiving instruction.
- Invite a dancer, an actor, a director, a dance teacher, a choreographer, a set designer, a lighting technician, an usher, or a comic (preferably a family member of a student) to provide a demonstration and show some of the tools he or she uses to do his or her art/craft/occupation/hobby.

Props and materials

Clear a large floor area for a stage or a studio. The area should be large enough for dancing and drama to take place. On a nearby table or shelf, include

- materials for writing scripts, dance steps, jokes, and music
- program booklet samples; materials for making program booklets
- varied colors of fabric (2 × 4) for children to tie, twist, drape, wrap, and fold into costumes
- tape recorder, various kinds of music on tape, blank tapes, musical instruments

Roles and perspectives

Before, during, and after play, explore the following with your children:

- Who performs on a stage? What materials and props do dancers/musicians/actors/comics/composers/choreographers/conductors use? What literacy tools do they use?
- What makes a performance enjoyable for an audience? What makes a good audience? Which kinds of performances do you prefer to participate in/watch/listen to?
- People interested in theatre and dance often have to raise money to pay for productions. How do they do this? How could we raise money to support our classroom theatre?

Video or Music Store

Building background knowledge

- Tour a video rental shop or a music store. Help children notice all the print in the environment.

- Invite a worker from a video or music store to come to your classroom and give a brief demonstration or show some occupational materials. Leave time for follow-up questions.
- Discuss the print material and packaging associated with videos, video games, compact discs, and cassette tapes.

Props and materials

Set up a cashier stand. Provide shelves for displaying merchandise. Place a table and chairs in the area so that children may develop props for the center. (Creating the materials for this center may be as educational and fun as playing in it.) Include the following items:

- video, video game, compact disc, and cassette cases to use as models
- materials for children to create their own merchandise: crayons, markers, magazines, glue, and very thick cardboard (to serve as cases)
- cash register and scanner, play money, checks, and credit cards
- tapes and a cassette player or CDs and a compact disc player for playing music in the store or for listening to music before purchasing
- music and video catalogs for ordering store materials; materials for creating order forms, scheduling workers, and making signs and advertisements

Roles and perspectives

Before, during, and after play, explore the following with your children:

- What do people in a video/music store do? What tools and materials do cashiers/managers/customers need to do their jobs? What literacy materials do they use?
- What roles are you taking in the video/music center? Why do you prefer these roles?
- What is on the cover of cassettes, videos, video games, and compact discs? Why do advertisers/promoters choose certain pictures and words? Whose attention are they seeking?

Weather Station

Building background knowledge

- View videotaped weather reports; listen to weather reports on the radio; listen to or read forecasts at <www.weather.com>.
- Go to <www.yahooligans.com>. Click on "Science and Nature" and then "Weather." This site contains child-friendly weather information. Print and share with your students.
- Observe and record the weather with your students; help them develop vocabulary to describe what they see, feel, hear, and smell outside. Read *Weather Words* by Gail Gibbons (1990), matching the kinds of weather described to what your children observe in your region.

- Invite a weather professional to your classroom to show occupational tools and materials.
- Tour a weather center. Help your children notice the environmental print.

Props and materials

Place a table and a magnetic whiteboard or chalkboard near an outdoor window. Stock with

- state and country maps (commercial or child-created); weather maps; pointers for reporting
- a pretend video camera
- magnets and pictures of weather with weather words to match
- nonfiction reference books on weather
- paper and pencils for writing weather reports and making weather maps

Roles and perspectives

Before, during, and after play, explore the following with your children:

- Who helps put together a weather report? What do weather reporters/meteorologists/camerapeople do? What tools help them do their jobs? What literacy materials do they use?
- What kinds of questions do meteorologists have about weather? How do they find answers?

Wildlife Sanctuary

Building background knowledge
- View wildlife videos/documentaries. On a second viewing, turn down the volume and invite students to provide the narration.
- Visit a natural history museum, a nature center, or a wildlife sanctuary. Many have walking tours and programs for children.
- Read literature about wildlife, particularly endangered species.
- Visit a website that has information about wildlife refuges and sanctuaries, for example, <www.nwf.org/kids>.

Props and materials

Use a rug or a mat (approximately 3 × 5 feet) to serve as the bounds of the sanctuary. Help your children understand that a sanctuary is an area devoted to the safety and security of wildlife. Place the following items in a container:

- yarn or tape for delineating trails; fabric shapes for delineating woodlands, wetlands, grasslands, and open water
- materials to make maps and brochures, write narratives for tours and documentaries, develop children's programs, and label exhibits
- miniature wild animals, miniature people, small blocks to build a picnic area

Roles and perspectives

Before, during, and after play, explore the following with your children:

- Who works at a wildlife sanctuary? What do wildlife biologists/naturalists/docents/rangers/animal handlers/veterinarians/people who raise funds do? What literacy tools and materials do they need to do their jobs?
- What do animals do? How do they survive? What health and safety issues do they face? Why do they need to be protected by sanctuaries and refuges?
- How do you feel about endangered species? What real-life actions could we take to help them? Who could we contact to help us make a difference for these living things? With whom could we share information?

A SERIES OF CENTERS

Some weeks, you may wish to make available a series of related play centers. To do so, think about the kinds of themes that (1) connect with your children's interests and (2) connect various elements of your curriculum. For example, a news theme could involve children in exploring the weather (science, math), sports (math, health, physical education), international, state, and local news (social studies), and human-interest stories. Although the centers in this chapter are described with a focus on literacy, they could easily be expanded to address mathematics, social studies, science, health, and physical education concepts. Following are some ideas for centers related by theme.

> *News:* weather center, sports center, international news, state news, local news, human interest
> *School:* school office, classroom, gym, library, kitchen, cafeteria
> *Grocery store:* cashier, office, photo processor, pharmacy, deli, bakery
> *Library:* checkout, shelf area, reading area, tables for writing, storytelling corner, crafts, computer area
> *Gas station:* gas pumps, car wash, oil change, repair shop, ministore with checkout
> *City street:* corner for street artists, food stand, sweepers, construction area, police station, fire station, hospital

PLAY ADAPTATIONS FOR OLDER CHILDREN

If you teach older children, you may wish to adapt some of the ideas in this chapter by providing structured scenarios in addition to open-ended possibilities. Older children's advanced logic and social skills make it possible for them to play within a set of guidelines and work with others toward a shared goal (Isenberg and Jalongo 2001). For example, when one group of fifth graders was exploring the Civil War, their student teacher invited them to pretend they were reporters and to prepare fact-based oral reports on current issues of the day. As a fun little twist, he encouraged the children to pretend there was television back then. The children worked in small groups to find relevant facts from the expository text they were reading, to write scripts, which included commercials, and to perform for their peers.

Jacquie Whitmore, in working with a multiage (first through fourth grades) group on an intensive study of pets, took her students to a veterinarian's office, read books about pets, invited family members to bring in pets, and watched a pet care video. When she and the children set up a veterinarian's office, they discussed possible roles (veterinarians, technicians, assistants, and clients); the reasons clients go to the veterinarian (checkups, injuries, illnesses); what clients do in a veterinarian's office (sign in, stay with their pets, ask questions); what office workers do (help clients sign in, fill out forms); what technicians do (examine specimens, help the vet); and what veterinarians do (examine and care for pets; provide diagnoses). The structured roles provided children with a scaffold for exploring issues of responsible pet care.

INQUIRE INTO CHILDREN'S PLAY

Children play about what they know. Therefore, play is an excellent context for inquiring into children's literacies. As with any inquiry, your overarching goal as you inquire into play is to develop understandings about your children and the ways in which they think, learn, and come to know the world. Following are examples of questions you might ask about play:

- What literacies are present in my students' play? What functions of written language are they exploring? How do children expand their literacies through play?
- How are children's identities reflected in and constructed through their play activity? What role does literacy play in this construction?
- What differences do boys and girls exhibit in their play? Does ethnicity or cultural orientation seem to make a difference in what and how children play? Are there differences in the roles children choose? In the themes they develop? In their ways of communicating through oral and/or written language?
- How do children who are learning a second language use and develop language as they play? How do they explore, use, and develop content knowledge?

Play is children's primary learning tool; it is their principal way of expanding their knowledge about the world. "Theory and research link play with a host of developmental virtues, including imagination, creativity, problem-solving, social competence, emotional well-being, and literacy development" (Johnson and Christie 2000, 9). These are essentials for living a healthy, happy, and fulfilling life—and play fosters their development. Perhaps the most wonderful aspect of play, though, is that it enhances children's lives *today*. As Evan expressed it to his teacher, Christian, one play-filled afternoon, "You give us the sunshine to our class every day."

APPENDIX
Books That Support Emergent Literacy

Aardema, V. 1981. *Bringing the Rain to Kapiti Plain*. New York: Dial.

———. 1992. *Who's in Rabbit's House?* New York: Dial.

———. 1992. *Why Mosquitoes Buzz in People's Ears*. New York: Dial.

Ada, A. F. 1997. *Gathering the Sun: An Alphabet Book in Spanish and English*. New York: Lothrop, Lee & Shepard.

Adler, D. 1993. *A Picture Book of Jesse Owens*. New York: Holiday House.

Adoff, A. 2000. *Touch the Poem*. New York: Blue Sky Press.

Alvarez, J. 2000. *The Secret Footprints*. New York: Alfred A. Knopf.

Anno, M. 1992. *Anno's Counting Book*. New York: HarperCollins.

Arnosky, J. 1996. *All About Deer*. New York: Scholastic.

———. 1999. *All About Owls*. New York: Scholastic.

Axelrod, A. 1997. *Pigs in the Pantry*. New York: Simon & Schuster.

Aylesworth, J. 1998. *The Gingerbread Man*. New York: Scholastic.

Baylor, B. 1994. *The Table Where Rich People Sit*. New York: Aladdin.

Bierhorst, J., ed. 1994. *On the Road of Stars: Native American Night Poems and Sleep Charms*. New York: Macmillan.

Bourgeois, P. 1999. *Postal Workers*. New York: Kids Can Press.

Branley, F. 1986. *What the Moon Is Like*. New York: HarperTrophy.

———. 1998. *Floating in Space*. New York: HarperCollins.

———. 1999. *The Planets in Our Solar System*. New York: HarperTrophy.

Brett, J. 1989. *The Mitten*. New York: G.P. Putnam's Sons.

———. 1994. *Town Mouse Country Mouse*. New York: G.P. Putnam's Sons.

———. 1999. *Gingerbread Baby*. New York: G.P. Putnam's Sons.

Brown, M. 1987. *Stone Soup*. New York: Aladdin.

———. 1999. *Arthur's Computer Disaster*. New York: Little, Brown.

Bruchac, J. 1995. *The Earth Under Sky Bear's Feet*. New York: Philomel.

———. 1998. *The First Strawberries: A Cherokee Story*. New York: Penguin.

———. 1998. *Many Nations: An Alphabet of Native America*. New York: Troll.

Brusca, M., and C. Wilson. 1995. *Three Friends, Tres Amigos*. New York: Henry Holt.

Bryan, A, ed. 1997. *Ashley Bryan's ABC of African American Poetry*. New York: Atheneum.

Cannon, J. 1993. *Stellaluna*. New York: Harcourt Brace.

Carle, E. 1969. *The Very Hungry Caterpillar*. New York: Philomel.

———. 1971. *Do You Want to Be My Friend?* New York: HarperCollins.

———. 1972. *Walter the Baker*. New York: Simon & Schuster.

———. 1984. *The Very Busy Spider*. New York: Putnam.

———. 1987. *Have You Seen My Cat?* New York: Simon & Schuster.

———. 1987. *A House for Hermit Crab*. New York: Scholastic.

———. 1993. *Today is Monday*. New York: Scholastic.

———. 1997. *From Head to Toe*. New York: HarperCollins.

Carlson, N. 1988. *I Like Me!* New York: Viking.

Carter, D., Ill. 1992. *Over in the Meadow: An Old Counting Rhyme*. Based on the original story by Olive A. Wadsworth. New York: Scholastic.

Cherry, L. 1990. *The Great Kapok Tree*. New York: Harcourt Brace.

Cole, J. 1990. *The Magic School Bus: Lost in the Solar System*. New York: Scholastic.

Coles, R. 1995. *The Story of Ruby Bridges*. New York: Scholastic.

Cooney, B. 1982. *Miss Rumphius*. New York: Puffin.

Cowen-Fletcher, J. 1994. *It Takes a Village*. New York: Scholastic.

Curtis, J. L. 1993. *When I Was Little: A Four-Year-Old's Memoir of Her Youth*. New York: Scholastic.

Demi. 1996. *The Empty Pot*. New York: Henry Holt.

———. 1998. *The Greatest Treasure*. New York: Scholastic.

de Paola, T. 1983. *The Legend of the Bluebonnet*. New York: Putnam.

———. 1988a. *The Legend of the Indian Paintbrush*. New York: Putnam.

———. 1988b. *Tomie dePaola's Book of Poems*. New York: Putnam.

Dorros, A. 1995. *Isla*. New York: Dutton.

Dragonwagon, C. 1990. *Home Place*. New York: Macmillan.

Dunbar, J., and D. Gliori. 1998. *Tell Me Something Happy Before I Go to Sleep*. San Diego, CA: Harcourt Brace.

Earle, A. 1995. *Zipping, Zapping, Zooming Bats*. New York. HarperCollins.

Ehlert, L. 1989. *Eating the Alphabet*. Orlando, FL: Harcourt Brace.

———. 1991. *Red Leaf, Yellow Leaf*. Orlando, FL: Harcourt Brace.

———. 1995. *Snowballs*. Orlando, FL: Harcourt Brace.

———. 1998. *Top Cat*. Orlando, FL: Harcourt Brace.

Emberly, B. 1987. *The Moon Seems to Change*. New York: HarperTrophy.

Florian, D. 1999. *Winter Eyes*. New York: William Morrow.

———. 2000. *Mammalabilia*. Orlando, FL: Harcourt Brace.

Flournoy, V. 1985. *The Patchwork Quilt*. New York: Dial.

Fox, M. 1987. *Hattie and the Fox*. New York: Simon & Schuster.

———. 1994. *Tough Boris*. New York: Harcourt Brace.

Galdone, P. 1973. *The Three Billy Goats Gruff*. New York: Clarion.

———. 1994. *The Three Little Pigs*. New York: Clarion.

George, K. O. 1997. *The Great Frog Race and Other Poems*. New York: Houghton Mifflin.

———. 1998. *Old Elm Speaks: Tree Poems*. New York: Clarion.

Gibbons, G. 1990. *Weather Words*. New York: Holiday House.

———. 1999. *Bats*. New York: Holiday House.

Giovanni, N. 1996. *The Sun Is So Quiet*. New York: Henry Holt.

Gollub, M. 1998. *Cool Melons—Turn to Frogs! The Life and Poems of Issa*. New York: Lee & Low Books.

Graham, I., and A. Graham. 1998. *The Best Book of Spaceships*. New York: Kingfisher.

Greenfield, E. 1978. *Honey, I Love and Other Poems*. New York: Harper & Row.

Grifalconi, A. 1995. *The Lion's Whiskers*. New York: Scholastic.

Grimes, N. 1984. *Meet Danitra Brown*. New York: Lothrop, Lee & Shepard.

Hall, Z. 1994. *It's Pumpkin Time!* New York: Scholastic.

———. 1996. *The Apple Pie Tree*. New York: Scholastic.

Hamanaka, S. 1994. *All the Colors of the Earth*. New York: William Morrow.

Harrison, M., and C. Stuart-Clark. 1999. *One Hundred Years of Poetry for Children*. Oxford, UK: Oxford University Press.

Harter, P. 1994. *Shadow Play: Night Haiku*. New York: Simon & Schuster.

Hartman, G. 1991. *As the Crow Flies: A First Book of Maps*. New York: Aladdin.

Hausherr, R. 1997. *Celebrating Families*. New York: Scholastic.

Heard, G. 1992. *Creatures of Earth, Sea, and Sky*. Honesdale, PA: Boyds Mills/Wordsong.

Heller, R. 1983. *The Reason for a Flower*. New York: Putnam.

Henkes, K. 1991. *Chrysanthemum*. New York: Greenwillow.

———. 1995. *Goodbye, Curtis*. New York: Greenwillow.

———. 1996. *Lilly's Purple Plastic Purse*. New York: Greenwillow.

Herrera, J. 2000. *The Upside Down Boy*. San Francisco: Children's Book Press.

Hesse, K. 1999. *Come On, Rain!* New York: Scholastic.

Himmelman, J. 1990. *Ibis: A True Whale Story*. New York: Scholastic.

Ho, M. 1996. *Hush!* New York: Orchard.

Hobbie, H. 1997. *Toot and Puddle*. New York: Little, Brown.

Hoban, R. 1995. *Bedtime for Francis*. Reprint edition. New York: Harper-Collins.

Hoberman, M. 1991. *Fathers, Mothers, Sisters, Brothers: A Collection of Family Poems*. Boston, MA: Little, Brown.

Hoffman, M. 1991. *Amazing Grace*. New York: Dial.

———. 1995. *Boundless Grace*. New York: Dial.

Hollander, C. 1994. *Why Bear Has a Short Tail*. New York: Scholastic.

Hopkins, L. B. 1995. *Good Rhymes, Good Times*. New York: HarperCollins.

———. 1996. *School Supplies: A Book of Poems*. New York: Simon & Schuster.

Howe, E. 1991. *Aunt Flossie's Hats (and Crab Cakes Later)*. New York: Clarion.

———. 1991. *Papa Tells Chita a Story*. New York: Simon & Schuster.

Hudson, W., ed. 1993. *Pass It On*. New York: Scholastic.

Hudson, W., and C. Hudson, eds. 1995. *How Sweet the Sound*. New York: Scholastic.

Hughes, L. 1994. *The Dreamkeeper and Other Poems*. New York: Knopf.

Intrater, R. 1995. *Two Eyes, a Nose, and a Mouth*. New York: Scholastic.

Jeunesse, G., and P. Bourgoing. 1989. *The Ladybug and Other Insects*. New York: Scholastic.

Jeunesse, G., and S. Perols. 1996. *The Human Body*. New York: Scholastic.

Jeunesse, G., and P. Valat. 1998. *Sports*. New York: Scholastic.

Johnson, A. 1989. *Tell Me a Story, Mama*. New York: The Trumpet Club.

———. 1990. *When I Am Old With You*. New York: Orchard.

Johnson, S. 1996. *Alphabet City*. New York: Viking.

Johnston, T. 2000. *It's About Dogs*. Orlando, FL: Harcourt Brace.

Katz, B. 1996. *Germs! Germs! Germs!* New York: Scholastic.

Keats, E. 1962. *The Snowy Day*. New York: Viking.

———. 1967. *Peter's Chair*. New York: Viking.

Kennedy, X. J., and D. M. Kennedy. 1999. *Knock at a Star: A Child's Introduction to Poetry*. New York: Little, Brown.

Kennedy, X. J., and D. M. Kennedy, eds. 1992. *Talking Like the Rain: A Read-to-Me Book of Poems*. New York: Little, Brown.

Kent, J. 1971. *The Fat Cat*. Parents Magazine Press.

Kitamura, S. 1992. *From Acorn to Zoo*. New York: Farrar, Straus & Giroux.

Kottke, J. 2000. *A Day with a Mail Carrier*. San Francisco: Children's Book Press.

Krauss, R. 1989. *The Carrot Seed*. Reprint edition. New York: Harper.

Kuklin, S. 1992. *How My Family Lives in America*. New York: Bradley Press.

Lester, A. 1996. *When Frank Was Four*. New York: Houghton Mifflin.

Lester, H. 1988. *Tacky the Penguin*. New York: Houghton Mifflin.

Leventhal, D. 1998. *What Is Your Language?* New York: Puffin.

Levine, E. 1989. *I Hate English!* New York: Scholastic.

Lewis, J. P. 1998. *Doodle Dandies*. New York: Simon & Schuster.

Lind, A. 1994. *Black Bear Cub*. Norwalk, CT: Trudy Corporation.

Lionni, L. 1964. *Tico and the Golden Wings*. New York: Alfred A. Knopf.

———. 1985. *It's Mine!* New York: Alfred A. Knopf.

———. 1987. *Alexander and the Wind-Up Mouse*. New York: Alfred A. Knopf

———. 1989. *Tillie and the Wall*. New York: Alfred A. Knopf.

Lobel, A. 1982. *Ming Lo Moves the Mountain*. New York: Greenwillow.

Lueders, E., and P. St. John, eds. 1976. *Zero Makes Me Hungry: A Collection of Poems for Today*. New York: Lothrop, Lee & Shepard.

Maass, R. 1992. *When Autumn Comes*. New York: Henry Holt.

———. 1993. *When Winter Comes*. New York: Henry Holt.

———. 1996. *When Spring Comes*. New York: Henry Holt.

———. 1996. *When Summer Comes*. New York: Henry Holt.

Marshall, J. 1988. *Goldilocks and the Three Bears*. New York: Dial.

Martin, B. 1967. *Brown Bear, Brown Bear, What Do You See?* New York: Henry Holt.

———. 1991. *Polar Bear, Polar Bear, What Do You Hear?* New York: Henry Holt.

Martin, R. 1989. *Will's Mammoth*. New York: G.P. Putnam's Sons.

———. 1992. *The Rough-Face Girl*. New York: Putnam & Grosset.

Marzollo, J. 1993. *Happy Birthday, Martin Luther King*. New York: Scholastic.

———. 1998. *How Kids Grow*. New York: Scholastic.

Mavor, S. 1997. *You and Me: Poems of Friendship*. New York: Orchard.

Mazer, A. 1991. *The Salamander Room*. New York: Alfred A. Knopf.

McCully, E. 1998. *Beautiful Warrior: The Legend of Nun's Kung Fu*. New York: Scholastic.

McGuffee, M. 1996. *The Day the Earth Was Silent*. Bloomington, IN: Inquiring Voices Press.

McKissack, P. 1988. *Mirandy and Brother Wind*. New York: Random House.

Medearis, A. 1994. *Harry's House*. New York: Scholastic.

Milton, J. 1993. *Bats: Creatures of the Night*. New York: Grosset & Dunlap.

Mora, P. 1996. *Confetti*. New York: Lee & Low Books.

———. 1998. *This Big Sky.* New York: Scholastic.

Morgan, A. 1995. *Sadie and the Snowman.* New York: Scholastic.

Morris, A. 1993. *Bread, Bread, Bread.* New York: William Morrow.

O'Neill, M. 1961. *Hailstones and Halibut Bones.* New York: Doubleday.

Paek, M. 1988. *Aekyung's Dream.* San Francisco: Children's Book Press.

Palotta, J. 1992. *The Icky Bug Counting Book.* Watertown, MA: Charlesbridge.

Panzer, N. 1999. *Celebrate America in Poetry and Art.* New York: Hyperion.

Paterson, K. 1990. *The Tale of the Mandarin Ducks.* New York: Lodestar.

Pilkey, D. 1996. *The Paperboy.* New York: Orchard.

Pinkney, S. 2000. *Shades of Black: A Celebration of Our Children.* New York: Scholastic.

Pinkwater, D. 1977. *The Big Orange Splot.* New York: Scholastic.

Polacco, P. 1990. *Thunder Cake.* New York: Putnam & Grosset.

———. 1992. *Mrs. Katz and Tush.* New York: Bantam.

———. 1993. *Babushka Baba Yaga.* New York: Philomel.

———. 1993. *The Keeping Quilt.* New York: Silver, Burdett & Ginn.

———. 1996. *Aunt Chip and the Triple Creek Dam Affair.* New York: Philomel.

Pomerantz, C. 1989. *The Chalk Doll.* New York: Lippincott.

———. 1993. *If I Had a Paka: Poems in Eleven Languages.* New York: Greenwillow.

Prelutsky, J., ed. 1983. *The Random House Book of Poetry for Children.* New York: Random House.

———. 1985. *My Parents Think I'm Sleeping.* New York: Greenwillow.

———. 1996. *A Pizza the Size of the Sun.* New York: Greenwillow.

———, ed. 1998. *Imagine That!* New York: Alfred A. Knopf.

Rand, G. 1992. *Prince William.* New York: Henry Holt.

Reiser, L. 1993. *Margaret and Margarita, Margarita y Margaret.* New York: Greenwillow.

Roberts, B. 1997. *A Mouse Told His Mother.* Boston: Little, Brown.

Royston, A. 1991. *What's Inside? My Body.* London: Dorling Kindersley Limited.

Rylant, C. 1982. *When I Was Young in the Mountains.* New York: Dutton.

———. 1993. *The Relatives Came.* New York: Aladdin.

Sandved, K. 1996. *The Butterfly Alphabet.* New York. Scholastic.

Sanfield, S. 1995. *Bit By Bit.* New York: Philomel.

Say, A. 1997. *Allison.* New York: Houghton Mifflin.

Schlein, M. 1996. *More Than One.* New York: Greenwillow.

Scieska, J. 1989. *The True Story of the Three Little Pigs!* New York: Penguin.

Serfozo, M. 1990. *Rain Talk*. New York: Macmillan.

Seuss, T. G. 1996. *My Many Colored Days*. New York: Alfred A. Knopf.

Shannon, D. 1998. *No, David!*. New York: Scholastic.

————. 1999. *David Goes to School*. New York: Blue Sky Press.

Sherrow, V. 1994. *Chipmunk at Hollow Tree Lane*. Norwalk, CT: Trudy Corporation.

Shulevitz, U. 1998. *Snow*. New York: Farrar, Straus & Giroux.

Silverstein, S. 1974. *Where the Sidewalk Ends*. New York: Harper & Row.

Smith, C. L. 2000. *Jingle Dancer*. New York: Morrow.

Soto, G. 1993. *Too Many Tamales*. New York: Putnam & Grossett.

Steptoe, J. 1987. *Mufaro's Beautiful Daughters*. New York: William Morrow.

————. 1997. *In Daddy's Arms I Am Tall: African Americans Celebrating Fathers*. New York: Lee & Low Books.

Swamp, C. J. 1995. *Giving Thanks*. New York: Lee & Low Books.

Sweeney, J. 1996. *Me on the Map*. New York: Crown.

Tanner, J. 1987. *Niki's Walk*. South Melbourne, Australia: Macmillan.

Tchana, K., and L. Pami. 1997. *Oh, No, Toto!* New York: Scholastic.

Turkle, B. 1976. *Deep in the Forest*. New York: Dutton.

Waddell, M. 1992. *Owl Babies*. Cambridge, MA: Candlewick Press.

Weisner, D. 1988. *Free Fall*. New York: William Morrow.

Wells, R. 1997. *McDuff Moves In*. New York: Hyperion.

————. 1998. *Yoko*. New York: Hyperion.

Widman, C. 1991. *The Lemon Drop Jar*. New York: Simon & Schuster.

Winkleman, B. 1998. *Flying Squirrel at Acorn Place*. Norwalk, CT: Trudy Corporation.

Wood, A. 1996. *The Flying Dragon Room*. New York: Scholastic.

Wyeth, S. D. 1998. *Something Beautiful*. New York: Bantam Doubleday Dell.

Young, E. 1989. *Lon Po Po: A Red Riding Hood Story from China*. New York: Philomel.

Zelinsky, P. 1986. *Rumplestiltskin*. New York: Dutton.

Zion, G. 1956. *Harry the Dirty Dog*. New York: HarperCollins.

Zoehfeld, K. 1994. *Dolphin's First Day*. Norwalk, CT: Trudy Corporation.

REFERENCES

Applebee, A. 1978. *The Child's Concept of Story: Ages Two to Seventeen*. Chicago: University of Chicago Press.

ASCD Advisory Panel on Improving Student Achievement. 1995. *Educating Everybody's Children*, ed. R. Cole. Alexandria, VA: Association for Supervision and Curriculum Development.

Bagert, B. 1992. "Act It Out: Making Poetry Come Alive." In *Invitation to Read: More Children's Literature in the Reading Program*, ed. B. Cullinan, 14–23. Newark, DE: International Reading Association.

Bissex, G. 1987. "What Is a Teacher-Researcher?" In *Seeing for Ourselves: Case-Study Research by Teachers of Writing*, ed. G. Bissex and R. Bullock Portsmouth, NH: Heinemann.

Bogdan, R., and S. Biklen 1998. *Qualitative Research in Education*. Needham Heights, MA: Allyn & Bacon.

Booth, D. 1991. "Drama Talk: Our Own Words and the Words of Others." In *The Talk Curriculum*, ed. D. Booth, and C. Hall, 89–105. Portsmouth, NH: Heinemann.

Bredekamp, S., and C. Copple. 1997. *Developmentally Appropriate Practice in Early Childhood Programs*. Washington DC: National Association for the Education of Young Children.

Brown, D., and L. Briggs. 1992. "What Teachers Should Know About Young Children's Story Awareness." *Reading Improvement* 29 (2): 40–44.

Bruce, J. 1997. "Family Treasures." In *Many Families, Many Literacies*, ed. D. Taylor, 190–91. Portsmouth, NH: Heinemann.

Bruner, J. 1983. "Play, Thought, and Language." *Peabody Journal of Education* 60: 60–69.

Busching, B. 1981. "Readers Theater: An Education for Language and Life." *Language Arts* 58 (3): 330–38.

Cecil, N., and P. Lauritzen. 1994. *Literacy and the Arts for the Integrated Classroom*. White Plains, NY: Longman.

Chenfield, M. 1985. *Creative Experiences for Young Children*. 2d ed. Orlando, FL: Harcourt Brace.

Clay, M. 1972. *Sand Test*. New Zealand: Heinemann.

———. 1975. *What Did I Write?* Auckland, NZ: Heinemann.

———. 1979. *Reading: The Patterning of Complex Behavior*. New Zealand: Heinemann.

———. 1985. *The Early Detection of Reading Difficulties*. 3d ed. Portsmouth, NH: Heinemann.

Cochran-Smith, M., and S. Lytle. 1993. *Inside/Outside: Teacher Research and Knowledge*. New York: Teachers College Press.

Cole, R., ed. 1995. *Educating Everybody's Children*. ASCD Improving Student Achievement Research Panel. Alexandria, VA: Association for Supervision and Curriculum Development.

Cooper, J. D. 2000. *Literacy*. 4th ed. New York: Houghton Mifflin.

Cordeiro, P., M. Giaccobe, and C. Cazden. 1983. "Apostrophes, Quotation Marks, and Periods: Learning Punctuation in the First Grade." *Language Arts* (60): 323–32.

Croft, D. 1990. *Activities Handbook for Teachers of Young Children*. New York: Houghton Mifflin.

Cronin, H., D. Meadows, and R. Sinatra. 1990. "Integrating Computers, Reading, and Writing Across the Curriculum." *Educational Leadership* 48 (1): 57–62.

Cullinan, B., and L. Galda. 1998. *Literature and the Child* 4th ed. New York: Harcourt Brace.

Cunningham, P., and R. Allington. 1999. *Classrooms That Work: They Can All Read and Write*. New York: Longman.

Dahl, L., and N. Farnan. 1998. *Children's Writing: Perspectives From Research*. Newark, DE, and Chicago, IL: International Reading Association and the National Reading Conference.

Davis, B., V. Resta, K. Miller, and K. Fortman. 1999. "Beginning Teachers Improve Classroom Practice Through Collaborative Inquiry." *Networks: An On-Line Journal for Teacher Research* (2): 2.

Derman-Sparks, L. 1989. *Anti-Bias Curriculum*. Washington, DC: National Association for the Education of Young Children.

Donmoyer, R. 1990. "Generalizability and the Single-Case Study." In *Qualitative Inquiry in Education*, ed. E. Eisner, and A. Peshkin, 175–200. New York: Teachers College Press.

Dudley-Marling, C., and S. Murphy. 1999. "Editors' Pages." *Language Arts* 76 (6): 456–58.

Duke, N. 2000. "3.6 Minutes Per Day: The Scarcity of Informational Texts in First Grade." *Reading Research Quarterly* 35 (2): 202–24.

Durkin, D. 1966. *Children Who Read Early*. New York: Teachers College Press.

Dyson, A. 1989. *Multiple Worlds of Child Writers*. New York: Teachers College Press.

————. 1993. "From Invention to Social Action in Early Childhood Literacy: A Reconceptualization Through Dialogue About Difference." *Early Childhood Research Quarterly* (8): 409–25.

Edelsky, C. 1983. "Segmentation and Punctuation: Developmental Data from Young Writers in a Bilingual Program." *Research in the Teaching of English* 17 (2): 135–56.

Fairclough, N. 1989. *Language and Power*. London: Longman.

Fecho, R. 1993. "Reading as a Teacher." In *Inside/Outside: Teacher Research and Knowledge*, ed. M. Cochran-Smith and S. Lytle, 265–72. New York: Teachers College Press.

Ferreiro, E. 1984. "The Underlying Logic of Literacy Development." In *Awakening to Literacy*, ed H. Goelman, A. Oberg, and F. Smith, 154–73. Portsmouth, NH: Heinemann.

Ferreiro, E., and A. Teberosky. 1982. *Literacy Before Schooling*. Portsmouth, NH: Heinemann.

Fischer, D., M. Mercado, V. Morgan, K. Robb, J. Sheehan-Carr, and M. Torres. 2000. "The Curtain Rises: Teachers Unveil Their Processes of Transformation in Doing Classroom Inquiry." *Networks: An On-Line Journal for Teacher Research* (3): 1.

Garcia, G. 2000. "Bilingual Children's Reading." In *Handbook of Reading Research, Volume III*, ed. M. Kamil, P. Mosenthal, P.D. Pearson, and R. Barr, 813–34. Mahwah, NJ: Lawrence Erlbaum Associates.

Gee, J. 1996. *Social Linguistics and Literacies: Ideology in Discourses*. Bristol, PA: Falmer Press.

Glazer, J. 1997. "Who Says?" In *Standards Consensus Series: Teaching Reading and Literature in the Early Elementary Grades*, 40–41. Urbana, IL: National Council of Teachers of English.

Goodman, K. 1986. *What's Whole in Whole Language?* Portsmouth, NH: Heinemann.

————. 1993. *Phonics Phacts*. Portsmouth, NH: Heinemann.

Goodman, Y. 1984. "The Development of Initial Literacy." In *Awakening to Literacy*, ed. H. Goelman, A. Oberg, and F. Smith, 102–109. Portsmouth, NH: Heinemann.

————. 1996. "Revaluing Readers While Readers Revalue Themselves: Retrospective Miscue Analysis." *The Reading Teacher* 49 (8): 600–609.

Goodman, Y., B. Altwerger, and A. Marek. 1989. *Print Awareness in Preschool Children: The Development of Literacy in Preschool Children*. Occasional Paper: Program in Language and Literacy. University of Arizona: Tucson, AZ.

Grady, M. 1998. *Qualitative and Action Research: A Practitioner Handbook*. Bloomington, ID: Phi Delta Kappa.

Grainger, T. 1999. "Conversations in the Classroom: Poetic Voices at Play." *Language Arts* 76 (4): 292–97.

Graves, D. 1983. *Writing: Teachers and Children at Work*. Portsmouth, NH: Heinemann.

———. 1989. *Exploring Nonfiction*. Portsmouth, NH: Heinemann

———. 1992. *Explore Poetry*. Portsmouth, NH: Heinemann.

Guba, E., and Y. Lincoln. 1981. *Effective Evaluation*. San Francisco: Jossey Bass.

Gundlach, R. 1982. "Children as Writers: The Beginnings of Learning to Write." In *What Writers Know: The Language, Process, and Structure of Written Discourse*, ed. M. Nystrand, 129–48. New York: Academic Press.

Hall, N. 1996. "Learning About Punctuation: An Introduction and Overview." In *Learning About Punctuation*, ed. N. Hall and A. Robinson, 5–36. Portsmouth, NH: Heinemann.

Halliday, M. 1975. *Learning How to Mean: Explorations in the Development of Language*. London: Edward Arnold.

Harste, J., C. Burke, and V. Woodward. 1981. *Children, Their Language and World: Initial Encounters with Print*. (Project NIE-G-79-0132). National Institute of Education.

Heard, G. 1989. *For the Good of the Earth and Sun*. Portsmouth, NH: Heinemann.

Heath, S. 1983. *Ways With Words: Language, Life, and Work in Communities and Classrooms*. Cambridge, England: Cambridge University Press.

Hendrick, J. 1997. "Reggio Amelia and American Schools: Telling Them Apart and Putting Them Together—Can We Do It?" In *First Steps Toward Teaching the Reggio Way*, ed. J. Hendrick, 41–53. Upper Saddle River, NJ: Prentice-Hall.

Houck, P. 1997. "Lessons from an Exhibition: Reflections of an Art Educator." In *First Steps Toward Teaching the Reggio Way*, ed. J. Hendrick, 26–40. Upper Saddle River, NJ: Prentice-Hall.

Hubbard, R., and B. Power. 1993a. *The Art of Classroom Inquiry*. Portsmouth, NH: Heinemann.

———. 1993b. "Finding and Framing a Research Question." In *Teachers Are Researchers: Reflection and Action*, ed. L. Patterson, C. Santa, K. Short, and K. Smith, 19–25. Newark, DE: International Reading Association.

———. 1999. *Living the Questions*. York, ME: Stenhouse.

Huston, B. 2000. "Teaching Written Language Through Developmentally Appropriate Practices." Action Research Project, Saginaw Valley State University, University Center, Michigan.

Isakson, M., and M. Boody. 1993. "Hard Questions About Teacher Research." In *Teachers Are Researchers: Reflection and Action*, ed. L. Patterson, C. Santa, K. Short, and K. Smith, 26–34. Newark, DE: International Reading Association.

Isakson, M., and D. Williams. 1996. "Allowing Space for Not Knowing: A Dialogue About Teachers' Journals." In *Research in the Classroom*, ed. Z. Donoahue, M. VanTassell, and L. Patterson, 10–35. Newark, DE: International Reading Association.

Isenberg, J., and M. Jalongo. 2001. *Creative Expression and Play in Early Childhood*. Upper Saddle River, NJ: Merrill/Prentice-Hall.

Ivener, B. 1997. "Examining Illustrations." In Standards Consensus Series: *Teaching Reading and Literature in the Early Elementary Grades*, 35–39. Urbana, IL: National Council of Teachers of English.

Janeczko, P. 1999. *How to Write Poetry*. New York: Scholastic.

Johnson, J., and J. Christie. 2000. "Draft of the Platform of the Play, Policy, and Practice Caucus." *Play, Policy, & Practice Connections: Newsletter of the Play, Policy & Practice Caucus of the National Association for the Education of Young Children*, IV (2): 9–11.

Johnson, N., and C. Giorgis. 2000. "Promoting Discussion." *The Reading Teacher* 54 (1): 106–13.

Kaser, S., and K. Short. 1997. "Exploring Cultural Diversity Through Peer Talk." In *Peer Talk in the Classroom: Learning from Research*, ed. J. Paratore and R. McCormack, 45–65. Newark, DE: International Reading Association.

Keene, E., and R. Zimmermann. 1997. *Mosaic of Thought: Teaching Comrehension in a Reader's Workshop*. Portsmouth, NH: Heinemann.

Kiefer, B. 1986. "The Child and the Picture Book: Creating Live Circuits." *Children's Literature Association Quarterly*, (11): 63–68.

Kieff, J., and R. Casbergue. 2000. *Playful Learning and Teaching: Integrating Play into Preschool and Primary Programs*. Needham Heights, MA: Allyn & Bacon.

Kilmer, S., and H. Hofman. 1995. "Transforming Science Curriculum." In *Reaching Potentials: Transforming Early Childhood Curriculum and Assessment*, ed. S. Bredekamp and T. Rosegrant, 43–63. Washington, DC: National Association for the Education of Young Children.

King, D., S. Crenshaw, and P. Jenkins. 1998. "Valuing Readers and Writers Through a Close Look at Assessment." *Talking Points* 10 (1): 13–15.

King, M., and V. Rentel. 1982. *Transition to Writing*. Final Report. Volume II. National Institute of Education-G-79-0039; G-79-0137.

Koch, K. 1970. *Wishes, Lies, and Dreams*. New York: Vintage.

Kohl, H. 1988. "Making Theater: Developing Plays with Young People." *Teachers & Writers* 20 (2): 1–6.

———. 1999. *A Grain of Poetry: How to Read Contemporary Poems and Make Them a Part of Your Life*. New York: Harperflamingo.

Koskinen, P., I. Blum, S. Bisson, S. Phillips, T. Creamer, and T. Baker. 1999. "Shared Reading, Books, and Audiotapes: Supporting Diverse Students in School and at Home." *The Reading Teacher* 52 (5): 430–44.

Kress, G. 1999. "Genre and the Changing Contexts for English Language Arts." *Language Arts* 76 (3): 461–69.

Landis, D. 1999. "Students' Stories About Reading Education." *Language Arts* 76 (3): 210–16.

Lindfors, J. 1991. *Children's Language and Learning*. Needham Heights, MA: Allyn & Bacon.

Luce-Kapler, R. 1999. "White Chickens, Wild Swings, and Winter Nights." *Language Arts* 76 (4): 298–304.

Luke, A., and P. Freebody. 1999. "Further Notes on the Four Resources Model." *Reading Online*. <http://www.readingonline.org/research/lukefreebody.html>.

Mardell, B. 1999. *From Basketball to the Beatles: In Search of Compelling Early Childhood Curriculum*. Portsmouth, NH: Heinemann.

Martens, P., and Y. Goodman. 1996. "Invented Punctuation." In *Learning About Punctuation*, ed. N. Hall and A. Robinson, 37–53. Portsmouth, NH: Heinemann.

Martinez, M., N. Roser, and S. Strecker. 1998/1999. " 'I Never Thought I Could Be a Star': A Readers Theater Ticket to Fluency." *The Reading Teacher* 52 (4): 326–34.

McCormack, R. 1997. Eavesdropping on Second Graders' Peer Talk About African Trickster Tales. In *Peer Talk in the Classroom: Learning from Research*, ed. J. Paratore and R. McCormack, Newark, DE: International Reading Association.

McFarland, K. P., and J. C. Stansell. 1993. "Historical Perspectives." *Teachers are Researchers: Reflection and Action*, ed. L. Patterson, C. Santa, K. Short, and K. Smith, 12–18. Newark, DE: International Reading Association.

McGee, L., and D. Richgels. 1996. *Literacy's Beginnings* 2d ed. Needham Heights, MA: Allyn & Bacon.

Meyer, S. 1998. A Play Script: Play, Language Development, Adult Interaction, and Young Children." Action Research Project, Saginaw Valley State University, University Center, Michigan.

Miller, H. 2000. "Teaching and Learning About Cultural Diversity." *The Reading Teacher* 53 (8): 666–67.

Milz, V. 1982. "A Psycholinguistic Description of the Development of Writing in Selected First Grade Students." ED259331.

Morrow, L. 1997. *The Literacy Center*. York, ME: Stenhouse.

Morrow, L., D. Tracey, D. Woo, and M. Pressley. 1999. "Characteristics of Exemplary First-grade Literacy Instruction." *The Reading Teacher*, 52 (5): 462–76.

Neill, M. 2000. "Transforming Student Assessment." In *Issues and Trends in Literacy Education*, 2d ed., ed. R. Robinson, M. McKenna, and J. Wedman, 136–52. Needham Heights, MA: Allyn & Bacon.

Neuman, S., C. Copple, and S. Bredekamp. 2000. *Learning to Read and Write: Developmentally Appropriate Practices for Young Children.* Washington, DC: National Education for the Association of Young Children.

Nieto, S. 1999. "Multiculturalism, Social Justice, and Critical Teaching." In *Education Is Politics*, ed. I. Shor and C. Pari, 1–32. Portsmouth, NH: Boynton/Cook.

Nikolai, C. 1999. *Reading Bookbags: Literacy Development at Home.* Action Research Project, Saginaw Valley State University, University Center, Michigan.

Ninio, A., and J. Bruner. 1978. "The Achievements and Antecedents of Labelling." *Journal of Child Language* (5): 5–15.

O'Connor, Y. 2000. *At-Home Literacy Packets Foster Parent Involvement in Children's Learning.* Action Research Project, Saginaw Valley State University, University Center: Michigan.

Owocki, G. 1999. *Literacy Through Play.* Portsmouth, NH: Heinemann.

Pappas, C., and E. Brown. 1987. "Learning to Read by Reading: Learning How to Extend the Functional Potential of Language." *Research in the Teaching of English* 21 (2): 160–84.

Pappas, C., L. Kiefer, and L. Levstik. 1999. *An Integratred Language Perspective in the Elementary School.* New York: Longman.

Patterson, L. 1996. "Reliving the Learning: Learning From Classroom Talk and Texts." In *Research in the Classroom*, ed. Z. Donoahue, M. VanTassell, and L. Patterson, 3–9. Newark, DE: International Reading Association.

Patterson, L., and P. Shannon. 1993. "Reflection, Inquiry, Action." In *Teachers Are Researchers: Reflection and Action*, ed. L. Patterson, C. Santa, K. Short, and K. Smith, 7–11. Newark, DE: International Reading Association.

Peterson, R. 1997. "Literature Groups." In Standards Consensus Series: *Teaching Reading and Literature in the Early Elementary Grades*, 35–39. Urbana, IL: National Council of Teachers of English.

Pickering, J. 1975. *Readers Theater.* Encino, CA: Dickenson Publishing Company.

Pinnell, G., and I. Fountas. 1998. *Word Matters.* Portsmouth, NH: Heinemann.

Pross, E. 1986. "Using Theater Games to Enhance Second Language Acquisition in Bilingual Education." *The Bilingual Review* 13 (3): 35–40.

Read, C. 1975. *Children's Categorization of Speech Sounds in English.* Urbana, IL: National Council of Teachers of English.

Routman, R. 2000. *Conversations.* Portsmouth, NH: Heinemann.

Salinger, T. 1998. "How Do We Assess Young Children's Literacy Learning?" In *Children Achieving*, ed. S. Neuman and K. Roskos, 223–49. Newark, DE: International Reading Association.

Schickedanz, J. 1999. *Much More Than the ABCs*. Washington, DC: National Association for the Education of Young Children.

Schultz, C. 2000. "How Partner Reading Fosters Literacy Development in First Grade Students." Action Research Project, Saginaw Valley State University, University Center, Michigan.

Sebesta, S. 1992. "Enriching the Arts and Humanities" In *Invitation to Read: More Children's Literature in the Reading Program*, ed. B. Cullinan, 50–63. Newark, DE: International Reading Association.

Shor, I. 1999. "Preface: Two Rivers of Reform." In *Education Is Politics: Critical Teaching Across Differences, K–12*, ed. I. Shor and C. Pari, vii–ix. Portsmouth, NH: Boynton/Cook.

Short, K., J. Harste, and C. Burke. 1996. *Creating Classrooms for Authors and Inquirers*. Portsmouth, NH: Heinemann.

Short, K., G. Kauffman, and L. Kahn. 2000. " 'I Just *Need* to Draw': Responding to Literature Across Multiple Sign Systems." *The Reading Teacher* 54 (2): 160–71.

Sims, M. 1993. "How My Question Keeps Evolving." In *Inside/Outside: Teacher Research and Knowledge*, ed. M. Cochran-Smith and S. Lytle. 283–89. New York: Teachers College Press.

Sloyer, S. 1982. *Readers Theatre: Story Dramatization in the Classroom*. Urbana, IL: National Council of Teachers of English.

Smith, K. 1993. "Meeting the Challenge of Research in the Elementary Classroom." In *Teachers Are Researchers: Reflection and Action*, ed. L. Patterson, C. Santa, K. Short, and K. Smith, 37–41. Newark, DE: International Reading Association.

Stasz, B. 2000. "The Road to Chiliseni: Collecting Stories to Read By." *The Reading Teacher* 53 (7): 560–63.

Sulzby, E. 1985a. "Children's Emergent Reading of Favorite Storybooks: A Developmental Study." *Reading Research Quarterly* 20 (4): 458–81.

———. 1985b. "Kindergartners as Writers and Readers." In *Advances in Writing Research, Vol. 1: Children's Writing Development*, ed. M. Farr, 127–99. Norwood, NJ: Ablex.

Sulzby, E., and W. Teale. 1991. "Emergent Literacy." In *Handbook of Reading Research Vol. 2*, ed. R. Barr, M. Kamil, P. Mosenthal, and P.D Pearson, 727–57. White Plains, NY: Longman.

Sweet, A., and J. Guthrie. 1996. "How Children's Motivations Relate to Literacy Development and Instruction." *The Reading Teacher* 49 (8): 660–62.

Taylor, D. 1997. *Many Families, Many Literacies: An International Declaration of Principles*. Portsmouth, NH: Heinemann.

———. 1998. *Family Literacy*. Portsmouth, NH: Heinemann.

Thomas, K., and S. Rinehart. 1990. "Young Children's Oral Language, Reading and Writing." *Journal of Research in Childhood Education* 5 (1): 5–26.

Tierney, R. 2000. "Literacy Assessment Reform: Shifting Beliefs, Principled Possibilities, and Emerging Practices." In *Issues and Trends in Literacy Education,* 2d ed., ed. R. Robinson, M. McKenna, and J. Wedman, 115–35. Needham Heights, MA: Allyn & Bacon.

Tierney, R., J. Readence, and E. Dishner. 1990. *Reading Strategies and Practices*. Boston: Allyn & Bacon.

Tompkins, G. 2001. *Literacy for the Twenty-first Century*. 2d ed. Upper Saddle River: Merrill/Prentice-Hall.

Tonjes, M., R. Wolpow, and M. Zintz. 1999. *Integrated Content Literacy*. Boston: McGraw-Hill.

Tower, C. 2000. "Questions That Matter: Preparing Elementary Students for the Inquiry Process." *The Reading Teacher* 53 (7): 550–57.

Van Hoorn, J., P. Nourot, B. Scales, and K. Alward. 1993. *Play at the Center of the Curriculum*. New York: Merrill.

Vygotsky, L. 1978. *Mind in Society: The Development of Higher Psychological Processes*, ed. M. Cole, V. John-Steiner, S. Scribner, and E. Souberman. Cambridge, MA: Harvard University Press.

Watts-Taffe, S., and D. Truscott. 2000. "Using What We Know About Language and Literacy Development for ESL Students in the Mainstream Classroom." *Language Arts* 77 (3): 258–65.

Wertsch, J. 1991. "A Sociocultural Approach to Socially Shared Cognition." In *Perspectives on Socially Shared Cognition*, ed. L. Resnick, J. Levine, and S. Teasley, 85–100. Washington, DC: American Psychological Association.

Whitmore, K., and Y. Goodman. 1995. "Transforming Curriculum in Language and Literacy." In *Reaching Potentials: Transforming Early Childhood Curriculum and Assessment, Vol. 2*, ed. S. Bredekamp and T. Rosegrant, 145–66. Washington, DC: National Association for the Education of Young Children.

Wilde, S. 1992. *You Ken Red This!* Portsmouth, NH: Heinemann.

Wink, J. 1997. *Critical Pedagogy: Notes from the Real World*. White Plains, NY: Longman.

Winston, L. 1997. *Keepsakes: Using Family Stories in Elementary Classrooms*. Portsmouth, NH: Heinemann.

Yenika-Agbaw, V. 1997. "Taking Children's Literature Seriously: Reading for Pleasure and Social Change." *Language Arts* 74 (6): 446–53.

INDEX

Another outstanding resource from **Gretchen Owocki**

Literacy Through Play

Gretchen Owocki

Foreword by Sue Bredekamp

Gretchen Owocki lets other teachers in on one of the best-kept secrets of early childhood education: play is a virtual gold mine for facilitating literacy learning. When children play in a purposefully designed, literacy-rich environment, teachers can discover and capitalize on some truly important, highly teachable moments.

Literacy Through Play is a resource for preschool and primary teachers who are looking for proven methods for preparing young children to become confident and flexible readers and writers. Owocki begins the book by establishing the theoretical rationale for the importance of play in literacy development, then outlines what teachers can do to set up a developmentally appropriate environment. She takes us inside two classrooms that use play in smart ways, offering proven ideas for developing the play environment; teaching literacy through play; assessing children's literacy knowledge as they play; implementing developmentally appropriate practices; and collaborating with families.

0-325-00127-8 / 136pp

The Beginning Reading Handbook
Strategies for Success

Gail Heald-Taylor

If you're looking for one comprehensive book featuring the best strategies for teaching reading, then your search has ended. Throughout *The Beginning Reading Handbook,* the emphasis is on the numerous, specific strategies that can be easily implemented with young children—not only to make learning to read a truly joyous experience, but to help build a strong foundation that will lead to long-term success in school.

Gail Heald-Taylor uses literature as the foundation for instruction. That is, everything—comprehension, the study of sentences, words, phonics, etc.—is conducted within the context of good literature, via contextual instruction and learning.

0-325-00333-5 / 208pp

Surprising Destinations
A Guide to Essential Learning in Early Childhood

Mary Kenner Glover *and* Beth Giacalone
Foreword by Bobbi Fisher

Developing a sense of adventure in learning can make all the difference between teaching incipient lifelong learners or struggling with apathetic students. In this engaging little book, Mary Glover and Beth Giacalone recount how a buddy-reading project between preschoolers and first/second graders became a yearlong vehicle for developing multiple literacies, life values, and enthusiasms of all sorts.

This book offers a model for a refreshing, thought-provoking approach to early childhood curriculum that integrates art, science, gardening, celebrations, intergenerational program involvement, community service projects, and human rights study.

0-325-00376-9 / 112pp

Emergent Literacy in Kindergarten
A Review of the Research and Related Suggested Activities and Learning Strategies

Violet B. Robinson, Gretchen Ross, *and* Harriet C. Neal

The past several decades have spawned considerable research on emergent literacy, much of which has been reported by the National Research Council (NRC). *Emergent Literacy in Kindergarten* makes that research available and accessible to early childhood educators.

By summarizing all of the relevant NRC research data and presenting related recommendations from IRA and NAEYC, this authoritative book helps teachers create instructional programs that are based upon sound thinking. Throughout the focus is on preschool and kindergarten children.

002054 / 112pp

The Research Workshop
Bringing the World into Your Classroom

Paula Rogovin

Any teacher can develop a research workshop. And in this new, reader-friendly book, Paula Rogovin shows how to do it. Demonstrating how young children's interests and questions become the central focus of the curriculum, she offers dozens of easy-to-use techniques for organizing the classroom and the school day to support student research. She also provides explicit guidelines for finding a wide range of resources, fostering family and community involvement, and dealing with assessment, home-work, and diverse student interests and abilities. As examples of how to follow the guidelines, two complete research studies are included.

0-325-00370-X / 224pp

Literacy from Day One

Pat Barrett Dragan

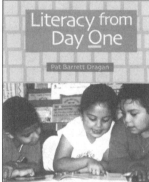

Pat Dragan has discovered that one of the best ways to begin a new school year is by putting an Overnight Book Program at the core of the literacy curriculum. The payoff is considerable. Everything developing readers and writers need to understand literacy can be learned easily and joyfully by taking books home to share with their families and returning to school the next day to participate in a range of engaging literacy activities.

Humor and innovation are also important ingredients in teaching young children. Dragan emphasizes throughout specific methods that promote joyful learning, creativity, integrated learning, and making connections.

0-325-00343-2 / 128pp

From Basketball to the Beatles
In Search of Compelling Early Childhood Curriculum

Ben Mardell
Foreword by Eleanor Duckworth

If you're a preschool or primary teacher looking for compelling curriculum, then your search has ended. According to Ben Mardell, the best ideas can be found with your students, and enthusiasm is the key ingredient. *From Basketball to the Beatles* describes some of the projects Ben created by tapping into children's interests—and the results are both instructive and galvanizing.

This entertaining and informative guide provides both the big picture about work in early childhood classrooms—the theory of teaching young children—and the details of developing and implementing preschool curriculum.

0-325-00194-4 / 172pp

To **save 10%** or for more information, visit us online: **www.heinemann.com**

Need help in other areas of **the curriculum?**

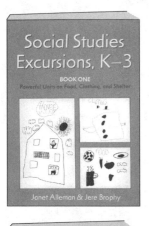

Social Studies Excursions, K–3
Book One: Powerful Units on Food, Clothing, and Shelter

Janet Alleman *and* Jere Brophy

The problem with most social studies textbooks is that they lack the content K–3 students need to develop basic social understandings—despite the fact that this is one of the goals of most state and district curriculum guides. With *Social Studies Excursions, K–3,* Alleman and Brophy offer a better alternative. They provide units structured around powerful ideas, developed in depth with applications to outside life, creating a far more substantive program than any major textbook can support.

0-325-00315-7 / 324pp

Primary Science
Taking the Plunge
SECOND EDITION

Wynne Harlen

When *Primary Science* was first published, it provided such valuable insight into the teacher's role in the science classroom that it quickly became the standard against which all other methods texts were measured. Now, sixteen years later, Wynne Harlen has revised her classic text, updating it with the most recent and pertinent research, while preserving the parts that have endured and need no change.

This book is particularly aimed at generalist teachers, who may not see themselves as "science teachers," yet have to teach science. The ideas Harlen presents are firmly grounded in classroom practice and illustrated by numerous classroom examples.

0-325-00386-6 / 160pp

Learning Through Problems
Number Sense and Computational Strategies
A RESOURCE FOR TEACHERS

Paul R. Trafton *and* Diane Thiessen

Learning Through Problems describes a powerful approach to mathematics instruction—one that honors young children's thinking and sense-making ability. Too often, the strands of mathematics (addition, subtraction, place value, and problem solving) are viewed as isolated topics. Trafton and Thiessen weave these strands together and offer a wide variety of contexts for genuine mathematical exploration.

While grounded in solid theory, *Learning Through Problems* is above all a practical resource. The book takes you into classrooms where students value challenges, reflect on their work, and participate in thoughtful discussions.

0-325-00126-X / 116pp

To **save 10%** or for more information, visit us online: **www.heinemann.com**